I0135813

AQA
Sociology
EXAM NOTES

For A Level (Year 1) & AS Level

Education

Research Methods (including Methods in Context)

Families and Households

BOOK 1

Published by Educationzone Ltd
P.O. Box 56829
London
N21 3YA
United Kingdom

© 2016 Educationzone Ltd

British Library Cataloguing in Publication Data.
A catalogue record for this publication is available from the British Library.

For more information:
Visit our website for more exam questions and answers.
www.sociologyzone.co.uk
Email us for further information:
info@sociologyzone.co.uk

About the Exam Notes

Written with examination success in mind!

- These exam notes have been written by Sociology examiners and experienced teachers, with only one purpose in mind— exam success. Using these exam notes will help students achieve the best possible grade in their Sociology exam.

- We have provided the depth of information required for your Sociology examinations, both in terms of knowledge and evaluation, which makes these exam notes more concise than general Sociology text books, and more comprehensive than standard revision guides (which often lack the depth of evaluation required to achieve an A grade).

We have focused on the 'evaluation' part.

- Contrary to popular belief, learning and memorising lots of facts and theories will not get you a grade A or B in your exam. The exam requires you to be able to 'analyse' and 'evaluate' sociological knowledge, this does not mean jotting down a few brief criticisms at the end of your essay. The analysis and evaluation that you make, needs to be expanded upon and explained in an effective manner. With this in mind, we have written a lot of the evaluation points using the three-step-rule: identify, expand and conclude. We have done this for you in this book to demonstrate what a 'developed' evaluation point looks like. Please try and remember this technique and demonstrate it in your exam.

Exam questions

- We have given you lots of exam questions at the end of each exam note to practise. We have covered most of the different types of questions you may be asked for each topic both at AS and at A Level. If you are taking the A level course, it is a good way of testing and practising both your knowledge and examination skills. You may realise some of the questions require the same answers, but are worded differently, this was deliberate, just so you are familiar with the different way the questions can be worded.

- Please visit www.sociologyzone.co.uk for exam notes, exam questions, mark schemes, model answers and much more.

Contents

Section 1 – Education

Section 2 – Research Methods (including Methods in Context)

Section 3 – Families and Households

Section 1

Education

AQA Specification

Education		
Students are expected to be familiar with sociological explanations of the following content:	•	the role and functions of the education system, including its relationship to the economy and to class structure
	•	differential educational achievement of social groups by social class, gender and ethnicity in contemporary society
	•	relationships and processes within schools, with particular reference to teacher/pupil relationships, pupil identities and subcultures, the hidden curriculum, and the organisation of teaching and learning
	•	the significance of educational policies, including policies of selection, marketisation and privatisation, and policies to achieve greater equality of opportunity or outcome, for an understanding of the structure, role, impact and experience of and access to education; the impact of globalisation on educational policy.

The AQA specification: **Education**

- The relationship the role and functions of the education system, including its relationship to the economy and to class structure.

The exam requires that you are able to:

▶ Describe and evaluate the functionalist perspective on education.

Keywords

- **Social solidarity** refers to the bonding/integration of people together into society through shared values, and a common culture and understanding.

- **Meritocratic** means that status or position in society is achieved through your own abilities and efforts rather than because of your class, ethnicity or gender, or the family you were born into or who you know.

Functionalist perspective on education

- Functionalists argue that for society to function effectively, there must be social order and stability (ie, an absence of disorder, conflict and tension), otherwise society will collapse. In order for society to survive, society needs **social solidarity** – everyone sharing the same norms and values (**value consensus**).

- Functionalism is seen as a **structural theory** because it claims that social structures (ie, social institutions) such as religion, family and school perform a number of positive 'functions/roles', both for society as a whole and for individuals, in order to help maintain social solidarity. Therefore, functionalists are mainly interested in the positive functions performed by education. There are two key functions::

  — *The socialisation function.* The school system helps socialise students into society by teaching individuals about the accepted behaviour and rules of society, which helps achieve social solidarity.

  — *The economic function.* The school system plays a key role in slotting people into 'appropriate' future occupational positions in society.

Durkheim: social solidarity

- **Education promotes social solidarity.** Durkheim (1903) claims that the education system teaches students the shared values and norms of society which create social solidarity. The school, with its rules, rituals and regulations, teaches students the importance of social constraints and cooperation; in some respects, school is 'society in miniature', creating tolerant and law-abiding future citizens who will cooperate with each other.

Parsons: universalistic values and meritocracy

- **Education teaches universalistic values.** Parsons (1961) argues that school helps prepare us for society by moving us from particularistic to universalistic values. Particularistic values are taught during primary socialisation within the family, in which parents treat their children as if they are special regardless of their achievement. Society cannot act in this way but must function on universalistic values: everyone has to be treated equally. Students must learn that success and achievement (or status with respect to the law) does not depend on where you come from or who you know, but on individual merit (see below). Learning these universalistic standards enables students to more easily make the transition from particularistic values (family) to universalistic values (society) which are essential for cooperation.

- **Meritocracy.** Parsons also sees the education system as playing the role of socialising individuals into accepting the shared values of a meritocratic society. Firstly, this means that everyone achieves their place in society through their own efforts and abilities, rather than through any inherited status. Secondly, every individual is given an equal opportunity to achieve their full potential without being discriminated against on grounds of social class, ethnicity or gender. Therefore, the education system teaches pupils to understand the values of achievement and of equal opportunity. Parsons sees the school as a miniature version of 'society', as both are meritocratic. In school, individuals succeed or fail depending on their own ability and effort. This prepares them for life in modern society and its economy, which is competitive and individualistic.

Davis and More: role allocation

- **Role allocation.** Davis and Moore (1945) see the education system's main function as one of selection and the allocation to students of their future work roles. It does this by carrying out a filtering process of 'sifting and sorting out' individuals so that the most talented get the best qualifications and are allocated to the most important jobs. Individuals have different abilities and skills. Davis and Moore see some work roles as more complex than others and requiring greater skill. For society to function efficiently, the most talented individuals need to be allocated to the most important jobs. Higher rewards are offered for these jobs to motivate everyone to strive for them. A meritocratic education system allows everyone to compete equally. As a result, society is more productive because the most able people do the most important jobs.

Human capital theory

- **Human capital theory** was developed by Schultz (1971) and suggests that high levels of spending on education and training (hence 'human capital') are required as these develop people's knowledge and skills which in turn helps produce an efficient and successful economy. Functionalists argue that greater investment in human capital has led to the expansion of higher education courses to meet the demands of modern technological advanced society. The meritocratic education system is more important than ever as it is the best way to make sure the best-qualified and most highly-skilled people get the best jobs. This ensures greater economic productivity for society and a higher financial return for the skilled individual.

✓✗ Evaluation

✗ **Meritocracy is a myth.** Marxists argue that the meritocratic education system is a myth. This is because, in reality, some social groups such as the working class and ethnic or gender groups are often discriminated against or under-achieve for reasons outside school influence (eg, material deprivation). This would suggest that the education system is not totally based on equal opportunity for everyone, as suggested by the functionalists, as the success of some students can be influenced by factors such as class, ethnicity and gender.

Marxists would also argue that the education system works in favour of the ruling class because it transmits the values and ideological views of that class rather than society's shared values, as claimed by the functionalists.

✗ **Social class, gender and ethnicity are influential.** Evidence has shown that most people in middle-class occupations have middle-class backgrounds, and that working-class jobs are often filled by people from working-class backgrounds. Equally, females and certain ethnic/colour groups (eg, Bangladeshi or Black) are less likely to be in well-paid jobs. This would suggest a person's class background, ethnicity and gender are more important in determining their income later in life than is their achievement in school.

✗ **Education is not linked to job skill.** It is difficult to see a direct link between the subjects studied at school and what is required of workers in their jobs. It could be argued that beyond basic standards of literacy and numeracy, and university courses in a few subjects, such as law or medicine, most formal education is not closely related to the skills required for an efficient workforce. This would suggest that education does not necessarily equip people for future work roles.

✗ **Most functional jobs are questionable.** Davis and Moore assume that the most important functional jobs are given to those best qualified for them, and that they are rewarded financially for them. However, in real life this is not the case. For example, footballers (eg, David Beckham) are exceptionally well-paid; does this mean that being a footballer is functionally more important for society than being a doctor, teacher or nurse, because they are paid less?

Practice exam questions

AS level exam questions

1. Define the term 'meritocracy'. [2 marks]

2. Define the term 'value consensus'. [2 marks]

3. Define the term 'social solidarity'. [2 marks]

4. Define the term 'universalistic norms'. [2 marks]

5. Outline **three** functions that the education system might perform according to the functionalist view. **[6 marks]**

6. Outline **three** ways in which school prepares pupils for work. **[6 marks]**

7. Outline and explain **two** criticisms that may be made of the functionalist view of the role of the education system. **[10 marks]**

8. Using material from **Item (...)** and your knowledge, evaluate the functionalist contribution to our understanding of the role of the education system in society. **[20 marks]**

A level exam questions

1. Outline and explain **two** roles that education fulfils according to functionalists. **[4 marks]**

2. Outline **two** ways in which schools are 'based on meritocratic principles'. **[4 marks]**

3. Outline **three** criticisms that sociologists may make of the functionalist view of the education system. **[6 marks]**

4. Outline **three** ways in which school prepares pupils for work. **[6 marks]**

5. Applying material from **Item (...),** analyse **two** ways in which education is 'based on meritocratic principles'. **[10 marks]**

The AQA specification: Education

- The relationship, role and functions of the education system, including its relationship to the economy and class structure.

The exam requires that you are able to:

▶ Describe and evaluate the New Right perspective on education.

Keywords

- **Marketisation** is a method of introducing competition into public services (eg, education and health) which were previously controlled and run by the state (eg, central government or local councils). It is effected by reducing state control and exposing services to the free market of supply and demand based on competition and consumer choice. In terms of education, this means that schools compete with each other to attract customers (ie, parents/pupils) and parents can choose which school they send their children to.

- **Meritocratic** means that status or position in society is achieved through your own abilities and efforts rather than because of your class, ethnicity or gender, or the family you were born into or who you know.

New Right perspective on education

- The New Right perspective (also known as the 'neoliberal perspective') was developed in the 1980s and is more a political (held by certain educationalists, politicians and academics) than a sociological perspective. The New Right has views on education and other aspects of society (eg, family, welfare and economy), which are in many ways similar to those of the functionalists; in fact, they are seen as a contemporary extension of functionalism. The New Right is of interest to sociologists because it has had the greatest influence on education policies in the UK and the USA, especially during the 1980s and 1990s.

The similarity with functionalism. The New Right believes:

— Education should socialise pupils into accepting shared values (eg, of British citizenship) which will help provide a sense of national identity and cohesion to ensure a stable society.

— Education is important for a successful economy as it trains student into the workforce.

— Some people are naturally more talented than others, and therefore future role allocation at work is based on educational meritocracy, that is, making sure that the most able students have their talents developed and are recruited into the most important jobs.

The problem

The New Right developed its educational perspective in response to a number of perceived concerns, summarised below:

1. **Britain has a declining and inefficient economy with many working-class people dependent on the welfare system which costs the government a lot of tax money.**

The New Right argues that too much state control of education has led the UK to become a declining and inefficient economy (as investment/jobs are going to other, more skilled countries). This is because state control crushes people's personal and business initiative and stifles their enterprise. This can be seen in the welfare system, where it has led to a culture of state welfare dependency – the poor have come to depend on welfare benefits rather than looking for work. State control means high government spending on education and other services such as the welfare system (benefits) which is a drain on a country's resources; it costs a lot of money, which has meant high taxes and less money to invest in industry.

2. **Education is failing to raise standards among some students and to provide the necessary skills required for a modern global industry.**

Chubb and Moe (1988) believe that an education system controlled and run by the government (central and local) is not the best way to raise standards and produce a skilled workforce. This is because a government-controlled education imposes one type of school system that government assumes is best for society without giving due consideration to students' different abilities, or the needs of parents and employers. This has led to a lack of the skills required to compete in an increasingly global economy, in which low-skilled workers will lose their jobs to more highly-skilled workers in other countries.

Furthermore, government-controlled schools are not accountable to parents and employers. This, according to the New Right, makes schools ineffective: schools which get poor results do not change because they are not answerable to their consumers (pupils, parents and employers). The results of state-controlled schools are lower standards and a less qualified workforce.

The solution: marketisation

- The New Right argues that implementing a market-style education (marketisation) will raise educational standards. This means schools should inhabit the free market and compete (like a business) with each other to attract customers (ie, parents/pupils) and parents should be able to choose which school they send their children to. The customer will choose the best products or services (ie, education). Therefore, schools competing with each for pupils will continually need to offer (or improve) high-quality services to ensure they attract customers. In theory, instilling competition between schools will raise educational standards in the UK. Private schools, for example, have to please their customers in order to survive and therefore standards are high and there is constant pressure for them to improve further. Creating a market-style education will:

  — *Improve the economic growth of the country.* An 'education market' will raise standards, which will give pupils better life opportunities as well as improve the economic efficiency and growth of the country. Furthermore, rising standards are essential in a global economy, where workers lacking high-level skills will lose their jobs to more highly-skilled workers from other countries.

  — *Improve society.* Raising standards means higher educational qualifications for those at the bottom (the working class), which in turn means better employment prospects, which will give working-class people a chance to escape from dependency on the welfare system.

Some state control is still required

- Although the New Right wants to reduce the role of the state in education, it does see some role for the state . The state should create the framework for competition between schools by, for example, publishing league tables of exam results (and setting a national curriculum that all schools must teach) as this would provide parents with the information required for them to make choices. The state also needs to ensure that the school transmits society's shared culture through a curriculum that emphasises a shared national identity (eg, through assemblies and lessons in citizenship, religious education and history).

✔X Evaluation

X Competition creates inequality. Halsey et al (1997) suggest that competition between schools does not raise standards but can create inequality. Those schools whose students mainly come from working-class areas will achieve poorer exam results than those whose students come from middle-class areas. This will attract fewer pupils, which means less money from the government, and thus a cycle of decline begins with the consequence of standards being lowered, not raised.

X Parental choice is a myth. Stephen Ball (1994) argues that educational changes have benefited middle-class more than working-class parents. This is because oversubscribed, popular schools are more likely to select middle-class children over working-class children or children with special needs or low ability levels (based on their SATs), to ensure that the school's examination results and position in the league table are not affected, and thus the school's popularity and strong financial position are maintained.

X Material capital denies consumer choices. Middle-class parents can afford to buy a property in a middle-class area where there is a successful school that is high in the league table, thus effectively reducing consumer choice.

X Does competition between schools raise standards? Levin & Belfield (2006) analysed schools which have made greater use of marketisation principles and found only modest improvements in student achievement (measured in terms of GCSE and A-Level results).

X Does marketisation lead to a lower quality of education? Critics of the New Right perspective argue that marketisation may lead to a lower quality of education. It could be argued that many schools, such as academies, place an intensive focus upon exam preparation in order to get good exam results (so they appear high in the league table) and too little on the content of education itself (ie, a deeper understanding of the subject). This means marketisation may not be a reliable guide to the quality or standard of the education that pupils have received.

Practice exam questions

AS/A level question

1. Using material from **Item (...)** and your knowledge, evaluate the contribution of the New Right view to our understanding of the role of education.   **[20 marks] or [30 marks]**

The AQA specification: **Education**

- The relationship, role and functions of the education system, including its relationship to the economy and class structure.

The exam requires that you are able to:

▶ Describe and evaluate the Marxist perspective on education.

Keywords

- **Ideological state apparatus (ISA)** is a term used for institutions such as education, churches, family, media and the law which serve to brainwash people into accepting that capitalist ideology (ideas, values and beliefs) as commonly-held and socially just. The main function of ISA is to justify the wealth and power of the ruling class.

- **Hidden curriculum** can be defined as the ideas and views that are taught informally, and usually unintentionally, in a school system. These include behaviours, attitudes and obedience that students pick up while they are at school. This is in contrast to the formal curriculum, such as the subjects, courses and activities in which students participate.

Brief introduction to Marxism

Marxism is known as a conflict theory because it sees capitalist society as consisting of two main classes, with one class exploiting the other. The two social classes are:

- **Ruling class (or bourgeoisie).** People who own the means of production (eg, factories, shops and land) whose aim is to make money by exploiting the labour of the working class. This group of people are often referred to by a number of names such as the capitalist class, capitalists or the minority class.
- **Working class (or proletariat).** People who work for the ruling class in return for a wage. Members of the working class are often paid far less than they deserve and are therefore seen as being exploited by the ruling class in order to maximise the latter's profit.

Marxism suggests that in a capitalist society, the relationship between the two classes is unfair. The working class demands to be paid more for their labour while the ruling class wants to keep wages to a minimum to maximise their profit, hence a conflict of interest occurs between the classes.

Marxist perspective on education

Marxists see the education system as an instrument of, or as being controlled by, the ruling class. Marxist thought on the role of education is summarised below and then expanded in the body of the exam notes:

— It largely agrees with the functionalists on the role of the schools, ie, that they play a socialisation and allocation role. It differs in claiming that the school system works in the interests of the ruling class and not for the benefit of society as a whole..

— It believes schools transmit the norms and values of the ruling class as the social norm, and from one generation to the next.

— It holds that school socialises students to believe that capitalistic values (materialistic values) can be viewed as the norm and something to aspire to.

— It believes that schooling reinforces class inequality; assessment systems (meritocracy) within schools ensure that working-class students are allocated to the jobs that reflect their class position.

— It prevents the working class from realising that the school system operates unfairly towards them.

Education as ideological state apparatus (ISA)

The Marxist philosopher Althusser (1971) disagrees with the functionalist view that education socialises students into accepting the common values of mainstream society. He sees education as benefiting the ruling class because the education system acts as an ISA. This means that the education system socialises students into accepting capitalistic ideology (ie, capitalistic ideas, values and beliefs). The main function of ISA is the continuation of the wealth and power of the ruling class. ISA does this by:

- **Reproducing class inequality.** The education system reproduces class inequalities between the ruling class and working class. This is because each generation of working-class pupils fails at school and is thus prepared for an appropriate role allocation and class position in society, thereby ending up in the same kinds of jobs as the previous one.

- **Legitimising class inequality.** The education system legitimises (justifies) class inequalities by socialising students into accepting capitalistic ideology (ie, capitalistic ideas, values and beliefs) as being common and just. It tries to convince people through the school's meritocracy, which is seen as a legitimate (just and fair) system, that everyone has an equal opportunity to succeed and that inequality is therefore inevitable, with failure being the fault of the individual, not the capitalist system.

ISAs such as education, religion, family and the media are instruments that help brainwash the working class to accept ruling-class ideology as the norm, helping the ruling class to maintain power without having to use force. This is important since no class can hold power for any length of time by using force alone. Brainwashing the working class allows the ruling class to achieve the same results: it exerts its influence subconsciously on the minds of working-class people so they see its ideology as reasonable and just.

The correspondence principle and the hidden curriculum

- Marxist such as Bowles & Gintis (1976) agree with the functionalists who see a close relationship between school and the world of work. Where Bowles & Gintis differ is that they see the education system as being controlled by capitalists and serving their interests, whereas functionalists see education as benefiting society as a whole.

- According to Bowles and Gintis, for capitalism to run efficiently it needs workers who are passive, obedient to authority and hardworking. They see schools as preparing pupils to be just that: obedient, exploitable workers for capitalist businesses. Bowles & Gintis developed the 'correspondence principle' from a study of high school children in the USA, and found that how schools are organised and run is mirrored in (corresponds to) the world of work. This similarity creates new generations of workers ready to be exploited by capitalist business.

How school mirrors work

	Schools	Work
Hierarchy	Schools teach the acceptance of hierarchy of authority; teachers give the orders and pupils obey.	There is a hierarchical structure in the workplace. Workers obey managers.
Rewards	Pupils are motivated by the external rewards of exam success rather than interest in the subject.	Workers are motivated by wages rather the satisfaction of the job itself.
Alienation	Pupils have no control over the educational curriculum.	Workers lack control over production or what goes on at work.
Fragmentation	Knowledge is fragmented, or broken into small pieces; subjects are unconnected to each other.	Work is fragmented into small meaningless tasks.
Conformity	Conformist pupils (eg, those who are obedient, hardworking and punctual) are awarded higher grades than those who challenge authority.	Workers who challenge authority, or are lazy or not punctual, are often dismissed or not promoted.

Bowles & Gintis argue that the correspondence principle is taught through the hidden curriculum, that is, not explicitly taught but informally learnt during everyday lessons and the workings of the school, eg, emphasis on punctuality, obedience, pupil acceptance of authority, rewards and so on.

The myth of meritocracy

- According to Bowles & Gintis, the education system sells the view that it works on meritocratic principles, that is, that everyone has an equal chance of doing well in life (eg, those who get the highest qualifications get the best-paid jobs). This makes people accept their educational failure and low wages as fair and justified ('I didn't work hard enough' or 'I wasn't clever enough'); it provides an explanation. Bowles & Gintis see the idea of meritocracy as a myth: people are conned into believing that success or failure is based on merit whereas in reality their class background determines how well they do in education. Therefore, the education system legitimates class inequalities in society because it prevents people from recognising their exploited position, and, in particular, prevents working-class people from rebelling against the capitalist system.

Role allocation

- Bowles & Gintis reject the functionalist view of role allocation, ie, that education allocates the most talented people, through the meritocratic process, to the most important and best-paid jobs in society. Their research found that students with high grades tend to be hardworking and obedient, rather than non-conformist, or creative thinkers. This would support their view that the education system rewards those who conform to the qualities required of the future workforce, ie, to be subordinate, obedient and disciplined.

Bourdieu – Cultural capital

- Bourdieu (1977) examined the role 'culture' plays in the education system. He argues that the education system (ie, teaching, books, exams and the language they employ) embody very middle- and upper-class cultural values (eg, literature, music) rather than those of the working class. Working-class pupils do not possess the cultural capital (ideas, language, tastes, values and lifestyle associated with a particular class) required for success. This means that middle-class pupils will generally do better than working-class pupils. This makes the school an institution that ensures middle-class dominance from one generation to the next.

Willis – learning to labour

Neo-Marxist sociologist Paul Willis (1977) used qualitative research (eg, observations and interviews) to study 12 working class boys (known as 'the lads') through their last 18 months at a comprehensive school and their first few months of work. Willis did not find that the lads were brainwashed by the education system into conforming to the norms and values of the school (eg, hard work, conformity and obedience to authority). Therefore, Willis rejects Bowles and Gintis' rejection of meritocracy and disputes the hidden curriculum. What he did find was that 'the lads' developed an anti-school culture, resisting and rejecting the norms and values supported by the school. They rejected the meritocratic ideology that claims working-class pupils can get on through hard work. Willis found:

- The counter-school culture. The lads formed an anti-school culture. They disobeyed the school's rules (eg, smoking, disrupting classes, truancy, sexism and racism). For the lads, such acts of defiance were ways of resisting the school's authority.
- Workplace. Willis followed the lads into their first jobs which were unskilled manual jobs, often in factories, where he found a shop-floor culture of male manual workers similar to the anti-school culture. They both involved lack of respect for authority, sexism and racism and 'havin a laff' to cope with boring and tedious work over which they had little control.

For Willis, the irony is that the lads' rejection of the school's ideology and their anti-school culture guarantee that they will fail at school, thereby ensuring that they end up in the manual work that capitalism needs someone to perform. Thus, their resistance to school ends up reproducing class inequality since they ended up in working-class jobs.

✔✗ Evaluation

✔ **Economy influences education.** The Marxist view that education is shaped by the economic system is still relevant today. Glenn Rikowski (2005), a Marxist, argues there has been a 'business takeover' of schools. For example, marketisation policies (eg, league tables and competition between schools), more emphasis on NVQs and BTECs, the privatisation of some educational services and business sponsorship of state schools (eg, academies) all point to the fact that the influence of business on education is stronger than ever.

✗ **There is non-supporting research evidence.** A limitation of Bowles and Gintis' correspondence theory/hidden curriculum is that Willis (1977) has produced research evidence that does not support it. Willis showed that many pupils actively resist authority, often forming anti-school subcultures, suggesting that the hidden curriculum is not always accepted by pupils who can show independent rather than conformist behaviour yet still end up in working-class jobs! Furthermore, Reynolds (1984) believes that some education encourages critical thinking of the education system, for example sociology, which teaches radical perspectives.

✗ **Willis's research is outdated.** A limitation of Willis's research study is that the study was carried out over thirty years ago and so is now outdated. With the decline in manual work, attitudes to education among working-class males have become more positive: they may not reject school as often today as they did in the past. Furthermore, his study of only 12 boys in one school is unlikely to be representative and therefore generalisations from the findings need to be treated with caution.

✗ It ignores gender and ethnicity. Marxist explanations have been criticised because they focus too much on the relationship between social class and education and ignore inequality based on gender or ethnicity. For example, feminists see education (like the family) as an instrument that socialises gender inequality.

✗ It does not take into account an upwardly-mobile working class. Marxist explanations fail to recognise the extent to which education has benefited some working-class pupils, allowing them to move upwards socially. For example, many Afro-Caribbean families have now moved from working-class to middle-class positions.

Practice exam questions

AS level type questions

1. Define the term 'myth of meritocracy'.   **[2 marks]**

2. Define the term 'cultural capital'.   **[2 marks]**

3. Define the term 'correspondence principle'.   **[2 marks]**

4. Define the term 'hidden curriculum'.   **[2 marks]**

5. Define the term 'reproduction of social inequality'.   **[2 marks]**

6. Using **one** example, briefly explain how education may mirror the workplace.   **[2 marks]**

7. Using material from **Item (...)** and your knowledge, evaluate the Marxist view of our understanding of the role of education.   **[20 marks]**

A level type questions

1. Outline **two** features of the Marxist view of education. (Jan 2001).   **[4 marks]**

2. Outline **two** criticisms that could be made of Marxist views of education.   **[4 marks]**

3. Outline **two** ways in which school mirrors features of the workplace.   **[4 marks]**

4. Outline **three** ways in which the correspondence principle operates within school.   **[6 marks]**

5. Outline **three** ways in which Marxists see school as being similar to the world of work.   **[6 marks]**

6. Applying material from **Item (...)**, analyse **two** ways in which schooling in capitalist society may mirror the world of work.   **[10 marks]**

7. Applying material from **Item (...)** and your knowledge, evaluate the view that 'while Marxist and functionalist approaches focus on similar issues, they reach different conclusions about the role of education'.   **[30 marks]**

8. Using material from **Item (...)** and your knowledge, evaluate the view that the main function of the education system is to reproduce and legitimise social inequalities.   **[30 marks]**

9. Using material from **Item A** and your knowledge, evaluate the view that the education system exists mainly to select and prepare young people for their future work roles.   **[30 marks]**

The AQA specification: **Education**

- The relationship, role and functions of the education system, including its relationship to the economy and class structure.

The exam requires that you are able to:

▶ Describe and evaluate the role of education in relation to the economy.

Introduction

There is a close connection between education and the economy, with the education system being shaped by the demands from the economy. Notably, many of the changes in the education system have come about when there has been fear about how well the British economy is doing compared to the economies of other countries. This has had an enormous impact on what is taught in schools and colleges (as you will see below). Theresa May (2016), the Conservative Party leader, included education in her important long-term economic plan by introducing many more apprenticeships and vocational training schemes for young people as a means to boost the economy to compete in a global market.

Education before 1988

- In Britain, the 1870 Forster Education Act introduced a basic system of primary education (religious matters, literacy and numeracy) for all children up to the age of 10. This was introduced as a direct response to industrialisation, with the hope that a basic education would create a more skilled and literate workforce, giving Britain a competitive edge in the growing industrial economy of the time. As the needs of the economy grew, elementary schooling became a compulsory requirement and the school leaving age rose gradually in the pre-war years. In 1889, it was raised to 12, and in 1918 to 14.

Education from 1940-1965

- In the post-war years, the education system was drastically reformed by the Butler Education Act (1944). This Act brought about a tripartite system of secondary education, so called because there were three different types of schools, each catering for different aptitudes and abilities, seen as the best way to prepare pupils for the world of work. The 11+ exam, a test to determine pupils' academic ability, was used to determine which secondary school pupils attended. Abler children, that is, those who passed the 11+ exam, were offered a place at a grammar school, whilst those who failed the 11+ were offered a place at a secondary technical or secondary modern school which favoured a more vocational training (preparing people for the world of work, eg, electricity, metalwork, woodwork or cookery). It was hoped that the academic/vocational divide would prepare young people for the range of occupational needs demanded by the economy.

Education from 1965-1979

- By the 1960s, opinions were beginning to change regarding the effectiveness of the tripartite system. As Giddens (1993) suggests, sociological research began to highlight how the system wasted talent by failing to allow all learners to reach their potential because of social class. So in 1965, the Labour government then in power abolished the tripartite system and replaced it with a comprehensive system. This single type of school educated all pupils, regardless of academic ability, and thus removed the class divide of the old tripartite system. The aim was to bring equal opportunity and allow all pupils to succeed by means of their own effort and abilities, thus providing the economy with a fairer 'fit' of skills and talent.

Education in the 1970s

- During the 1970s, the British economy faced a period of economic stagnation (recession). Politicians were concerned about the rising levels of employment this created and, in particular, rising youth employment. The then Labour Prime Minister, James Callaghan, gave a famous speech at Ruskin College (1976) which was critical of the role of the education system. Callaghan argued that the education system needed to be improved and that more vocational training was needed in schools and colleges in order to meet the requirements of industry. This speech was written in response to increasing pressure from industry to respond to their needs (Jones 1996). This initiated the 'Great Debate' (between politicians, teachers, educationalists and parents) on the future role of education, which subsequently led to a broader range of educational and vocational training schemes 'to improve relations between industry and education'. It was the belief at that time that a skilled workforce would help improve the failing British economy.

Education in the 1980s

- During the 1980s, the British economy was still in recession, with a decline in the heavy industrial and manufacturing sectors, and rising unemployment. The then Conservative government, under Margret Thatcher (1979-1997), felt that high unemployment was the result of schools failing to teach appropriate work skills. This 'skills crisis' led to the introduction of the New Vocationalism policy aimed at combating youth unemployment and increasing young people's level of skills. Under New Vocationalism, a number of schemes were introduced, such as Apprenticeships and Training Schemes which essentially combined 'on the job' training and studying with the aim of achieving a qualification or certification (eg, YTS, TVEI, NVQs and GNVQs).

Education from 1997 to 2010

- Between 1997 and 2010, a Labour government was in power. Many of the policies began by the previous Conservative government were continued with the aim of forging closer links between education and the economy, for example:
- Specialist schools (schools with a special focus on certain subject areas (technology, languages, science, business, music, etc) and Academies were introduced, partly to provide a skilled workforce. Essentially the aim was to improve standards of learning as well as to raise the aspirations and career prospects of pupils from all backgrounds, including the most disadvantaged. It was hoped that specialist schools would provide pupils with a broader range of skills suited to the needs of the economy. Academies strengthened relationships with the wider community by connecting with local businesses which gave schools the opportunity to provide their pupils with specialist education and work-related training experiences.

- Vocational GCSE's and the 14 -19 diploma programmes/qualifications (these replaced GNVQs) were phased in from 2009 alongside the traditional GCSE/A level route. The aim was to create parity of esteem with academic courses and thus bridge the vocational/academic divide by offering improved vocational programmes. It was hoped that these courses would raise standards and produce the more highly-skilled workers needed by the economy.

- The Increased Flexibility Programme (IFP) was introduced in 2002 for 14 to 16 year olds (Key Stage 4) to provide vocational learning opportunities by allowing young people to attend college for one or two days per week to follow vocational qualifications not available at school.

Education from 2010 to 2015

- From 2010 to 2015, the coalition government in power (Conservatives and Liberal Democrats) was concerned at the downward trend in the number of unskilled jobs available in the UK. One way to ensure that Britain had a suitably-skilled workforce was the extension of compulsory education, which raised the age at which children were allowed to leave education or training to 17 in 2013 and 18 in 2015. This brought with it various initiatives to allow schools and colleges more options in providing vocational education and training in the hope that many more young people would leave education in a much better position to find skilled employment.

Sociological Perspectives

- Functionalists and Marxists have different opinions on the relationship between education and the economy. Functionalists consider the relationship between education and the economy as positive, as education has a key role in socialising and preparing young people for their future roles in society and the economy. Marxists, on the other hand, see education as preparing young people for exploitation in a capitalist society and reinforcing social conflict. Marxists argue that the relationship between education and the economy is presented as fair and natural when in reality it serves to justify inequality and unequal power relationships.

Functionalism

- Durkheim (1857-1917) sees education as a 'miniature society' that prepares young people for their future role in society by equipping them with the right behaviour and attitudes necessary for their future jobs. For example, schools help develop social skills, such as the ability to interact and cooperate with each other, as this promotes social solidarity, which is important in the world of work.

  Parsons (1952) argues that education teaches young people the principle of meritocracy, ie, that everyone is given an equal chance to do well, and that those who succeed do so due to their own hard work and ability. The principle of meritocracy is important because it helps young people make the transition from particularistic standards (in the family) to universalistic standards (society) (see exam notes for Functionalism); that is, a person's status is mainly achieved not ascribed, or, in other words, is not defined by who you are or where your family is from. This is essential for cooperation in society.

Davis and Moore (1945) see the education system as selecting students for their future work roles, known as role allocation. It does this through a filtering process which assesses children's ability (via streaming, setting and examination), so that the most able get the best qualifications and are allocated to the most important Jobs.

Marxism

- Marxists argue that education prepares young working-class people to be exploited in capitalist society. They argue that the education system appears to be meritocratic by offering everyone an equal chance to do well, but that this is a myth. They see education as continuing to reproduce class inequality from one generation to the next, through the practice of streaming and labelling, which denies working-class children equal opportunity. Differences in achievement can be blamed on the individual (eg, 'not working hard enough') rather than on a system which makes unequal achievement seem fair and just. According to Marxists, the education system legitimises class inequality by making it appear that working-class children have an equal chance in the economy, when in reality they do not. The majority of working-class people, with low or no qualifications and skills, will end up in poorly-paid jobs to be exploited by the capitalist (educated) class.

Bowles and Gintis (1976) suggest that the relationship between education and the economy is based on the correspondence principle, whereby education is organised and run in the same way as the world of work. They argue that the correspondence principle is taught through the hidden curriculum, ie not explicitly taught but informally learnt during everyday lessons and the workings of the school (eg, punctuality, obedience, pupil acceptance of authority, rewards and so on). Therefore, the similarity between education and the world of work, according to Bowles and Gintis, creates new generations of workers ready to be exploited by the capitalist class.

Paul Willis (1977) in 'Learning to Labour' takes a neo-Marxist approach to analyse the relationship between education and the economy. The study of 12 working-class boys (known as the 'lads') through their last 18 months at a comprehensive school and the first few months of work found that the lads' experience of school led them to accept that 'education was not for them' and the formation of an anti-school subculture (disobeying school rules and authority). Willis concludes that working-class culture contributes to kids getting working-class jobs. The lads' anti-school culture guarantees that they will fail at school, thereby ensuring that they end up in the manual work that capitalism needs someone to perform. Thus, their resistance to school ended up reproducing class inequality since they ended up in working-class jobs.

Working-class identity, education and the economy

- Louise Archer et al (2010) apply the concept of habitus, which refers to a person's social identity (their outlook on life, interest, tastes and lifestyle) to explain why the social identity of working-class pupils is linked to educational failure. Schools devalue and stigmatise working-class identities as worthless (eg, 'hoodies', 'onesies', Nike tracksuits, 'chav-like behaviour') and not conducive to educational success. As a result, according to Archer et al, working-class pupils who invest in 'Nike-style' identities, actively choose to reject school because it does not fit in with their identity: it is 'not for them'. This limits their chances of academic success and, consequently, prepares them for lower-level unskilled jobs in the economy.

Feminism

- Feminism has focused on how a patriarchal society has dominated the relationship between education and the economy. In the 1970s, the feminist movement had considerable success in changing social attitudes and legislation towards women (eg, the Equal Pay Act of 1970 and the Sex Discrimination Act of 1975), especially their economic position in society. This transformation has led to reforms in the education system (eg, the introduction of the National Curriculum) and raised aspirations and expectations. Where girls were once excluded from schooling, they are now doing better than boys in most subjects and at all levels. However, women are still under-represented in certain types of jobs and in senior positions.

- According to Mary Hamilton (2003) many jobs still reinforce gender inequality, being perceived as either 'female' or 'male' (eg, nursing = female; engineering = male), which can influence boys' and girls' job aspirations. This is reinforced by gender-specific vocational courses, such as 'health and social care' which is dominated by female students, reinforcing the idea that care work is 'women's work'.

✔✗ Evaluation

✗ **Tripartite system.** The tripartite system failed to address a social class divide in education. Two-thirds of middle-class boys were likely to go to grammar schools, compared to one-third of working-class boys (Halsey et al 1980). This meant working-class pupils were more likely to be labelled a 'failure', resulting in low motivation and subsequently low educational achievement and, thus, less likely to go to university. This suggests that the tripartite system maintained class inequality by allocating the different classes to different types of schools offering different life opportunities, and thus allowing the loss of potential talent that could be beneficial to the economy.

✗ **Comprehensive system.** A major criticism of the comprehensive system is that pupils were streamed or set according to their ability. The problem with this is that a clearly disproportionate number of middle-class pupils were placed in high-ability streams or sets, whereas a disproportionate number of working-class pupils were placed in the bottom groups. This meant the comprehensive system was reinforcing occupational aspirations based on social class, with middle-class pupils being rewarded with better jobs than working-class pupils, something the comprehensive system was attempting to avoid.

✗ **Functionalism.** Some critics argue that Davis and Moore's theory, that the most important functional jobs are given to the best-qualified who are therefore rewarded more financially, is not relevant in contemporary British society. For example, football and the birth of 'celebrity culture' (eg, Big Brother contestants) have provided some individuals with fame and fortune without formal training or qualifications.

✘ **Vocational training/ New Vocationalism.** Phil Cohen (1984) questions the real purpose of vocational training, and argues the real aim was to create 'good' attitudes and 'work discipline' rather than actual job skills. In this way, young people came to accept a likely future of low-paid and -skilled work. New Vocationalism has been criticised by Finn (1987), a neo-Marxist, who claims that there was a hidden political agenda to vocational training. He argues that it provided cheap labour for employers of young people and also helped the government by reducing politically embarrassing unemployment statistics.

✘ **Upwardly-mobile working class.** Marxist explanations fail to recognise the extent to which education has benefited some working-class pupils, allowing them to move upwards both economically and socially. For example, many Afro-Caribbean pupils who have done well academically have now moved from being working-class to being middle-class.

✘ **Paul Willis's research.** A limitation of Willis's research study is that the study was carried out over thirty years ago and so is now outdated. With the decline in manual work, attitudes to education among working-class males have become more positive: they may not reject school as often today as they did in the past. Furthermore, his study of only 12 boys in one school is unlikely to be representative and therefore generalisations from the findings need to be treated with caution.

Practice exam questions

AS level type questions

1. Define the term 'vocational' education.   **[2 marks]**

2. Applying material from **Item (...)**, outline and explain two ways in which educational institutions can contribute to the economy.   **[10 marks]**

3. Applying material from **Item (...)** and your knowledge, evaluate the different ways in which educational institutions can contribute to the economy.   **[20 marks]**

A level type questions

1. Applying material from **Item (...)**, and your knowledge, evaluate the Functionalist and Marxist approaches to the relationship between education and the economy   **[30 marks]**

The AQA specification: **Education**

- Differential educational achievement of social groups by social class, gender and ethnicity in contemporary society.

The exam requires that you are able to:

▶ Describe and evaluate the relationship between class and educational achievement.

Introduction

There is a clear relationship between a person's social class and their educational achievement. Upper/middle-class children have continuously outperformed working class-children in education. This has been the case throughout the 20th century, regardless of how the education system has been organised. For example:

— Primary school children. Middle- and upper-class children do much better in National Curriculum Tests (NCTs or SATs) than working-class children.

— GCSE and A level performance. About three quarters of children from middle- and upper-class backgrounds get five or more GCSE A*– C, whereas less than a third of working-class children achieve this. Working-class pupils are more likely to take vocational courses then academic AS and A-Level subjects and are less likely to do better than middle-class pupils.

— University. Middle- and upper-class children are approximately five times more likely to go to university than working-class children.

Sociologists have suggested several different explanations for why upper- and middle-class pupils do better than working-class pupils. They have grouped their explanations into two broad categories:

— External factors—factors outside school

— Internal factors—what goes on inside the school

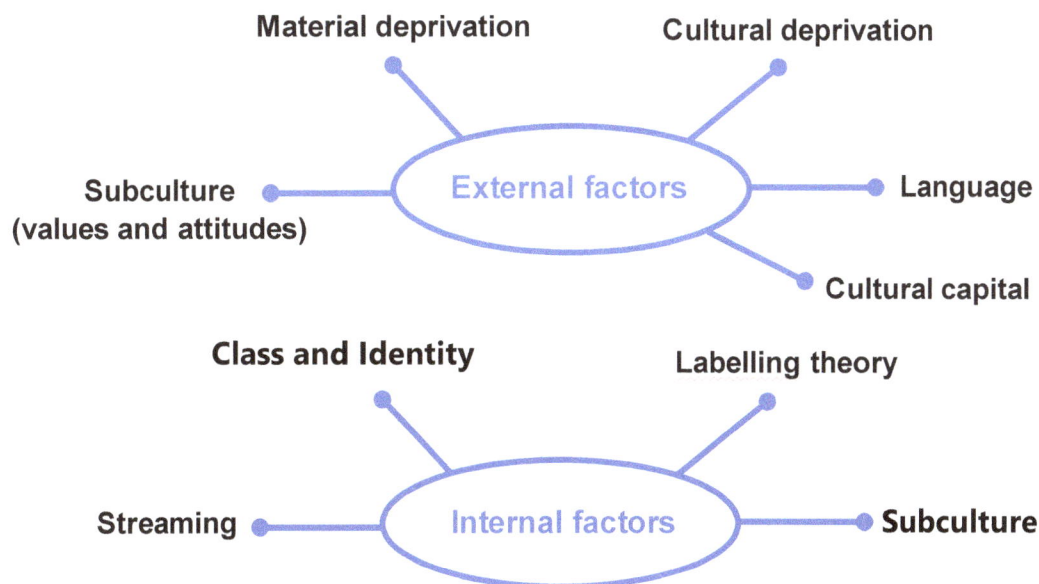

External factors

Some sociological theories as to why working-class children do not perform as well as middle-class children link to the home environment. Such theories suggest that the education system itself is not to blame, but that certain types of home environments are a key contributory factor to the under-achievement of many working-class children.

Cultural deprivation theory

Sociologists argue that there is a link between the right type of culture and educational success. 'Culture' refers to having the values, beliefs, behaviour, attitudes and knowledge that society regards as important for educational success, which are transmitted during primary socialisation, ie, that from parent to child. Therefore, cultural deprivation theory suggests that working-class children perform less well academically because they are socialised differently to those from the upper and middle classes. This means the working class 'lacks' or is 'deficient' in the culture required for educational success, and is thus at a disadvantage in the educational system. There are many aspects to cultural deprivation theory, but they can be broadly broken into three main categories:

— Cognitive development (intellectual development, eg, learning, reasoning and problem-solving).
— Linguistic deprivation (language development).
— Working-class subculture (values and attitudes).

- **Cognitive development.** Research evidence suggests that intellectual development is closely linked to social class. One explanation is that working-class parents do not engage with and stimulate their children as much as middle-class parents, partly because of the lack of books and educational toys, and partly because of the quality of interaction between the parent and the child. The child's intellect is therefore not developed. This explanation suggests that certain working-class parenting styles can have an impact on the child's cognitive development.

- **Linguistic deprivation.** The quality of language may account for class differences in educational achievement. Members of the working class are socialised into a particular type of language code which is inadequate in the education system, and which can contribute to their low educational success. Bernstein (1971) distinguishes between two distinct linguistic codes:

   — Elaborated code, which involves having a wide vocabulary and sophisticated grammar and which means explanations, verbal or written, are clearly understood by everyone.

   — Restricted code, which is characterised by a limited vocabulary and limited use of grammar which means explanations, verbal or written, are not clearly understood by everyone, and thus will often require more description and/or need to be supplemented by non-verbal cues, such as gestures, for other people to make sense of what they are saying.

Middle-class children can readily switch from one code to the other, while working-class children are limited to the restricted code. The elaborated code is the one used in the educational system by teachers, exams, textbooks, university interviewers, etc. This gives the middle class an educational advantage.

- **Working-class subculture.** Sugarman (1970) argues different social classes have different values and attitudes towards education. He argues that middle-class parents value education in a way which underpins educational success and that working-class values are different from those of the middle class. He has identified three major features of working-class values. Each of these 'subcultural' values places children from a working-class background at a disadvantage in the education system.

  — Immediate gratification. Members of the working class tend to want rewards (gratification) 'now' rather than making sacrifices for future rewards, eg, job = equals money = immediate material benefits. The middle class, on the other hand, practises deferred gratification (putting off today's pleasure for future gains), eg, investment in their children's education = good career progression = greater financial rewards.

  — Fatalism. Working-class children accept their social and economic position in life: they do not believe they can change or improve it with individual effort put into school. (Think of the 'lads' in the study by Paul Willis 'Learning to Labour' (1977)).

  — Low parent interest. The working class is less likely to look at the long-term benefits of being in the education system, and therefore less likely to value the importance of education. For example, working-class parents show less interest in their child's education than middle-class parents (eg, they are less likely to attend parents' evenings, less interested in their child's studies and progress and less likely to have interaction with teachers by phone or email).

Material deprivation theory

Some sociologists have argued that it is not that children are culturally deprived, but that they lack sufficient resources (ie, they are materially deprived). Material deprivation theory argues that poorer pupils fail at school because they come from environments that are deficient in certain factors which are important for educational success, such as:

  — Low income, meaning a lack of educational books, toys, trips, computer/internet access, or inability to afford extra private tutoring, or university fees.

  — Poor housing such as overcrowded or cramped homes, meaning children do not have somewhere quiet to study. Homeless children or those living in temporary accommodation are more likely to be absent from school.

  — Poor diet which can lead poor health, entailing illnesses and absences from school, and lack of concentration in class due to hunger.

Cultural capital theory

- **Cultural capital** can be understood as having two components. There is 'cultural capital' (eg, having the right knowledge, attitude, values, skills and behaviour) and 'economic capital' (wealth). Bourdieu (1977), a Marxist, who coined the term 'cultural capital', claims that in order to do well in the education system, students must possess a certain level of cultural capital. It is for this reason that middle-class families have higher educational success than working-class families, because they have a greater 'quantity' of cultural capital.

— According to Bourdieu, the middle class uses its economic capital to convert this into educational capital which helps their children to obtain good educational qualifications (eg, by sending them to private schools or paying for extra tuition). This, in turn, leads to their children obtaining highly-paid jobs. This 'cultural capital' is then passed onto their own children, thus reproducing the advantages of the middle-class from one generation to the next.

✓✗ Evaluation

Cognitive development

✔ **Supporting research study.** A longitudinal study, 'The Effective Pre-School and Primary Education' (2007, Institute of Education), found that the 'home learning' climate strongly predicts a child's intellectual development by the age of ten - even after five full years in primary school). The study suggests that upper- and middle-class parents stimulate and engage more in terms of dialogue and play than working-class children, which helps children and thus affects later educational achievement.

✗ **School factors.** The view that working-class parents do not stimulate or challenge their children intellectually has been criticised. Some sociologists would agree that parenting style may play a part but there are school factors which can also contribute to working-class under-achievement, eg, teachers' low expectations lead to low performance (negative labelling).

✗ **Poverty.** Working-class students may drop out of education earlier because their parents earn a low income rather than because of a lack of motivation and parental encouragement.

Linguistic deprivation

✔ **Supporting research evidence.** There is supporting research evidence for linguistic deprivation. Davie et al (1972), in the National Child Development study, found that the parent's social class was strongly related to the child's reading attainment at the age of 7, with significant different reading abilities between working-class and middle-class children. This shows that children's reading ability is strongly related to class, suggesting literacy deficiency should be tackled at home and not be left until the child reaches the education system.

✗ **Just different.** Labov (1973) criticises the linguistic deprivation explanation as a reason for differences in educational achievement. He investigated low-income Afro-Caribbean American children from Harlem. He concluded that their speech patterns were not inferior, just different, and found that working-class children were more effective in making their point whereas middle-class children tended to 'waffle' and add irrelevant details.

✗ **Language distinction too simplistic.** Gaine and George (1999) argue that Bernstein's language distinction is too simplistic; there are differences in the use of elaborated language codes within middle-class families as well as in the use of restricted language codes within working-class families. This suggests that it is difficult to make generalisations about working- and middle-class families because they use language in a variety of ways.

Different types of cultural values

✔ **Supporting research study: 'Pushy' middle class parents.** A study by Gianni De Fraja (2010) found the level of parental involvement has a greater impact on a pupil's achievement than the efforts of the school. He found that middle-class pupils do better at school than working-class pupils because middle-class parents are more 'pushy' about their education. Parents from middle-class backgrounds are prepared and able to put in the extra effort to help children with homework, read bedtime stories and regularly attend parents' evenings, which all encourage children to work hard and do well at school. However, schools and teachers also put more effort in with pupils from better-off homes, because of the pressure exerted by pushy middle-class parents. The implications of this study suggest that policies aimed at improving parental effort could be effective in increasing children's educational attainment.

✘ **Does the working class have different values?** The view that working-class families have different values to those of the middle class has been questioned The idea that working-class values are fixed is wrong; not all working-class families have fatalistic and 'immediate gratification' values but hold the same educational values as the middle class: they are just as concerned and ambitious for their children's success in education. Many working-class parents work long hours, and have less flexibility and choice in their working hours. Not spending as much time interacting with their children or visiting a school is not due to lack of interest or encouragement among working-class parents but purely due to the constraints imposed by their jobs: they do not have the luxury of time that middle-class parents may have!

Cultural capital

✔ **Supporting research study.** There is supporting research evidence to show that cultural capital can improve educational achievement. Alice Sullivan (2001) carried out a self-completion questionnaire on 465 Year 11 pupils in four schools to assess their cultural capital. A range of questions included determining parents' social class (eg, by educational qualifications and occupations); reading (type and amount); type of TV programmes watched; and whether they visited art galleries, museums and theatres. She also tested their vocabulary and knowledge of famous cultural figures. She found that those who read complex fiction and watched serious TV documentaries developed wider vocabulary and cultural knowledge, indicating higher cultural capital. These pupils were more likely to be successful at GCSE level and more likely to be middle class. This shows that cultural capital is transmitted by higher-class parents to their children which, in turn, provides them with educational success.

Internal factors

There are factors within the education system that can also influence class differences in educational achievement. Sociologists known as interactionists have focused on the small-scale interactions between teachers and pupils and argue that such interactions can have an impact on the student's achievement. They have identified a number of related causes of under-achievement, such as labelling, self-fulfilling prophecy, streaming and pupil subcultures.

Labelling theory

- Labelling refers to how teachers categorise pupils as 'bright', 'troublesome', 'lazy', 'enthusiastic', etc. The labelling theory states that how teachers 'label' a student can affect their educational performance. Becker (1951) interviewed 60 teachers from Chicago high schools about their attitudes towards pupils, such as their ideal type of student (eg, work ethic, conduct, appearance and behaviour). He found that teachers held a positive and ideal view of middle-class pupils and preferred to teach them, whereas they held a negative view of working-class pupils and were less willing to teach them. Becker argues that the holding of such stereotypes would affect teachers' perceptions of pupils, their interaction with them, and subsequent educational achievement.

  Interactionists have generally concluded that teachers have often failed to assess their working-class pupils' academic potential objectively and instead have been very likely to assess students' academic potential in terms of such variables as their appearance, language, social skills and social class background rather than in terms of their real intellectual abilities. Working-class children have thus often been perceived by teachers as being on average less intelligent than middle-class children. Labelling can work through:

- **Self-fulfilling prophecy.** Teachers have a profound role in guiding their students into success or failure, and this is partly affected by their own mindset about the student. In the context of education, a 'prophecy' is a prediction a teacher will make at the start about a student by attaching a label, eg calling a boy a 'troublemaker'. This affects the teacher's perception of and behaviour towards the student (eg, their interaction with them). The boy picks up on this; his self-perception is influenced by the teacher's label and his behaviour reflects it: he slowly sees himself as a troublemaker. This confirms his teacher's labelling as accurate (hence, self-fulfilling prophecy). Teachers create self-fulfilling prophecies through labels they attach to pupils. Studies have shown that negative labels can easily promote under-achievement, whereas positive labels promote success. In terms of social class and educational achievement, teachers believe middle-class pupils are bright and will therefore succeed; working-class pupils tend to be given negative labels and are thus more likely to fail.

- **Subculture.** A subculture can be defined as a group whose beliefs, values and attitudes are different from those of mainstream culture, or the wider society. As a response to the way that pupils have been labelled and streamed, pupils may seek out others who have been similarly labelled and form their own subculture. Colin Lacey (1970) found that streaming can lead to:

  — Pro-school subculture being formed by pupils in higher-stream classes. They accept the school's rules, values and goals, such as homework, attendance and respect to teachers, and enjoy and conform to school life, lessons, activities, etc.

  — Anti-school subculture often being formed by those in lower-stream classes. They will engage in behaviour that rejects the school's rules, values and goals and often turns them upside-down, eg, disrespect towards teachers and a dislike of school, breaking school rules, avoiding doing schoolwork, playing truant and sabotaging their uniforms. Lacey argues that pupils form anti-school subcultures as a means of gaining status among their peer friends by, for example, rudeness, vandalism, smoking, bullying, and not doing their homework.

Working-class pupils tend to join an anti-school subculture which is likely to lead to educational failure. This becomes a self-fulfilling prophecy whereby schools and teachers will continue to deem working-class pupils as having lower ability when in reality they may have academic potential.

- **Streaming** (or setting) is the act of putting students with similar abilities in the same class and teaching them together for some or all subjects (eg, top set for the bright pupils, bottom set for the 'thick' pupils). Lacey (1970) argues that when streaming, setting or banding systems are in operation at school, working-class students were more likely to be consigned to lower streams, sets or bands even when in reality they often had very good academic potential. A study by David Gillborn and Deborah Youdell (2001) examined teachers' ideas of ability to decide which pupils have the potential to achieve five GCSE A*-C. They found that working-class and black pupils are less likely to be perceived as having the potential, and are more likely to be in a lower stream and be entered for lower-tier GCSEs. This process of institutional labelling and streaming not only widens the class gap between the working and middle class in terms of educational achievement but also creates a self-fulfilling prophecy: poor exam performance confirms the teacher's initial predication.

Pupil class identities and the school

Sociologists are also interested in how pupils' identities and educational success are shaped by social and cultural influences outside school. Louise Archer et al (2010) analysed the relationship between working-class pupils' self-identity and school, and how this can have an impact on their achievement. She shows that young people who subscribe to youth culture and working-class styles are limiting their own access to routes to academic success and that working-class young people are shown as belonging to a culture in which they recognise that educational success is not for them. To understand this relationship, she draws on Bourdieu's concepts:

- **Habitus** refers to a person's social identity, ie, who they are, which is made up of thoughts, values, how they speak, interest, lifestyle preferences and tastes (eg, fashion, music and socialising) and outlook on life. Social groups are formed with those who share a similar habitus—a person's habitus reflects a person social class. More importantly, habitus is developed by class. Habitus can be used to explain why middle classes do well in education: they belong to a class whose 'habitus' is similar to that of the school. For example, middle-class students often do not even have to make a decision about going to university because they simply expect to go. Working-class students, however, often feel out of place and uncomfortable and thus may drop out of education.

- **Symbolic capital and symbolic violence.** Schools and the middle class share a very similar habitus; therefore, middle-class pupils would have been socialised at home into sharing the school's habitus. Such a similar outlook on life would give middle-class parents 'symbolic capital' (eg, status and recognition) and schools will view the habitus of the middle class as correct. In comparison, the working-class habitus is viewed as worthless by the school. Bourdieu calls this rejection of working-class symbolic capital 'symbolic violence'. Defining the working-class lifestyle and tastes (habitus) as inferior will result in working-class students experiencing the world of education as alien and unnatural.

- **Education stigmatises working-class habitus.** Louise Archer et al (2010) examined the relationship between social identity and the aspirations of working-class students who were identified as being at risk of dropping out of education or unlikely to progress into post-16 education. Archer argues that many working-class pupils were conscious that society and school looked down on them. This symbolic violence led them to seek alternative ways of creating self-worth, status and value. They did so by investing heavily in 'style' (eg, clothing, hairstyle, make-up and jewellery), especially through consumer brands such as Nike which they associated with being 'cool' or 'hard' or having 'street cred'—which brought status recognition—or earned approval from peer groups. However, buying into such lifestyles brings conflict with schools and colleges (eg, dress codes). The school's middle-class habitus stigmatises working-class identities as rule-breakers and having 'poor' taste to the point where certain items of clothing associated with working-class youth such as 'hoodies' have become linked with criminality. Archer, believes that working-class pupils' investment in 'Nike-like' identities, not only caused them to be marginalised at school; but they also actively choose to reject education because it does not fit in with their identity or way of life.

- **The working class rejects higher education as undesirable and unrealistic.** 'Nike-style' identities also play a part in working-class pupils' rejection of higher education. This is because working-class pupils want to earn good money and reject education because they are keen to join the job market: being a student would mean not having the cash to pay for street styles. In addition, there is an underlying feeling for many young people that higher education was for others. Middle-class students are seen as unstylish and working-class students felt unable to access 'posh', middle-class spaces such as university and professional careers, which are seen as 'not for the likes of us.'

✔✗ Evaluation

Interactionist theory

✔ **Explains how teacher-student relations have an impact on education.** A positive contribution is that the interactionists highlight how the everyday running of a school can have an impact on a pupil's educational performance. This assumption suggests that students can be streamed on the basis of the teacher-student relationship, regardless of ability.

✔ **Can improve teaching methods.** Interactionist explanation has real-life application. It has highlighted important implications for the way teachers should be trained. As Wood (1983) explains, schools could improve teaching methods by reducing stereotyping and labelling, and thus reduce deviance in school.

✔ **Does not only deal with social background:** A strength of the interactionist explanation is that it can provide a detailed insight into the day-to-day life of educational institutions and show that educational attainment is not just based on external factors, eg, home background.

✔ **Supporting research evidence on labelling and self-fulfilling prophecy:** Rosenthal and Jacobson (1964) carried out a field experiment to investigate whether the effects of teachers' expectations on pupils' behaviour can affect their performance. In an elementary school in San Francisco, an IQ test was administered to all children from grades 1 to 6. At the beginning of the school year, teachers were told that in each class, 20% of the children were identified as being more academically able (known as 'spurters'). Unknown to the teachers, they were just randomly chosen. The way teachers interacted with these 'spurters' had an effect on their intelligence tests: the 'spurters' made more progress than their classmates a year later. This is explained by the 'self-fulfilling prophecy': pupils are defined by the teacher in a particular way (eg, 'bright'), and predictions are made about their future behaviour. The teacher then applies the label to the student, and the student responds and absorb that new identity and will act accordingly.

✔ **Supporting research evidence for the effects of streaming.** There is supporting research evidence by Ireson & Hallam (2001). They found that streaming and setting can have a negative effect on a child's educational performance, especially among low achievers. They found that setting may raise attainment in the top groups but not in the lower groups. For example, they found that low achievers in streamed groups in mathematics perform less well than similar pupils in mixed-ability groups. This suggests that streaming and setting for lower groups can have a negative effect on educational attainment.

✗ **Too many subject teachers mean labels cannot be used consistently.** Some sociologists have questioned exactly how the labelling process is conducted in school. A negative label from one subject teacher does not necessarily mean that the label will be passed on to all other subject teachers. Pupils are taught by a number of different teachers and the interaction between pupil and teacher will be different for each subject, so it is difficult to see how the labelling process can be applied consistently.

✗ **Ignores outside factors.** The interactionists have been criticised for placing too much emphasis on what goes on in school and ignoring outside factors such as home background (eg, poverty or marital discord), which might have a significant influence on what goes on in school.

✗ **Too deterministic.** The labelling approach is too deterministic; once pupils receive a label, the outcome is determined. However, pupils do not all react to labelling in the same way. Sometimes the student may choose to ignore, negotiate or reject the given label. For example, Mirza (1992) studied two South London comprehensives, focussing on 62 young black females aged 15-19. She challenges the idea that the labelling process can cause the under-achievement of black female students. She concludes that there is some racism within the school but denies that this has any effect on the self-confidence of black female students. Most black girls rejected the label and were determined to work hard for educational success. Additionally, Fuller (1984) demonstrated that black girls are more likely to reject negative labels given to them and will try to prove the teacher wrong.

AS level type questions

1. Define the term 'cultural capital'. [2 marks]

2. Define the term 'cultural deprivation'. [2 marks]

3. Define the term 'compensatory' education. [2 marks]

4. Define the term 'immediate gratification'. [2 marks]

5. Define the term 'material deprivation'. [2 marks]

6. Define the term 'deferred gratification'. [2 marks]

7. Using **one** example, briefly explain how the restricted speech code may lead to underachievement. [2 marks]

8. Using **one** example, briefly explain how cultural deprivation may affect educational achievement. [2 marks]

9. Outline **three** material factors that might cause working-class educational underachievement. [6 marks]

10. Outline **three** ways in which a child's cultural background may fail 'to equip them to meet the demands of schooling'. [6 marks]

11. Outline **three** features of the restricted speech code. [6 marks]

12. Outline and explain **two** ways in which the labelling process may lead to educational under-achievement for some pupils. [10 marks]

13. Outline and briefly explain **two** reasons why labelling theory may be 'an inadequate explanation of class differences in achievement'. [10 marks]

14. Outline and explain **two** ways in which pupils' home and family circumstances may affect their educational achievement. [10 marks]

15. Outline and explain **two** factors or processes within the school system that may influence working-class pupils' levels of achievement. [10 marks]

16. Applying material from **Item (...)** and your knowledge, evaluate the view that middle-class pupils' higher levels of achievement are the product of outside-school influences. [20 marks]

17. Applying material from **Item (...)** and your knowledge, evaluate the importance of cultural factors in causing social class differences in educational achievement. [20 marks]

A level type questions

1. Outline **two** material factors that may affect social class differences in educational achievement.

   [4 marks]

2. Outline **two** factors in pupils' home background which may affect their educational achievement, other than language spoken or parental aspirations.

   [4 marks]

3. Outline **three** reasons why some working-class parents fail to attend parents' evenings at their children's school.

   [6 marks]

4. Outline **three** ways that 'laddish' behaviour may make it difficult for boys to do well in school.

   [6 marks]

5. Applying material from **Item (...)**, analyse **two** factors outside school that contribute to working-class under-achievement.

   [10 marks]

6. Applying material from **Item (...)**, analyse **two** ways in which cultural deprivation may lead to educational under-achievement for working-class pupils.

   [10 marks]

7. Applying material from **Item (...)**, analyse **two** ways in which the role of language may lead to educational under-achievement for working-class pupils.

   [10 marks]

8. Applying material from **Item (...)** and your knowledge, evaluate the claim that factors outside the school are the main causes of working-class under-achievement.

   [30 marks]

9. Applying material from **Item (...)** and your knowledge, evaluate the claim that factors inside the school are the main causes of working-class under-achievement.

   [30 marks]

The AQA specification: **Education**

- Differential educational achievement of social groups by social class, gender and ethnicity in contemporary society.

The exam requires that you are able to:

▶ Describe and evaluate the relationship between ethnicity and educational achievement.

Keywords

- **Ethnic group (ethnic minority)** refers to a group of people that share the same culture, religion, language or geographic origin, that is different from the main culture of a country (eg, Pakistani, Somali or Polish).

Introduction

- It was only from the late 1970s that the relationship between ethnicity and education began to be systematically investigated by sociologists, partly because the ethnic population in Britain was very small, and the major focus of attention was then social class and educational achievement. The main crux of this topic is that sociologists want to know why some ethnic groups do better than others.

Problem of measuring educational achievement in ethnic groups

- One difficulty of investigating ethnicity and educational achievement is the UK is who we include in each ethnic group. Incorrect classification of ethnic minorities can often produce unreliable and distorted pictures of educational achievement in certain ethnic groups. For example, should all Asians be classified together? If so, this would not distinguish between Sikh, Indian, Pakistani and Bangladeshi pupils. This would be misleading, as there is a large difference among 'Asians' with regards to educational achievement. For example, Indians outperform white British pupils, whilst Bangladeshi pupils do not. So it is important that when talking about ethnicity and educational achievement that we clearly define which ethnic groups we are referring to.

Class and gender differences in educational achievement in ethnic groups

- We must also take into account the social class and gender differences within and between ethnic groups as these play a part in educational achievement; for example, middle-class pupils from ethnic groups perform better than working-class pupils from the same ethnic background. Girls do better than boys in some ethnic groups, for example Caribbean girls do better than Caribbean boys, whereas Indian boys do better than Indian girls.

The pattern and trends of ethnic educational achievement

The government's Department for Education (2013) found that the percentage of pupils achieving 5 or more GCSEs at grade A* to C or equivalent varies between different ethnic groups:

— Chinese and Indian pupils consistently have the highest five or more GCSEs (A* to C) of all ethnic groups, including White British.

— Black Caribbean, Pakistani, Bangladeshi and Gypsy/Roma and Traveller children consistently have the lowest five or more GCSEs (A* to C).

— The poorest White British pupils (on free school meal-indicators of low income) are now the worst performing group, and do not obtain five or more GCSEs (A* to C).

Reason for ethnic differences in educational achievement

When assessing reasons for differences in educational achievement between ethnic groups we need to consider:

— External factors—factors outside the school (eg, family, home and background)

— Internal factors—what goes on inside the school (eg, interaction between pupils and teachers)

External factors: outside school explanations

Cultural deprivation theory

Cultural deprivation theory suggests that certain ethnic groups are 'deprived' of inadequate socialisation in the home which puts them at a disadvantage in the educational system. Cultural deprivation has three explanations:

— Cognitive and linguistic skills.

— Attitudes and values.

— Family structure and parental support.

- **Cognitive development**. Cultural deprivation theory suggests that one reason ethnic-minority pupils do not do as well academically is that their intellectual and linguistic skills may be under-developed. The theory argues that parents of children from low-income backgrounds (eg, Bangladeshi and Black families) do not engage and stimulate their children, and thus the child's cognitive development (reasoning and problem-solving skills) will be underdeveloped which leaves them poorly equipped for school.

- **Linguistic skills.** Those Asians and Afro-Caribbeans who use 'Creole' (Caribbean English) or who do not have English as their first or main language will often have lower educational attainment than those whose first language is English. A study by Bereiter & Engelmann (1966) of black American children from low-income families found that their language skills were inadequate (eg, poor use of grammar, sentence formation and expression of ideas) which prevented the progression of intellectual ability, ie, educational progress.

- **Attitudes and values.** Cultural deprivation theorists argue that different ethnic minority groups have different values and attitudes towards education. Most parents value and have a positive attitude towards education, with many ethnic minority parents having high aspirations for their children. Parents socialise their children with values that underpin educational success (eg, hard work and sacrifice). Cultural deprivation theorists argue that Afro-Caribbean children are socialised into a 'subculture' which is fatalistic and focuses on immediate gratification, resulting in the lack of motivation to succeed.

- **Family structure and support.** The type of family structure and parental support (eg, socialisation and attitudes towards education) can affect the pupils' levels of educational attainment.

  — Family structure. Afro-Caribbean families have a high rate of one-parent households, which leads to an absence of male role models and a family life described by Pryce (1979) as 'turbulent'. This has a negative effect on the educational performance of Afro-Caribbean students. This is supported by the New Right, such as Murray (1984) who sees the high level of single-parent households and a lack of male role models as being a major factor in the under-achievement of some ethnic groups.

  — Parental support. Parental support can play an important role in the pupil's educational attainment. Some ethnic minority parents are more involved and have higher aspirations and expectations of their children's education. For example, Driver and Ballard (1981) found that Indian families are seen as tight-knit, supportive and placing great value and expectations on their children's education, as compared to working-class Afro-Caribbeans. Sewell (2009) argues that black pupils, especially boys, need to have greater expectations placed on them to raise their aspirations.

  Lupton (2004) suggest that lower working-class White British families have fairly indifferent or negative attitudes towards education and that, in turn, their children will have low aspirations towards their own education which explain why they under-achieve.

Social class and material factors

Material deprivation (or poverty) refers to the lack of physical or economic resources. Material deprivation theory suggests that some ethnic minorities under-achieve because they are deficient in important resources for educational success (eg, books, toys, computers and space). According to the Swann Report (1985), difference in ethnic educational achievement is due to 'socio-economic' factors (class and economic wealth). For example:

- **Social class.** The lowest-achieving education ethnic groups—Afro-Caribbean, Bangladeshi and Pakistani - have a much higher proportion of pupils from working-class backgrounds than White British people. The highest-achieving ethnic groups—Chinese, African and Indians - have a higher proportion of pupils from wealthier families and a middle-class background.

- **Economic factors.** Social class is closely linked to economic factors. The lower the person's class position, the lower the income. Bangladeshi, Pakistani and Afro-Caribbean pupils are more likely to be raised in low-income families than members of other ethnic groups (Pilkington, 2003). This means they are more likely to be unemployed, live in the poorest areas, face poor-quality housing and over-crowding and, generally, material disadvantage (lack of educational books and computer/internet access, inability to afford extra private-tutoring).

Therefore, educational under-achievement can be explained in terms of social class and economic disadvantage rather than ethnicity.

✓✗ Evaluation of external factors

✗ **Language skills may not play a part.** There is research evidence that does not support the view that poor linguistic skills are the cause for differences in educational achievement. Evidence suggests that the impact of language declines as children get older. For example, the Department of Education (2013) found that pupils with English as a second language did nearly as well in their GCSEs (A* –C) as those pupils who spoke English as their mother tongue. For example, Indian pupils do very well despite often not having English as their home language.

✗ **Afro-Caribbeans do not have different attitudes and values.** Afro-Caribbean parents are more likely to provide supplementary schooling at weekends and in school holidays and make more contact with schools than white or Asian parents. Afro-Caribbean parents are also more successful than other ethnic minorities and White British in getting their children to stay on in education at the end of their compulsory schooling, and to enter some form of higher education. This shows that Afro-Caribbean parent do not have different attitudes or values (ie, subcultural values) but in fact have high levels of aspiration for and interest in their children.

✗ **Minorities are culturally different not culturally deprived.** Keddie (1973) argues that ethnic-minority children are not culturally deprived but just culturally different. They under-achieve because schools are ethnocentric: biased in favour of white culture and against minorities.

✗ **Social class does not override ethnicity.** There is contradictory evidence from Gillborn and Mirza (2000) who argue that social class does not override the influence of ethnicity. Pupils from the same social class background but from different ethnic groups still show significant differences in achievement. For example, White middle-class pupils will always do better at GCSE than black Afro-Caribbean pupils; Chinese and Indians will always do better at GCSE than Pakistani and Bangladeshi pupils, even if they are from the same social class.

Internal factors: inside school explanations

Some sociologists argue that what happens within schools can have an impact on the experience of schooling for some ethnic pupils, which can influence their educational achievement. Some internal factors are:

— Teacher's labelling.

— Racism.

— Pupil response.

Teacher's labelling

Interactionists have focused on the small-scale interaction between teachers and pupils and argue that such interactions can have an impact on the student's achievement. They see labelling attached to certain ethnic minorities as the cause of under-achievement. Some ethnic-minority pupils' under-achievement has been attributed to teachers' negative labelling. Teachers may reflect in their behaviour and teaching some degree of conscious or unconscious racism (prejudices and discrimination) in the form of low expectations and negative attitudes which bring about feelings of low self-esteem and inferiority in pupils.

Black pupils

Research by Gillborn and Youdell (2000) found that some teachers gave 'unintentional 'racist labels to Afro-Caribbean pupils. White teachers expected black pupils to be less motivated and worse-behaved and saw them as 'troublemakers'. Black pupils felt that their teachers under-estimated their ability and picked on them. Gillborn and Youdell, argue that the impact of this was that:

- **Black pupils were placed in lower sets.** Teachers were more likely to enter a disproportionate number of black pupils in lower tiers of GCSE examinations than other boys of similar ability, which prevents them achieving higher grades in their examinations. This has a spiralling effect as the pupils will develop low-esteem and become less motivated to work hard in order to improve their grades. This will become a self-fulfilling prophecy as it confirms the teacher's initial expectation.

- **Pupil exclusion.** The consequence of negative labels attached to black pupils is that they are more likely to be disciplined (even when their behaviour is similar to that of other ethnic groups). This may explain the high exclusion rate for black students. The impact of this is that Afro-Caribbean pupils' absences from school put them at disadvantage as their education becomes disrupted and fragmented, and they cannot catch up on missing work, especially at GCSE level.

Asian pupils

Wright's (1992) study of four inner city primary schools examined the relationship between teachers and Asian children. He found evidence of negative stereotyping:

- Teachers often perceived them as a problem because of their limited or poor English skills. This meant that teachers would use simplistic language when speaking to them.

- They saw the learning and social difficulties of Asian pupils (eg, speaking English and interacting with other pupils) as something they could ignore, or paid less attention to them in class activity.

As a result, Asian pupils were marginalised and prevented from participating fully in class activity which affected their self-esteem and thus impacted their learning.

- Connolly's (1998) study of a multi-ethnic inner city primary school found that teachers saw Asian pupils as conformist, hard-working, obedient and producing high-quality work. When Asian boys misbehaved it was seen as more silliness than challenging the authority of the teacher. As a result, they were not punished as much as Afro-Caribbean boys who, if they behaved similarly, were viewed as more threatening. The study suggests the teachers' general stereotyping of Asian pupils is as high-achieving and well-behaved.

Pupil subcultures

- Pupils may react in different ways to the racist labelling in schools, such as by forming or joining a pupil subculture. Sewell (1998) carried out a study of Afro-Caribbean students and found that black pupils adopted a range of responses to teachers' racist labelling of them, including

- *Conformists* - black pupils who are keen to succeed academically, accept the goals of education and see good behaviour as the key to academic success.
- *Innovators* - black pupils who accept the goals of education and want to succeed academically but reject the school system or teachers' approval.
- *Retreatists* - black pupils who are disconnected from both the school and black subculture.
- *Rebels* – black pupils who reject the school's goals and conform instead to the stereotypical image of aggressive masculinity (the 'black macho lad').

Sewell's study is important because it shows the variety of black pupils' responses to racism in school varies considerably: not all pupils react in a negative way to teachers' labelling. However, regardless of how the pupils responded, Sewell found teachers tended to see them all in the same way (negatively). As result of the discrimination, many boys under-achieved.

Institutional racism

Some sociologists argue that although the racist labelling practised by some teachers is important, it is not an adequate explanation for the widespread ethnic differences found in achievement. Instead they argue that we must focus on institutional racism—that is, the whole education system may be institutionally racist. Institutional racism refers to a system in which, policies and practices unintentionally discriminate against ethnic minorities, for example in the following ways.

- **The ethnocentric curriculum.** Many sociologists argue that the British school curriculum in ethnocentric. This means that school teaches a curriculum that is based on one single (British white) culture, gives priority to white culture and the English language, and ignores or downgrades other cultures. For example:
  - *Foreign Languages.* Foreign languages taught in school are primarily European, rather than from ethnic minorities.
  - *History.* The history curriculum often covers only white history or history from a white perspective. For example, in the past, the history of the British Empire was presented mainly from the colonisers' point of view and created a view of a glorified past empire (British Imperialism) while at the same time ignoring the history of black and Asian culture.
  - *Religion.* Although Religious Studies covers other faiths than Christianity, the balance is still in favour of the Judeo-Christian heritage.
  - *Physical Education.* Physical Education usually only deals with contemporary Western sports.
  - *School holidays/assemblies.* The timing of school holidays or the nature of school assemblies may reflect Christian celebrations and beliefs rather than those of other faiths.
  - *Books.* Textbooks such as history and geography books still frequently carry degrading stereotypes of people from non-white races, who are often portrayed in a negative light as, for example, primitive' or 'uncivilised savages', in subservient roles or as people needing constant help and assistance to run their lives and country.
  - *Hidden curriculum.* Uniform and dress requirement or arrangements for changing in the shower for PE or games may conflict with the cultural norms (such as requirements for modesty in Islam).

- **Setting and streaming.** The CRE (Commission for Racial Equality, 1992) study of 'Jayleigh' school (not the real name) found that the school used setting as a barrier to a large number of Asian pupils: Asian pupils were consistently placed in lower sets than their ability warranted and were less likely to be entered for GCSE exams. A study by David Gillborn and Deborah Youdell (2001) found that black pupils are less likely to be perceived as having potential, are more likely to be in a lower stream, and are entered for lower-tier GCSEs.

- **Ethnic minority teachers.** Research by the Commission for Racial Equality (1988) showed that teachers from ethnic minority backgrounds are significantly under-represented in schools in Britain, particularly at the top of school organisational hierarchies. This offers few positive role models to pupils.

- **Marketisation.** Marketisation is a method of introducing competition between schools to raise educational standards, such as publishing league tables of exam results and having control over their selection procedures. Gilborn (1997) argues that negative stereotypes of certain ethnic groups may influence the schools' admission procedures. The selection procedure can be used by schools to filter out minority groups that are under-achievers or liability pupils, leading to ethnic segregation, with minority pupils failing to get into better secondary schools. For example, Moore and Davenport (1990) found that primary school reports were used to screen pupils with language difficulties.

✔✘ Evaluation of internal factors

✘ **Racism not linked to low achievement.** There is opposing research evidence by Fuller (1980) who argues that that not all labelling can lead to such negative outcomes. She studied a group of high-achieving black girls in year 11 of a London comprehensive and found that the girls resisted the negative labelling the teachers had imposed on them, and formed a pro-school subculture. They worked hard to succeed academically but without the appearance of doing so, and did not seek the teacher's approval. This study shows that some Afro-Caribbean girls may react in a positive manner which shows that teacher perception does not always lead to a negative outcome, for example low educational achievement.

✘ **Methodological issues.** There are methodological limitations on the studies by Wright, Gilborn and Mac an Ghaill which support the view that racism/negative labelling affects students' educational achievement. The studies used a research method known as ethnography which involves direct observation of a small group. Because the sample is small, it is not possible to make generalisations from the findings. This applies to all multi-ethnic schools.

✘ **Teachers are not racist.** Another limitation of the labelling theory is that not all teachers are racist. Hammersley (1998) found that even those teachers who were racist in private did not bring racism into the classroom. Smith & Tomlinson (1989) conclude that the school a child went to (whether it was in an inner-city or suburban area) was much more important in determining exam results than the child's ethnic background. Taylor (1981) identified many teachers as being very sensitive to multi-cultural issues and actively concerned about developing a fair policy towards ethnic minorities.

✗ **Ethnocentric curriculum.** Maureen Stone (1981) is critical of multicultural education as this produces further racial stereotypes. The change from an ethnocentric curriculum to a multicultural curriculum where Afro-Caribbean pupils are encouraged to pursue their own cultural awareness by means such as steel bands and sports pursuits during normal timetable confirms the old stereotypical racial views that Afro-Caribbean blacks are good at 'music' and 'sports' and made no real further advancement. This would suggest that multicultural education may be failing Afro-Caribbean boys by challenging boys away from academic mainstream education and into sports.

✗ **Multicultural education.** Attempts have been made to address the ethnocentric curriculum by introducing multicultural education. The aim of multicultural education is based on the view that learning about their own and different ethnic cultures and languages would raise the self-esteem of ethnic-minority groups and encourage better educational results. However, sociologists argue that Black or Asian culture is trivialised or represented in a 'token' way by recognising music, dance, religious ceremonies, customs and cuisine at a superficial level and ignoring deeper cultural/historical values.

✗ **Postmodernists.** A further limitation has been put forward by postmodernists who argue that, in a fragmented postmodern world, an individual constructs their own identity not only from their ethnic culture but also from among other major social sources of influences (eg, media, peers, and the internet). These different experiences mean that ethnic background becomes less important and may not play such a negative role such as low esteem and expectations of ethnic-minority pupils as suggested by sociologists.

Practice exam questions

AS level type questions

1. Define the term 'ethnocentric curriculum'. [2 marks]

2. Using **one** example, briefly explain how 'multicultural education' may reduce ethnic differences in achievement. [2 marks]

3. Outline **three** ways in which processes within schools may contribute to educational under-achievement among some ethnic groups. [6 marks]

4. Outline **three** ways in which an ethnocentric curriculum may operate in education. [6 marks]

5. Identify and briefly explain **two** reasons for ethnic differences in educational achievement. [10 marks]

6. Outline and explain **two** forms of pupil responses to teachers' racism and negative labelling. [10 marks]

7. Applying material from **Item (...)** and your knowledge, evaluate sociological explanations of ethnic differences in educational achievement. **[20 marks]**

8. Applying material from **Item (...)** and your knowledge, evaluate the view that ethnic differences in educational achievement are primarily the result of factors outside the school. **[20 marks]**

A level type questions

1. Outline **three** ways in which processes within schools may contribute to educational under-achievement among some ethnic groups. **[6 marks]**

2. Outline **three** examples of ways in which school is organised that may be ethnocentric. **[6 marks]**

3. Applying material from **Item (...)** analyse **two** factors inside school that lead to ethnic differences in educational achievement. **[10 marks]**

4. Applying material from **Item (...)** analyse **two** reasons why pupils from some minority ethnic groups achieve above average results in school. **[10 marks]**

5. Applying material from **Item (...)** and your knowledge, evaluate sociological explanations of ethnic differences in educational achievement. **[30 marks]**

6. Applying material from **Item (...)** and your knowledge, evaluate the claim that 'ethnic differences in educational achievement are primarily the result of school factors'. **[30 marks]**

The AQA specification: Education

- Differential educational achievement of social groups by social class, gender and ethnicity in contemporary society.

The exam requires that you are able to:

▶ Describe and evaluate the relationship between gender and educational achievement.

Introduction

These exam notes focus on the difference in educational achievement between female and male students. Sociologists are interested in:

— Why girls do better than boys at most subjects at all levels (eg, SATs, GCSE, A-Level).

— Why boys are under-achieving.

— Why girls and boys opt to study different subjects.

— How school helps to reinforce gender identities.

Gender patterns of educational achievement

In the past, boys have outperformed girls in their educational achievements at all levels, but since the 1980s the trend had shifted: girls are now doing better than boys in most subjects and at all levels. For example, in 2013, 66 % of girls achieved 5 or more GCSE or equivalent passes at grades A* - C, compared to 56 % of boys. Similarly, at A Levels, in 2013, 47% of girls achieved A or B grades as compared to only 42% of boys. Such important differences have led researchers to shift their focus to male under-achievement. This has become known as the gender gap: boys failing in education, or under-achieving in comparison with the educational achievements of girls.

Reasons for improvements in girls' educational achievement

Reasons for the improvements in girls' educational achievements can be divided into external and internal factors:

— External factors: factors outside the educational system (eg, the home and the family).

— Internal factors: factors within schools and the educational system (eg, coursework).

External factors: reasons for girls' improved achievement

The influence of feminism

- From the early 1970s, feminists attempted to improve the position of women in society by lobbying the government for legislative changes in order to bring about more equality for women in all areas of life, and raise awareness of gender inequality. The education system became more aware of gender inequalities, attempting to bring in a more 'girl-friendly' education. Greater gender awareness was reflected in teacher practices, such as avoidance of sexist gender-stereotyping; educational resources minimised sex bias and promoted more images of girls and women. The influence of feminism can offer a partial explanation for girls' improvement in education as it led both to reforms to the education system and the raising of aspirations and expectations.

Changes in women's employment

- **Changes in the law.** Over the last 30 years, there has been a major increase in women's employment. In 1971, 53% of women were employed, as compared to over 67% in 2013. This is partly due to changes in employment law. For example, the Equal Pay Act of 1970 meant it was illegal to pay women less than men for the same job or a job of equal value. The Sex Discrimination Act of 1975 made it unlawful to discriminate in employment on the grounds of sex or marital status, opening up many opportunities for women in the employment sector. As a result, female students are more optimistic about their future careers and are encouraged to do well academically.

- **The decline of traditional manual jobs.** Changes in industry over the last 50 years have meant a decline in traditional 'manual' male manufacturing jobs (eg, mining, shipping and manufacturing) and an increase in service sector, welfare and communications jobs, which value what women can bring to the economy (eg, interpersonal and conflict-resolution skills) and are therefore more likely to be taken up by females rather than males. As consequences of these changes in the economy, girls have become more ambitious as they can see better opportunities, and therefore work harder at school. This is supported by Francis (2001) who carried out research (interviews and observations) of twelve classes of 14-16-year-old girls in three London secondary schools in 1998-1999 and found that girls were more ambitious and aspired to a high-level professional career (eg, doctor, lawyer) rather than the traditional female occupations (eg, clerical work, hairdressing or beauty therapy) and so needed good educational qualifications.

Changes in the family

There have been major changes in the family since the 1970s. These include:

- An increase in divorce rates—about 40% of marriages now end this way.
- An increase in lone-parent families, over 90% of which are female-headed.
- Smaller families and more women staying single.

These changes are having an influence on girls' attitudes towards education. For example, the increase in female-headed lone-parent families requires girls to be more economically independent; women need to take on the responsibility as income-earners. This creates a new financially-independent, career-minded role model for girls and gives the message that they need to do well academically and get good qualifications to secure a good income.

Internal factors: reason for girls' improved achievement

- **Equal opportunities policies.** Feminist ideas of equality also influenced the education system, encouraging the belief that boys and girls should have equal opportunities in school. This is now widely accepted and has become the social norm in education. This has led to a range of policies to encourage greater opportunities for girls and to raise their academic performance in subjects like sciences and technology. For example, equal opportunity polices to help girls saw the implementation of programmes such as:

— GIST (Girls into Science and Technology) and WISE (Women into Science and Engineering), which aim to raise aspirations (through strategies such as visits from female scientists) of girls in science and technology.

— The National Curriculum, introduced in 1988, which meant it was compulsory for boys and girls to study the same common core set of subjects (eg, science). This prevented schools from 'filtering' students into 'relevant' subjects by gender and ensured that girls had access to the same academic opportunities as boys.

Boaler (1998) argues that equal opportunities policies meant schools have become more meritocratic, which means girls now have more equal opportunities than in the past. They are able to do better, because girls in general work harder than boys, and achieve more.

Coursework

- The National Curriculum of 1988 saw the introduction of a coursework assessment which contributes to exams at GCSE and A 'level in most subjects and which has helped female students achieve higher grades. (However, although girls outperform boys in coursework, they also outperform them in examinations.) Mitsos and Browne (1998) argue that girls are more successful in coursework because they tend be more conscientious and hard-working: they are more likely be better-organised when it comes to their coursework and spend more time on the content of the material and the way it is presented than boys. (However, there is a free choice after 16 and at that point, traditional gender choices still seem to happen.)

Role models

- Another explanation of why girls are doing much better academically is that there are more female teachers and head teachers in schools and these provide a positive, pro-educational role model for girls. Furthermore, the presence of female teachers also 'feminises' the learning environment; as a result, girls come to perceive educational success as a desirable feminine characteristic.

Teacher interaction

- The different ways in which teachers interact with boys and girls may be among the reasons girls do better than boys: teachers respond more positively to girls than boys. Croll and Moses (1990) found that girls receive less of the teacher's time than boys do, and that boys were more likely to be involved in negative interactions with the teacher, (telling-off, punishment), suggesting some boys may be labelled in a negative way which may affect their educational achievement. Howe (1997) found that teachers respond more positively to girls than boys because they see girls as more cooperative, and boys as more disruptive. This may have an impact on the girls, as positive interactions will raise girls' self-esteem and thus have an effect on their levels of educational achievement.

Selection and league tables

- Marketisation policies such as the publication of exam 'league tables' and the use of student selection has created a more competitive climate amongst schools. Marketisation has meant that girls are seen as more desirable recruits than boys, as they achieve better exam results. Boys are seen as a liability because they are low-achieving and more likely to be badly-behaved, which will affect the school image, just as poor exam results will affect their position in the league tables. As a result, girls are more likely to secure a place in a good school and, in turn, are more likely to achieve better exam results.

Explanations for the under-achievement of boys

Sociologists are concerned as to why boys have failed to improve their educational achievements at the same rate as girls. Some possible explanations why boys are under-achieving are:

Literacy differences

- Poor language and literacy skills: according to the DfEE (Department of Education), the gap between boys and girls in terms of literacy is already established by the age of 7. By the time pupils reach secondary school, girls are ahead of boys.

  — *Early socialisation.* During early stages of their life, children are encouraged to display gender-appropriate behaviour and are given gender-appropriate toys: boys will spend more time playing (eg, with mechanical toys) and are less likely to be read to by parents, whereas girls are more likely to read and be read to by parents.

  — *Leisure interests.* During primary and secondary schooling, boys' leisure interests are focused more on video games and sports activities, which do not encourage the development of language and communication skills, whereas girls are more likely to focus on, for example, reading, writing and conversing.

This suggests that boys' poorer literacy and language skills hinder them in their exams as many subjects are literacy-based.

The decline of traditional male jobs

- Since the 1980s, globalisation has led to the decline of traditional manufacturing industries in the UK (eg, steel, shipping, car plants and mining). Mac an Ghaill (1994) argues that de-industrialisation led to working-class men experiencing high levels of unemployment, and as a result no longer being the 'breadwinners' within the family. The led to a male crisis of masculinity: an identity crisis of what men's role or purpose is in the family and society. Working-class boys may see little point in striving for qualifications since the jobs they would have traditionally gone into have disappeared. This undermines their self-esteem and motivation and so they give up trying to achieve.

Laddish subculture

Some sociologists argue that the growth of laddish subcultures (being 'macho' and 'anti-learning') has contributed to boys' under-achievement. According to Forde et al (2006), in order to maintain their masculinity, boys will often adopt four strategies:

— Withdrawal of effort.

— Rejection of academic work.

— Avoidance of the appearance of work.

— Disruptive behaviour.

Forde et al found that laddish behaviour was based on the idea that working hard at school is uncool and undermining of masculinity, and those who did work were viewed as 'swots' or described as 'keeno'. He found that boys based their laddish behaviour on the dominant view of masculinity: they acted tough, messed around, disrupted lessons and rejected schoolwork as feminine. This explanation suggests that poor behaviour and lack of effort is the reason some boys under-achieve.

Feminisation of schooling

According to Sewell (2006), another possible factor in boys' falling behind in education is that schools have become feminised. This means they no longer nurture 'masculine traits', eg, competitiveness and leadership. Evidence for 'feminisation' comes from:

— Female teachers. Most classroom teachers are likely to be women, who often outnumber men by a ratio of 6 to 1 in primary schools. The shortage of male role models gives the perception that educational success is feminine.

— Coursework. Educational assessment has been feminised by the introduction of coursework which disadvantages boys.

— Feminine styles of teaching. The way in which the curriculum is delivered by female teachers in the classroom, eg, the use of discussion, creativity, elaboration, expression of ideas and abstract concepts rather than the mechanical 'hands-on' approach which boys prefer.

Gender and subject choice

Despite the introduction of the National Curriculum, which attempted to remove bias in subject choice, there continues to be a difference in the subjects chosen by boys and girls.

• **The National Curriculum.** Some subjects are compulsory for boys and girls to study at GCSE, but where choice is possible, boys and girls choose differently. Boys are more likely to study technological and science-based subjects (eg, Design and Technology) whereas girls tend to choose arts, humanities and social science subjects (eg, Drama, Psychology).

• **Post-16 education.** All the sciences, engineering and technology are still dominated by males, whereas all the humanities, languages and arts are dominated by females. This has important implications as it has a considerable effect on the type of employment for which individuals are qualified.

Explanations of gender differences in subject choice

Sociologists have put forward a number of reasons for gender differences in subject choice:

- **Early socialisation.** Murphy and Elwood (1998) argue difference in subject choice has its roots in early differences in how boys and girls are socialised. As a results of differences in early socialisation, boys and girls have different tastes in reading. Boys tend to read hobby books, which develops an interest in the sciences, whereas girls tend to read stories about people. This may explain why boys are attracted to science-based subjects and girls are attracted to subjects like English.

- **Gender domains.** Gender domains are tasks and activities that are seen as either male or female territory; for example, looking after the elderly or sick will be seen as a female task while fixing cars will be seen as a male task. Children's beliefs about gender domains are shaped by early experiences and they subsequently tend to be more confident in engaging in tasks which they see as part of their gender domain. For example, Browne and Ross (1991) found that when children were set an open task, they were more comfortable when taking part in activities of their choice and gender domain. This could explain why girls are attracted to arts and humanities subjects and boys prefer sciences.

- **Gendered subject images.** Kelly (1987) identifies two main reasons that science tends to be seen as masculine. Firstly, the way science subjects are packaged makes them appear to be a boy's subject: science teachers tend to be male and the examples used in textbooks and by teachers tend to be linked to boys' experiences rather than the interests of girls. Secondly, students themselves make the greatest contribution to turning science into a boy's subject: boys dominate the science classrooms and grab science apparatus first.

- **Peer pressure.** Some boys and girls choose subjects because of peer pressure. Because of concerns about masculinity, some boys are reluctant to opt for subjects such as Child Development and Dance as to do so would open them up to ridicule and mean they may be seen as effeminate. For similar reasons, some females feel under pressure to opt out of subjects such as Physics. Dewar (1990) found that male students would call girls 'lesbian' or 'butch' if they appeared interested in sports.

- **Career aspirations.** Many jobs are seen as either 'female' or 'male' and tend to be dominated by one gender (eg, nursing = female; engineering = male). This inevitably shapes which subjects males and females choose to do, especially when selecting vocational courses.

Gender identities and schooling

Pupils' experiences of school can help to reinforce (or construct) their gender identities. This is what Connell (1995) calls hegemonic masculinity – the dominance of heterosexual masculine identity and the subordination of female and gay identities. It does this by:

- **Verbal abuse.** According to Connell, abusive language between pupils reinforces dominant gender identities. Boys use name-calling to put girls down if they behave in certain ways (eg, slags, tight, frigid). Paetcher (1998) found that name-calling helps to shape gender identities and male dominance. The use of negative labels such as 'gay', 'queer' and 'lezzie' are ways in which pupils can control each other's sexual identities. Parker (1996) found that boys were called 'gay' if they were friendly and polite, and got on well with girls or female teachers. Paetcher notes that pupils control one another's sexual identities though negative labels.

- **Teachers and discipline.** Teachers play a part in reinforcing gender identities. Hayward and Mac an Ghaill (1996) found that male teachers told boys off for 'behaving like girls' and teased them when they achieved lower marks than female students.

- **The male gaze.** Mac an Ghaill refers to the 'male gaze' as the way male pupils look girls up and down, seeing them as sexual objects and making judgements about their appearance. He argues that the male gaze is a form of surveillance through which dominant masculinity is reinforced and femininity devalued. This is often combined, for example, through telling stories of sexual conquest.

- **Double standards.** Boys will boast about their own sexual exploits but if girls do the same they will be called 'slags'.

✓✗ Evaluation

Cognitive development

✗ **Gender gap.** Although a gender gap has developed, statistics have shown that both girls and boys have gained better GCSE and A level examination results; boys, therefore, are doing badly relative to girls' performance. However, sociologists are still concerned as to why boys have failed to improve at the same rate of girls.

External factors

✗ **Radical feminists.** Radical feminists argue that although girls are now achieving more, the education system remains patriarchal (male-dominated). For example, sport education tends to focus on the achievements of boys than girls (eg, football and cricket). Subject choices made by boys (eg, maths) and girls (eg, sociology) often mean that girls' subjects are seen as 'soft' and those of boys as 'hard', which carries the perception that girls' subjects have lower status and market value in the real world. More men than women still occupy the senior management levels of schools and colleges (head teacher, deputy head etc.). They argue that the school produces/reinforces gender inequalities and 'female' and 'male' roles, and that this must be challenged and dealt with.

✗ **Maturation differences.** Some critics argue that the difference in educational achievement is due to biological rather than sociological factors. The difference in the maturation process of boys and girls may account for their difference in educational achievement. Girls mature earlier than boys and are more likely to be receptive to learning . For example, tests of 7-year-olds have shown that girls achieve better grades than boys in English, maths and science and technology. The implications for this are that girls will academically achieve more during their early years which set a better foundation for later on in school.

✗ **Gender linked to class and ethnicity.** Postmodernists such as Heaton (1998) argue that gender differences in educational achievement cannot be fully understood by looking at gender alone. We must consider other factors such as class and ethnicity which interact with gender to determine educational outcomes. For example, if when we link class and ethnicity, middle-class Asian boys do better than white working-class girls, demonstrating the relationship between gender and educational achievement is not straightforward as it may seem.

Internal factors

✗ **Coursework has little impact.** Murphy (1980) argues that females have been out-performing males long before the introduction of GCSE coursework such as in the days of the 11+ exams. Elwood (2005) argues coursework has less influence than the examination component on the overall final grade, in fact it she notes that the coursework has more influence on boys results than girls results, suggesting coursework has a limited effect on why girls do better than boys.

✗ **Teacher's attention.** Teacher-pupil interaction has not been supported by teachers who argue that their treat both sexes fairly and equally. Also there is no evidence that the difference in teacher-pupil interactions is the reason for the difference in educational achievement between girls and boys.

Boys-underachievement

✗ **Boys-underachievement exaggerated.** Wiener et al (1997) argue that the issue of male under-achievement has been exaggerated into a 'moral panic' fuelled by politicians and educationalists. Girls and boys have both made improvements in their GCSE and A level examinations, however the level attainment is slowly in boys than those of girls. Furthermore, under-achievement is mainly to do with working class boys, a major concern because this can lead to deviant subcultures and the formation of the underclass.

✗ **Decline of traditional men's job explanation questioned.** It could be argue that the decline in traditional manual working class jobs, many of them unskilled or semi-skilled require few qualification. Traditionally, many of these jobs would have been filled by working class boys with few if any qualifications. It therefore seems unlikely that the disappearance of such jobs would have much of an impact on boys" motivation to gain qualifications.

✗ **Feminism critique.** Feminist have raised concerns that educational policy recently on boy's underachievement. They argue that focusing on attempts to raise boys' underachievement can have a negative consequence for girls. By prioritising boys' needs can be damaging to girl's self-image sending a message that their achievement is not as important as the boys which can lower their self-esteem and aspirations. They argue that we should spend more time dealing with gender subject choices, educational underachievement of many girls and of boys domination of school space and teachers time.

Practice exam questions

AS level type questions

1. Define the term 'gender domains'. **[2 marks]**

2. Using **one** example, briefly how the 'male gaze' may affect pupils experience of schooling. **[2 marks]**

3. Outline **three** reasons why girls generally achieve more highly then boys in education. **[6 marks]**

Practice exam questions

4. Outline and explain **two** reasons for gender differences in subject choice. **[10 marks]**

5. Outline and explain **two** ways in which factors outside the education system have resulted in improved educational achievement for girls. **[10 marks]**

6. Outline and explain **two** policies or practices in schools that have helped to raise girls' educational achievement. **[10 marks]**

7. Outline and explain **two** reasons why girls are "now generally out-performing boys at all levels of schooling". **[10 marks]**

8. Applying material from **Item (...)** and your knowledge, evaluate sociological explanations of gender differences in achievement and in subject choice. **[20 marks]**

9. Applying material from **Item (...)** and your knowledge, evaluate sociological explanations for the educational underachievement among boys. **[20 marks]**

A level type questions

1. Outline **two** ways in which schools may produce a 'gender regime'. **[4 marks]**

2. Outline **two** ways in which schools may reinforce existing social class inequalities. (June 2008) **[4 marks]**

3. Outline **three** reasons for the educational under-achievement of boys. (specimen paper 2007/ June 2010) **[6 marks]**

4. Outline **three** examples of 'laddish' behaviour that may make it difficult for boys to do well in school. **[6 marks]**

5. Outline **three** reasons for gender differences in subject choice. **[6 marks]**

6. Outline **three** reasons why girls' examination performance has improved in recent years. **[6 marks]**

7. Applying material from **Item (...)**, analyse **two** reasons for boys' underachievement compared with girls.. **[10 marks]**

8. Applying material from **Item (...)**, analyse **two** factors within the education system that may have contributed to improvements in girls' achievement. **[10 marks]**

9. Applying material from **Item (...)** and your knowledge, evaluates the claim that although girls outperform boys in term of achievement, the experience of schooling reinforces traditional gender identities. **[30 marks]**

10. Applying material from **Item (...)** and your knowledge, evaluate the view that gender differences in both subject choice and educational achievement are mainly the result of the influence of wider society. (Jan 2010) **[30 marks]**

The AQA specification: Education

- The relationships and processes within schools, with particular reference to teacher/pupil relationships, pupil identities and subcultures, the hidden curriculum, and the organisation of teaching and learning.

The exam requires that you are able to:

▶ Describe and evaluate the relationships and processes within schools.

Note: The information presented here does not really represent new information as such, as this has been covered in the other exam notes. All we have done is collect all the relevant points to help you know how to answer this in the exam.

Introduction

Sociologists have argued that what goes on inside school (ie, processes and relationships) can have an important impact on the child's experience and educational achievement. The terms 'processes' and 'relationships' refer to:

— *Teacher and student relationships.* This involves the labelling theory: how teachers label children's academic ability and behaviour.

— *Pupil identities.* How a pupil's identity (how others see him/her) can ultimately have an impact on their educational achievement.

— *The formation of school subcultures.* The development of subcultures within schools can affect children's educational achievement and experience of school.

— *The hidden curriculum.* Ideas and views that the schools do not directly teach the children, but which the children learn during their everyday routine at school.

— *How the school is organised for teaching and learning.* The way students are organised into ability sets can have implications for their educational achievement.

This section examines the internal factors which can influence how well pupils do at school. All the points above are inter-related, and should not be seen in isolation. For example, how the teacher interacts with the pupils can lead to their being streamed into lower-ability groups, which can lead to the development of anti-school subcultures.

Teacher/pupil relationships

- Interactionists argue that how a teacher interacts with a pupil can affect the child's experience and educational achievement at school. Interactionists have put forward the labelling theory which explains this in more detail. The labelling theory states that teachers in their day-to-day interaction with pupils will often make judgements about a particular student, known as labels (eg, lazy, troublemaker, intelligent or 'thick').

- Interactionists argue that labelling students can affect their achievement by creating a self-fulfilling prophecy in the teacher. A 'prophecy' is a prediction made by a teacher at the start about a student by attaching a label, eg, 'troublemaker'. This affects the teacher's perception and subsequent behaviour towards the student. The child picks up on this, and their self-perception is influenced by the teachers' label; the child's behaviour now begins to reflect the new label— they slowly see themselves as a troublemaker. This confirms the teacher's initial labelling as accurate, and is therefore a self-fulfilling prophecy. Negative labels can easily promote under-achievement as they are more likely to be placed on lower-ability groups. Those given a positive label are more likely to succeed. Studies have shown that social class, ethnicity and gender can have impact on a child's experience at school.

Teachers' expectations and social class

- **Middle-class pupils.** Teachers have an 'ideal pupil' which tends to be one who conforms to white middle-class standards of behaviour, as they see such pupils as well-behaved, motivated and more academically able. This is not because teachers are racist, but because they tend to judge pupils by their own cultural standards as teachers tend to be white middle-class themselves. This means teachers are more likely to give a positive label to middle-class pupils, such as being 'bright' or 'more able' and therefore more likely to academically succeed.

  This is supported by Becker (1951) who interviewed 60 teachers from Chicago high schools and found that teachers held a positive and ideal view of middle-class pupils and prefer to teach such students, whereas they held a negative view of working-class pupils and were less willing to teach them. Becker argued that the holding of such stereotypes would affect teachers' perceptions of pupils, their interaction with them, and subsequent educational achievement.

- **Working-class pupils** are often perceived by teachers as being, on average, less intelligent than middle-class children and are therefore more likely to be labelled negatively and placed in lower-ability groups, regardless of their academic ability. This is because teachers often fail to assess working-class pupils' academic potential objectively and instead are more likely to assess students in terms of appearance, language, social skills and social class background. Gillborn and Youdell (1999) suggest that teachers discriminate against working-class pupils by failing to recognise their intelligence because they do not exhibit it in the right way, or in the same way as middle-class pupils.

  This is supported by Rist (1970) who carried out an observational study in an American kindergarten. He found the teacher used the children's socio-economic background (social class) and physical appearance (clothes and cleanliness) and not their academic ability to assign them into three different groups after eight days. The 'fast learners', mostly middle-class and of clean appearance, were grouped at the front of the class and received more teacher time (encouragement and support), while the two groups of 'slow learners' sat at the back, tended to be working-class, and received less teacher time. Rist concluded that each child's journey through school was determined by the eighth day of kindergarten. The labels given to these children by their kindergarten teacher set them on a course of action that could possibly affect the rest of their lives.

Teachers' expectations and gender

- The different ways teachers interact with boys and girls may be partly why girls do better than boys. Howe (1997) found that teachers respond more positively to girls than boys because they see girls as more cooperative and boys as more disruptive. This may have an impact on the girls, as positive interactions will raise a girl's self-esteem and thus have an effect on her educational achievement. Croll and Moses (1990) found that boys were more likely to be involved in negative interaction with the teacher, (telling off, punishment) suggesting boys are labelled in a negative way which may be affecting their educational achievement.

Teachers' perception and ethnicity

- Research studies suggest that certain ethnic minorities are more likely to experience racial discrimination, and thus be labelled in a negative way by teachers, which puts them at a disadvantage. Gillborn and Youdell (2000) found that white teachers expected black pupils to be less 'motivated' and saw them as 'troublemakers'. They argue that this negative label meant that teachers were likely to enter a disproportionate number of black pupils in lower tiers of GCSE examinations, compared to other boys of similar ability, which prevents them from achieving higher grades. This has a spiralling effect as the pupils will develop low self-esteem and become less motivated to work hard in order to improve their grades. This will become a self-fulfilling prophecy and thus confirm the teacher's initial expectation.

Connolly's (1998) study of a multi-ethnic inner-city primary school found that teachers saw Asian pupils as conformist, hard-working, obedient and producing high-quality work. When Asian boys misbehaved it was seen as more silliness than challenging the authority of the teacher. As a result, they were not punished as much as Afro-Caribbean boys whose misbehaviour was viewed as more threatening.

✔✘ Evaluation of teacher/pupil relationships

✘ **Too many subject teachers mean labels cannot be used consistently.** Some sociologists have questioned exactly how the labelling process is conducted in school. A negative label from one subject teacher does not necessarily mean that the label will be passed on to all other subject teachers. Pupils are taught by a number of different teachers and the interaction between pupil and teacher will be different for each subject, so it is difficult to see how the labelling process can be applied consistently when the pupil has many teachers.

✘ **Ignores outside factors.** The interactionists have been criticised for placing too much emphasis on what goes on in school and ignoring outside factors such as home background, which might have a significant influence (eg, poverty or marital discord).

✘ **Too deterministic.** The labelling approach is too deterministic: once pupils receive a label, the outcome is determined. However, pupils do not all react to labelling in the same way. Sometimes the student may choose to ignore, negotiate or reject the given label. For example, Mirza (1992) studied two South London comprehensives, focussing on 62 young black females aged 15-19. She challenges the idea that the labelling process can cause the under-achievement of black female students. She concludes that there is some racism within the school, but denies that this has any effect on the self-confidence of black female students. Most black girls rejected the label and were determined to work hard for educational success. Additionally, Fuller (1984) demonstrated that black girls were more likely to reject negative labels given to them and would try to prove the teacher wrong.

Pupil identities

- **Identity** refers to how pupils see and define themselves, and how other people see and define them. Sociologists have tended to focus on how a pupil's identity can ultimately have an impact on their educational achievement. Sociologists believe two factors shape pupils' identity.
  - Inside school factors. What goes on inside school, such as the teacher-student relationship, labelling/self-fulfilling prophecies, subculture and streaming/setting can all contribute to how pupils see themselves, which can subsequently affect their level of educational achievement.
  - Outside school factors. Outside factors such as social and cultural influences can also shape pupils' identity and have an impact on their achievement.

Inside school factors

- The type of identity students have is often linked to different levels of educational achievement. Becker (1971) argues that all teachers have an 'ideal pupil' in their mind. This type of pupil is well-behaved, motivated and academically able. As noted above, such pupils tend to come from white middle-class backgrounds. Teacher are more likely to give a positive label to middle-class pupils such as being 'bright' and therefore they are more likely to academically succeed as they will perceive themselves as 'academic'. Working-class students, on the other hand, are often perceived by teachers as being 'less able' and therefore more likely to label negatively, and place in lower-ability groups. This can lead students to have a low opinion of themselves which may account for their low educational achievement. As Rist (1970) and others have pointed out, a number of non-academic factors often influence teachers' labelling, such as speech, dress, appearance, personality and parents' socio-economic background.

Outside school factors

- **Habitus** refers to a person's social identity — their outlook on life, interests, lifestyle preferences and tastes (eg, fashion, clothing, music, socialising). Louise Archer et al (2010) apply the concept of habitus to explain why the social identity of working-class pupils produces under-achievement: their 'identity' is linked to educational failure. Archer argues that working-class and middle-class pupils have a different 'habitus'.

- Schools and the middle class share a very similar habitus. In comparison, conflict occurs between the school's habitus and the working-class habitus (identity). The school's habitus devalues and stigmatises working-class identities as worthless (eg, 'hoodies', 'onesies', Nike tracksuits, chav-like behaviour) and not conducive to educational success. Bourdieu calls this rejection of working-class values symbolic violence. As a result, working-class pupils may experience school, college and university as alien and 'not for them'. According to Archer et al, working-class pupils who invest in 'Nike-style' identities are not only marginalised at school, but also actively choose to reject school because it does not fit with their identity or way of life, and thus limit their chances of academic success.

✓✗ Evaluation of pupil identities

✗ **Supporting research evidence for 'habitus'.** There is supporting research evidence to show how working-class identity (habitus) can lead to educational failure. A study by Nicola Ingram (2009) focussed on working-class boys from a deprived neighbourhood who were academically able and attended a selective grammar school (which had a strong middle-class habitus). She found that the boys experienced a conflict between the middle-class school habitus and the habitus of their working-class background. The working-class boys were forced to reject aspects of their working-class identity. One example is that boys wearing tracksuits on non-uniform day were ridiculed and made to feel worthless by their friends and by the grammar school. They felt they had to abandon their working-class identify in order to fit in with the school habitus in order to succeed academically

Pupil subcultures

- A subculture can be defined as a group whose beliefs, values and attitudes are different from mainstream culture. Often the teachers' expectation of certain pupils can lead to the development of subcultures. As a response to the way that they have been labelled and streamed, pupils may seek out others who have been similarly labelled and form their own subculture. Colin Lacey (1970) found that the consequences of labelling and streaming can lead to pro-school or anti-school subcultures:

  — Pro-school subcultures are formed by pupils in higher streams. They accept the school's rules, values and goals such as homework, attendance and respect for teachers, and enjoy and conform to school life, lessons, activities, etc.

  — Anti-school subcultures are often formed by those in lower streams. They will engage in behaviour that rejects the school's rules, values and goals and often turns them upside-down, eg, disrespect towards teachers, breaking school rules, (eg, vandalism, smoking and bullying) avoiding doing school work, playing truant and sabotaging their uniforms. Lacey (1970) argues that pupils who form an anti-school subculture do so as a means of gaining status among their peers.

Class and subcultures

- Hargreaves (1967) argues that working-class pupils placed in low streams or sets in secondary school tend to form an anti-school subculture. He argues that this is a response to being labelled as 'failures'. Unable to achieve status in terms of the mainstream values of the school, these pupils replace school values with their own set of 'delinquent values', by which they can achieve the success and status in their eyes of their peers which has been denied by the school. Participation in such anti-school subcultures is likely to lead to educational failure, so this becomes a self-fulfilling prophecy whereby schools and teachers will continue to deem working-class pupils as being of lower ability.

- Hollingworth and Williams (2009) argue that when it comes to middle-class pupils, there is not a single type of subculture, but a great variety, depending on the leisure pursuits they enjoy. For example, they may be 'goths', 'hippies', 'emos' or 'poshies'. Although there are variations, middle-class pupils tend to form a pro-school subculture, having a positive attitude towards the values of school, whereby teachers have a positive view of them.

Gender and subcultures

- Male subcultures. Some sociologists argue that anti-school cultures are more likely to be formed by boys than girls, most notably boys from working-class backgrounds. The famous 1970s study by Paul Willis showed 12 working-class boys (known as the 'lads') at a comprehensive school who developed an anti-school culture, showing disrespect for authority by, for example, smoking, disrupting classes, truancy, sexism, racism, etc. Mac an Ghaill (1994) argues the lads' rejection of school was because they saw being studious students (swots) as undermining their masculinity, and 'pointless', as they viewed their masculinity as shaped by the traditional manual industry their fathers worked in and knew they were destined to follow in their fathers' footsteps.

  However, Mac an Ghaill suggests that Willis' study is no longer applicable to today's society, given the decline of manual work. As a result, Mac an Ghaill suggests that the formation of boys' subcultures is now based on connecting factors: the relationship between school, masculinity and sexuality. His analysis of school subcultures has led him to identify the following different types of boys' subcultures within the school system today:

  — *Macho lads.* The 'macho lads' are similar to the 'lads' in Wallis' study: white working-class boys who are anti-school because their 'masculine identity' is based on the manual jobs their working-class families performed. The 'macho lads' are undergoing a 'crisis of masculinity' as the traditional manual jobs are no longer available, making their future employment insecure. The consequences of this 'crisis' is that such working-class boys react by forming anti-school subcultures and leaving school with few academic qualifications.

  — *Academic achievers.* A pro-school subculture group from a working-class background, who have adapted to working hard as they see their educational qualifications as a route to a successful future. This group can be seen as a pro-school subculture, often placed into higher-ability classes, which receives favourable treatment from teachers.

  — *New enterprisers.* Another pro-school subculture group from a working-class background that focused on 'new vocationalism' subjects (eg, business, technology and computing) in the 1980s and 1990s. Such pupils rejected academic subjects as being less relevant to industry, and focused on vocational subjects, as they felt these gave a greater chance of career success by providing a real practical learning skill that could be applied in the job market.

  — *Real Englishmen.* A group of students from a liberal educated middle-class professional background who displayed a sense of superiority towards the education system by challenging or refusing to accept the academic authority of teachers. They saw the pursuit by other groups such as 'academic achievers' and 'new enterprisers' of a financial, materially rewarding career as shallow, compared to their own academic purism which they regarded as more 'prestigious' and believed would lead to a top professional career. The 'real English' group were neither pro- or anti-school but simply had ambivalent (conflicting) attitudes towards school such as displaying a lack of school values whilst achieving academic success with minimum effort.

- **Female subcultures.** Female pupils tend to have a positive attitude towards school and to affiliate themselves with pro-school subcultural groups. Mirza (1992) studied two South London comprehensives, focussing on 62 young black females aged 15-19. Even when black female students were exposed to labelling and racism within the school, most rejected the labels and would often form a pro-school subcultural group based on their ethnicity (Afro-Caribbean) which was determined to work hard for educational success.

Ethnic subculture

- Ethnic-minority pupils often join a school sub-culture as a reaction to what they perceive as racism and negative labelling by teachers (consciously or unconsciously), such as low expectations and negative attitudes. Pupils may react in different ways to such negative experiences; some students counter-react by succeeding academically and proving the negative labelling wrong (and forming a pro-school subculture). Others react negatively by joining an anti-school subculture.

- **Afro-Caribbean subculture.** Sewell (1998) carried out a study of Afro-Caribbean students and found that black pupils adopted a range of responses to teachers' racist labelling of them. They were:

  — *Conformists.* Black pupils who are keen to succeed academically, accept the goals of education and see good behaviour as the key to academic success.

  — *Innovators.* Black pupils who accept the goals of education and want to succeed academically but rejected the school system or teachers' approval.

  — *Retreatists.* Black pupils who are disconnected from both the school and black subculture.

  — *Rebels.* Black pupils who reject the school's goals and conform instead to the stereotypical image of aggressive masculinity (eg, the 'black macho lad').

Sewell's study is important because it shows the variety of black pupils' responses to racism in school varies considerably: not all pupils react in a negative way to teachers' labelling. However, regardless of how the pupils responded, Sewell found teachers tended to treat them all in the same way (negatively). This discrimination resulted in the under-achievement of many Afro-Caribbean boys.

Sewell (1997) suggests that there is considerable pressure on Afro-Caribbean boys by their peers to adopt the behaviour of 'street' subculture. Equally, more 'respect' is given to unruly and disruptive behaviour towards school, teachers and other pupils than to high achievement or effort to succeed.

- **Asian anti-subcultures.** South Asian pupils (Pakistani and Bangladeshi) are also likely to form anti-school subcultures which adopt similar attitudes and behaviours as their Afro-Caribbean peers. For example, Louise Archer (2003) found that Muslim boys in four schools in North England sometimes drew upon African American 'gangsta' culture which valued talking tough and having a macho identity. One possible explanation is given by Fordham and Ogbu (1986) who argue that notions of 'acting white' include doing well at school, while 'acting black' necessarily implies not doing well in school and is a respected status amongst peers.

Female subcultures

- **Female Afro-Caribbean subcultures.** Although some black boys reject school and education in favour of a culture of conspicuous consumption and street credibility, this is not always the case for black girls, who reject their teachers' low expectations and strive to achieve educational success. For example, Mary Fuller (1980) found that Afro-Caribbean girls did not form anti-school subcultures, like Afro-Caribbean boys. They would form a pro-school subculture that valued hard work in order to succeed academically and to prove the negative labelling by teachers wrong, demonstrating that teacher perception does not always lead to a negative outcome.

✓✗ Evaluation of subcultures

✗ **Too simplistic view of subcultures.** Peter Wood (1983) disagrees (with Willis and Hargreaves) that schools essentially have either pro-school cultures or anti-school subcultures, as this is far too simplistic a view. He argues that pupils use a variety of adaptations. Some pupils may accept some aspects of school values but reject others. He also argues that working-class and middle-class pupils' responses will differ in different school situations. The study of school subcultures is therefore more complex than it used it be.

✗ **Working-class subcultures are not always deviant.** Mac an Ghaill's analysis of the different school subcultures shows that the 'new enterpriser' subculture demonstrates that not all working-class pupils are prone to deviate into anti-school subcultures, suggesting that working-class pupils can form pro-school subcultures and aspire to successful careers.

The hidden curriculum

- **Hidden curriculum** can be defined as the ideas, behaviours and views that schools do not directly teach to the children, but which children learn during their everyday routine at school. This is contrasted with the formal curriculum, such as the teaching of subjects (eg, maths, English and history). The term 'hidden' is used by sociologists as the learning process which goes on in school is without the pupil being fully aware of it taking place. These learning practices can be a number of things such as correct attitudes, obedience, expectations, holding certain values and ideas, for example, being respectful to authority, acceptance of hierarchy, obedience to school rules and punctuality. The importance of the hidden curriculum is that it has an impact on the pupils' experience; it not only shapes their behaviour but also their educational achievement, often working in favour of middle-class pupils and less so for the working class. The hidden curriculum is transmitted in every aspect of school life. Below are some examples:

  — Generally speaking, power in schools tends to conform to the following pattern: at the top, white males as the head-teacher and deputy, then teachers, usually female, then non-academic stuff (eg, cleaners and cooks) who tend to be black and working-class, then pupils at the bottom. This teaches pupils to accept the different levels of status and power in society.

  — The everyday reinforcement of rules and importance of punctuality teaches the importance of keeping to a rigid and routine system.

  — Wearing school uniform imposes the identity of the school over that of the individual and teaches pupils to conform to group identity rather than express individuality, which can lead to dissent.

  — The organisation of different sets and levels by ability and by certain social groups (eg, working-class and some ethnic groups) teaches children that the difference of intelligence is just and fair.

  — Pupils are motivated by the external rewards of exam success rather than interest in the subject.

— Those who are conform by being obedient, hardworking and punctual are awarded higher grades than those who challenge authority.

- **Functionalism.** According to functionalists, the 'official' and hidden curriculum are important in school because they prepare students to accept social values and rules when they integrate in society as adults – which is important to have a healthy functioning society, both economically and socially.

- **Marxism.** Marxism sees the 'hidden curriculum' as an instrument of social control because it teaches that children who are obedient, conformist and hardworking are more likely to be rewarded and succeed in life than those who do not conform, as they are less likely to succeed academically.

Research has shown that working-class pupils are less likely to conform to school rules, more likely to form anti-school subcultures and therefore less likely to do well in school. Therefore, according to Marxists, the hidden curriculum prepares the working class to be subservient for their future working-class jobs. Anyon (1988) claims the hidden curriculum not only creates a docile and subservient individual, but allows working-class students to show resistance and conflict which may mirror itself in the world of work. In relation to middle-class pupils, the hidden curriculum is teaching the correct attitudes and behaviour needed for their successful professional jobs in the world of work.

✔✗ Evaluation of the hidden curriculum

✗ **The hidden curriculum.** The hidden curriculum has been questioned as a concept. Sociologist Henry Giroux (1984) argues it is wrong to view the hidden curriculum as being a single and coherent message that the school transmits. Instead he sees the school as a place where individual teachers have competing political and moral views, regardless of the overall ethos of the school. Teachers have different views and give different messages about what is important in education and life. For example, some teachers may place greater value and importance on punctuality and obedience, while others may disregard conformity and school rules and see equality and creatively as more important.

The organisation of teaching and learning

- How schools group students for teaching in terms of ability groups – in terms of steaming, setting or mixed ability - can have an effect on a student's self-esteem and ultimately a consequence on their educational achievement and career opportunities. The main methods of grouping students are:

  — Streaming (or banding) – this is where pupils are grouped by similar ability for most of their subjects. The top stream is the most academic group who will be taught at that level in all their subjects. The bottom stream contains the lowest groups who will be taught at that level in all their subjects.

  — Setting – this is where pupils are placed in ability by subject groups. For example, a pupil can be in set 3 for English, but set 1 for maths.

  — Mixed ability groups – this is where pupils of all abilities are taught together.

Studies that looked into social class, ethnicity and ability groups

- Sociologists have found that when streaming or setting is in operation at school, working-class students and certain ethnic groups were more likely to be consigned to low-ability groups. This can prevent them from obtaining the knowledge required for a high grade in examinations, for example, at GCSE level. In contrast, a disproportionate number of white middle-class pupils are placed in the upper sets/streams.

  It is also important to note that gender and certain ethnicities can play a part. For example, there is a disproportionate number of boys in lower sets , as well as of certain ethnic groups.

  A study by David Gillborn and Deborah Youdell (2001) examined teachers' 'idea of ability' to decide which pupils have the potential to achieve five GCSE A*-C. They found that working-class and black pupils are less likely to be perceived as having potential and are more likely to be in a lower stream and be entered for lower-tier GCSEs. Tikly et al (2006) evaluated the DfE African Caribbean Achievement Project (Aiming High) and found that Afro-Caribbean pupils are under-represented in higher-ability sets and examination tiers, and in gifted and talented cohorts. Smyth et al (2006) found that students in lower streams/sets have a more negative attitude to school, find the teaching pace too slow, spend less time on homework and are more likely than other students to disengage from school life.

Causes and consequences of having different ability groups

- One of the main reasons is the process of labelling (as well as external factors (home backgrounds) see exam note 5), rather than academic ability. Lacey (1970) argues working-class pupils often have very good academic potential but tend to be ignored. The process of labelling not only widens the class gap between working class and middle class in terms of educational achievement; it also creates a self-fulfilling prophecy in that poor exam performance confirms the teacher's initial predication.

- The low expectations of teachers of lower set groups can cause low self-esteem, leading to demotivation and higher absenteeism which may account for low educational achievement. This becomes a vicious circle as it in turn gives credence to the labelling theory and self-fulfilling prophecy process, ie, that working-class students are less able than middle-class ones, further confirming the teachers' low expectations of them.

Studies that show ability groups have a positive effect on educational achievement

- Those in favour of ability groups argue that pupils have different abilities and therefore need to be taught differently, for example, at a faster speed, in different ways or at a higher level. Some research does suggest that those in high-ability groups do tend to make more improvement then those in mixed-ability groups. For example, Ireson et al (2002) found that setting tends to be beneficial for the more able students in the top sets, although those in the bottom sets generally receive little challenge or stimulation and so can easily be demoralised, disruptive and disaffected.

Studies that show ability groups have a negative effect on educational achievement

- Hallam (2001) found that low-ability students are likely to score lower attainment levels when they are placed in similar attainment groupings than when they are placed in mixed ability groups. One explanation is that teachers usually set the 'disruptive' pupils together in the lower set as a form of social control. This allows the more able class to let the teacher teach. This is supported by Tennant (2004) who explored classroom interactions between teachers and pupils from different ethnic origins. He found that Afro-Caribbean pupils were placed in lower sets because they consumed more teacher time than other children, mostly for behavioural reasons, which was unsuitable for higher sets.

Studies that show ability groups have no effect on educational achievement

- Sukhnandan & Lee (1988) carried out a meta-analysis review and found that, in general, setting or streaming (whether high or low groups) has neither a negative nor a positive impact on pupils' educational achievement in comparison to mixed ability teaching, in both primary and secondary schools and across all subject areas. However, Sukhnandan and Lee do claim that streaming and setting 'reinforce social divisions' with a high portion of middle-class pupils in higher sets and bands and working-class pupils more likely to be in lower-ability groups.

Practice exam questions

AS level exam type questions

1. Define the term 'self-fulfilling prophecy'. **[2 marks]**

2. Define the term 'labelling'. **[2 marks]**

3. Define the term 'educational triage'. **[2 marks]**

4. Define the term 'hidden curriculum'. **[2 marks]**

5. Using **one** example, briefly explain how pupils' identities may lead to under-achievement. **[6 marks]**

6. Outline **three** ways in which pupils' experiences of schooling help shape their identities. **[6 marks]**

7. Outline **three** ways in which the labelling process may lead to educational under-achievement for some pupils. **[6 marks]**

8. Outline **three** ways in which pupils may respond to labelling and under-achievement. **[6 marks]**

9. Outline **three** ways in which the concept of 'self-fulfilling prophecy' might be criticised. **[6 marks]**

10. Outline and explain **two** forms of pupils' responses to teachers' racism and negative labelling. **[10 marks]**

11. Outline and explain **two** reasons put forward by sociologists as to why children from different social classes are likely to be treated differently by teachers. **[10 marks]**

12. Outline and explain **two** reasons why girls may be less likely than boys to be affected by anti-school subcultures. **[10 marks]**

13. Outline and explain **two** aspects of the hidden curriculum and describe how each one may influence the behaviour or progress of pupils of different genders. **[10 marks]**

14. Applying material from **Item (...)** and your own knowledge, evaluate the view that 'labelling and other processes within schools are what determine who succeeds and who fails in education'.

[20 marks]

A level exam type questions

1. Outline **two** possible effects of being placed in the lower sets. **[4 marks]**

2. Outline **two** features of 'anti-school subcultures'. **[4 marks]**

3. Outline **three** ways in which teachers' attitudes can affect the educational achievement of pupils

[6 marks]

4. Applying material from **Item (...)** analyse **two** reasons why pupils form subcultures in schools.

[10 marks]

5. Applying material from **Item (...)** and your knowledge, evaluate the view that pupil subcultures are the key to understanding educational under-achievement. **[30 marks]**

6. Applying material from **Item (...)** and your knowledge, evaluate the view that the 'hidden curriculum' can affect the behaviour and educational performance of pupils. **[30 marks]**

7. Applying material from **Item (...)** and your knowledge, evaluate the view that differences in educational achievement between social groups are the result of factors and processes within schools. **[30 marks]**

The AQA specification: Education

- The significance of educational policies, including policies of selection, marketisation and privatisation, and policies to achieve greater equality of opportunity or outcome, for an understanding of the structure, role, impact and experience of, and access to, education; the impact of globalisation on educational policy.

The exam requires that you are able to:

▶ Describe and evaluate the main educational policies that have been introduced (ie, tripartite system, comprehensive system and marketisation).

▶ Describe and evaluate educational policies that have attempted to improve equal opportunity for all pupils.

Key term

- **Educational policies** are initiatives/strategies introduced by governments to achieve a particular outcome in schools or education systems (often referred to as Acts).

- **Marketisation** is a method of introducing competition into the public services (eg, education and health) that were previously controlled and run by the government, with the aim of raising educational standards by creating competition between schools.

The aim of educational policies

- Politicians and educational advisors aim to introduce educational policies which will improve and raise the standard of education for all students regardless of social class, ethnicity and gender, and improve young people's skills in order to compete successfully in a global economy.

The debate about educational policies

- **Equal opportunities?** Many of the educational policies introduced have focused on reducing inequalities in the education system, so those from a less advantaged background, ethnicity or gender should have the same chance to gain good qualifications. However, some critics argue that some educational policies have actually made inequalities greater between classes, genders and ethnic groups.

Education policy before 1988

- Before 1870 there were no state school. Children of the wealthy were educated either through private tutors or at fee-paying schools. Working-class children had a very basic education which was run by churches and charities, with many not being educated at all. The need for an educated workforce led to the first significant education legislation, the 1870 Education Act (or Foster Act, named after William Foster), which established the first schools for all children up to the age of 10. The type of education received was basic, focusing mainly on religious matters, literacy and numeracy.

Education policy from 1944-1965

- The second significant legislation was the 1944 Education Act (the Butler Act) which introduced free secondary education for all pupils up to the age of 15. This Act brought about the tripartite system of secondary education, so called because there were three different types of schools, each catering for different aptitudes and abilities. The aim of the 1944 Education Act was to bring equal opportunity for all pupils to succeed in life through their own effort and abilities, rather than because of their social background. The 11+ exam was used to determine which secondary school students attended. Three types of schools were:

  — Grammar schools which offered an academic curriculum and access to higher education. They were for academic students who passed the 11+ exam.

  — Secondary modern schools which offered a more practical curriculum and access to manual work for those who failed the 11+.

  — Technical schools which existed in some areas to provide explicitly vocational education (eg, electricity metalwork, woodwork and cookery) for those who failed the 11+.

✓✗ Evaluation of the tripartite system

✗ **Reproduced class inequality.** A limitation of the tripartite system is that the 11+ examination questions were biased towards white, middle-class pupils (eg, the vocabulary and content were geared more towards middle-class culture) which meant working-class children did not have a real chance to do well and go to grammar school. This meant middle-class pupils were more likely to go to a grammar school (and university) while working-class pupils were more likely to go to a secondary modern and be labelled 'failures', resulting in low motivation, and subsequently low educational achievement, and thus, less likelihood of going to university. This suggests that the triplicate system, rather than promoting equal opportunity, maintained class inequality by allocating the different classes into different types of schools that offered different life opportunities.

✗ **Reproduced gender inequality.** The tripartite system reproduced gender inequality because it discriminated against girls: there were more grammar school places for boys than girls (as many grammar schools were single-sex), which meant girls with higher IQs than boys were often denied places at grammar schools in favour of boys with lower IQs.

✗ **Middle-class parents still had choices.** In addition to the tripartite system of schooling, there still existed private schools (fee-paying) for those from a more wealthy background who could afford to pay for a more privileged education for their children. This means that wealthy parents still had choices because parents whose children failed the 11+ could still obtain a good academic education for them by sending them to private school.

Education policy from 1965-1979

- The tripartite system was seen as failing to provide equal educational opportunities for all, especially those from a working-class background. So in 1965, the new Labour government abolished the tripartite system (ie, 11+ exam, grammar schools and secondary moderns) and replaced it with a comprehensive system. This single type of school aimed at educating all pupils under one roof, regardless of ability, and at removing the class divide of the tripartite system. Admissions into local comprehensive schools were based on catchment areas, that is, living within a certain distance of the school.

✓✗ Evaluation of the comprehensive system

✔ **Better examination results for all.** Some sociologists believe that the comprehensive system did reduce the class gap in educational qualifications as more working-class students achieve more examination passes in this type of school; the pass rates at GCSE and A-level have been steadily rising year by year.

✔ **Functionalists** argue that the comprehensive system brings children from different social backgrounds together and therefore promotes social integration of the different classes. However, Ford (1969) in his study found little social mixing between working-class and middle-class pupils, largely because of streaming (setting students by ability). Functionalists also see the comprehensive system as more meritocratic because it gives pupils a longer period in which to develop and show their abilities, unlike the tripartite system, which sought to select the most able pupils at the age of eleven.

✗ **Grammar schools still exist.** Not all schools managed to become fully comprehensive at it was up to the local authority to decide if they want to introduce the new system, with some refusing. Others allowed for the co-existence of grammars and comprehensive schools. As a result, the grammar - secondary modern divide still existed in many areas, giving wealthy parents a greater choice by allowing them to attempt to send their children to grammar schools and thus reproducing class inequality.

✗ **Exam results are not the same across all classes.** The comprehensive system did not reduce differences in educational achievement between working-class and middle-class children because middle-class pupils do better in examinations than working-class pupils, and go to university: the gap has remained. This shows that the idea that the comprehensive system would reduce class differences in educational attainment has failed.

✗ **Class barriers remained.** The comprehensive system failed to break down class barriers. This is because the school reflected the local population. For example, Knightsbridge has more middle- class than working-class, whereas Neasden has the opposite. Therefore, the intake of pupils attending their local comprehensive will depend on the socio-economic makeup of the catchment area.

✗ **Streaming and setting.** A major criticism of the comprehensive system is that pupils at school were streamed according to their ability. The problem with this is that a clearly disproportionate number of middle-class pupils were placed in high-ability streaming/sets, whereas a disproportionate number of working-class pupils were placed in the bottom groups. Furthermore, sociologists have shown that even where streaming is not present, teachers may continue to label working-class pupils negatively and restrict their opportunities. This would suggest that the comprehensive system continued to reproduce class inequality through setting and labelling.

✗ **Marxists** argue that the comprehensive system appears to be meritocratic by offering everyone an equal chance to all, but this is a myth. They argue that the comprehensive system continues to reproduce class inequality from one generation to the next, through the practice of streaming and labelling, which denies working-class children equal opportunity. Differences in achievement can be blamed on the individual (eg, 'not working hard enough') rather on the system representing unequal achievement as fair and just. Therefore, according to Marxists, the comprehensive system legitimises class inequality, by making it appear that working-class children have an equal chance when they do not.

Education policy from 1979-1997

- The Conservative governments of Margret Thatcher (1979-1997) saw education as failing to provide a sufficiently skilled workforce. Britain's lack of industrial competitiveness was partly blamed on schools. They also believed that schools were failing pupils and needed to raise the standard of education. Therefore, the Conservative Party introduced the 1988 Education Reforms Act (ERA), heavily influenced by New Right Policies whereby schools compete with each other, creating an 'education market', with the aim of raising educational standards. This concept is known as the marketisation of the education system.

- **Marketisation** is a method of introducing competition into public services (eg, education and health) that were previously controlled and run by the state, that is, central government or local councils. The aim of introducing marketisation principles is to raise standards in education by creating competition between schools. Policies to promote marketisation include:

  — More control for schools. Schools are able to opt-out of LEA control in order to give them more independence and more choices, for example in the employment of staff, curriculum and the way pupils are selected for entry. Having more control meant schools can respond to the wishes of parents and the local community, with the aim of improving the quality of education and exam results.

  — Parental choice. Parents can choose which school they send their children to. The right to choose will encourage schools to aim for the highest possible standards, as schools will compete to attract pupils as more pupils means more money for the school.

  — League tables. The publication of league tables (exam results e.g. GCSE and A Level) and Ofsted inspection reports gives parents the information they need to choose the right school. This puts pressure on schools to improve their performance to attract pupils.

  — Formula funding. Schools were allocated funds by local authorities based on the number of pupils: the more pupils, the greater budget the school received.

✓✗ Evaluation of marketisation

✗ **Criticism of parental choice.** It is claimed that the quality of a child's education is dependent on how powerful the parents are, which is referred to as parentocracy. Brown (1995) argues that middle-class families have greater 'parentocracy' than working-class parents because they have greater understanding of the education system: they are able to shop around for the best school, move into the catchment area of high-performing schools, and use this influence on the school to their advantage for their children. Thus, educational inequality can still exist as middle-class parents gain most from parental choice.

✗ **Criticisms of league tables and funding formula.** Ball (1994) argues that marketisation reproduces and legitimises inequality through league tables and the funding formula. League tables ensure that schools that achieve good results are in more demand, because parents are attracted to those with good rankings. This allows these schools to be more selective and to recruit high-achieving (eg, middle-class) pupils. As a result, middle-class pupils get the best education. The opposite occurs for less successful schools. These are unable to select, and tend to be full of less able children (mainly working-class). The overall effect of league tables is to produce unequal schools that reproduce social class inequalities. Funding is determined by pupil numbers; the more popular a school is, the higher funding received. These schools can afford to attract better-qualified teachers and better facilities. Unpopular schools lose income and find it difficult to match the teacher skills and facilities of their more successful rivals.

New Labour Government (1997-2010)

- The Labour government (known as New Labour) of Tony Blair and Gordon Brown came into power in 1997. They maintained the policy of marketisation but their main aim was to continue to reduce educational inequality. One way was to 'pump' more money into mainly deprived inner-city areas where pupils were under-achieving. Some of the implementations were:

  — Sure Start programme. This was introduced to help pre-school children and their families living in disadvantaged areas, as children from such areas are at risk of doing poorly at school, by providing better childcare support, early education, and health and family support while the child is growing up.

  — Education Action Zones (EAZ). These were introduced to help in areas of deprivation with low levels of educational achievement, usually under-performing secondary schools and their feeder primary schools). The aim was to provide additional support and resources (eg, improving attendance, employing better-qualified teachers, enhancing learning and teaching, and introducing Saturday classes).

  — City Academies. City Academies were set up in deprived inner-city areas (were the pupils came from working-class families) where schools were seen as failing. The aim was to knock down the old buildings and build new modern schools. This would help deprived children see their new education environment as exciting and important, and help raise educational achievement.

— **Educational Maintenance Allowance (EMAs).** EMAs are payments of £30 a week to students from low-income backgrounds to encourage them to stay on in post-16 education.

— **National literacy strategy.** This introduced literacy and numeracy hours in all primary schools and reduced class sizes; it was claimed that such policies are of greater benefit to disadvantaged children, and thus help reduce inequality.

✔✗ Evaluation of New Labour

✗ **They failed to deal with social inequality.** Marxists have criticised the New Labour policies for not dealing with social inequality adequately. For example, by retaining the idea of 'marketisation' and through the introduction of policies such as student fees, New Labour perpetuated class inequalities in education.

✗ **Tuition fees discouraged working-class children.** Benn (2012) criticised the New Labour policies on educational inequality. On the one hand, they introduced EMAs to encourage poor students to stay on at school and on the other, they introduced tuition fees for higher education which discourage pupils from working-class backgrounds from continuing their education at university.

✗ **Compensatory education was not effective.** The New Labour polices such as Sure Start and EAZ may not have been effective in terms of raising educational achievement. Research studies have shown that children in secondary school who were part of the Sure Start programme in primary school are still academically still falling behind, and not reaching the expected levels that were expected. This suggests those early interventionist programmes are not as effective in raising educational levels in children in deprived neighbourhoods because external factors play a part (eg, cultural capital, low income, language and cultural deprivation).

Coalition government policies from 2010-215

- From 2010 to 2015, a coalition government was in power (Conservative and Liberal Democrats). The coalition government continued with polices from previous governments but reformed many of them to further tackle educational inequality. They did this by reducing further the role of the LEA and continuing the principle of marketisation by giving greater powers to parents and pupils to choose schools. Some of the main polices to increase choice were:

  — **Academies.** From 2010, all state schools were encouraged to become academies, which would free them from LEA control and the National Curriculum. By 2014, over 56% of secondary and 11% of primary school in England were academies. New Labour's City Academies were focused exclusively on poor areas to replace under-performing comprehensives, whereas the coalition government allowed any school to become an academy, and thus arguably removed the focus on reducing educational inequality.

  — **Free schools.** Free schools are funded by the government (although not controlled by the LEA), do not need to teach the National Curriculum and can be set up by parents, teachers, and charities, often in response of what the local community wants with regards to education. The aim of the free schools programme is to give parents and teachers the chance to create a new school if they are unhappy with state schools in a local area, in the belief that competition will drive up standards and thus help reduce educational inequality.

— **The pupil premium.** The pupil premium is extra money (£600) that the school receives for each pupil who comes from a poor home. The aim is to attract disadvantaged children and help narrow the educational gap and thus reduce social inequalities in education.

— **Help with university fees.** In terms of university education, children from families with low to medium incomes could get help to cover the cost of living while at university, and larger loans were available for those from low-income families. Students were not required to repay anything until they started earning £21,000 and all debts were wiped out after 30 years. Students who did not end up in well-paid jobs would therefore be unlikely to repay the full amount of loans for tuition and maintenance, which would encourage those from poorer family backgrounds to go to university.

✔✘ Evaluation of Coalition government policies

✘ **Free-schools reinforced inequality.** Wiborg (2015) found that children from 'highly-educated' families were the ones who did well in free schools. She argues that free schools actually widen this educational gap between the middle and working class, because popular free schools end up developing selective admissions systems in order to manage demand and thus attract the bright pupils (usually from middle-class). Therefore, she concludes that free schools can lead to greater inequality.

✘ **The pupil premium was ineffective.** Ofsted (2012) found that in many cases the pupil premium made little or no difference to support poorer children as the money is often spent on other matters within the school and thus did not help reduce the educational gap.

Education policies of selection

Schools, given the opportunity, would select bright, motivated and well-behaved pupils in order to achieve the best possible results and remain in a high positon in the league table. However, government policies determine how schools must select their pupils. The main types of selection are:

- **Selection by ability.** Under the tripartite system, schools could select their pupils on academic ability, assessed by an intelligence test at the age of 11 (the 11+ exam). The 11+ exam was the main form of selection for which secondary school pupils attended (grammar or secondary modern). Those who passed the 11+ attended grammar and those who failed attended secondary modern schools. Selection by ability is now forbidden (see below under The Schools Admission Code policy) for all state-funded schools (except for the few remaining state-funded grammar schools). Selection by ability is still commonly used by private, fee-paying schools.

- **Open enrolment.** One policy introduced under the 1988 Education Act was the policy of 'open enrolment'. This gave parents the power to apply to any state-funded school . Schools could only reject applicants if they were physically full. If schools were over-subscribed, they had to follow the over-subscribed criteria (see below).

- **The School Admission Code** introduced in 1998, this must be complied with by all state-funded schools (eg, Academies, free faith, community and foundation schools). The aim of the Admission Code policies is to operate in a fair way and not to discriminate against pupils because of their social, economic, religious or ethnic background. Every child has the same equal opportunities to access a place at a school they desire. If the school is under-subscribed (not full), the school must accept that child. If a school is over-subscribed (more applications than actual places) it must follow set criteria used to allocate places. They are:

  — Priority must be given to children who have a brother or sister at the school.

  — Priority must be given to those who live in the catchment area of the school.

  — Schools can select up to 10% of their intake by aptitude in permitted subjects. Over-subscribed faith schools can prioritise those with the same religious faith.

  — Some over-subscribed state-funded schools pursue a 'fair banding' admissions policy. The school admits a fixed proportion of bright, average and weak students determined by Cognitive Ability Tests (CATs).

This means not all parents are able to get their first choice of school if it is over-subscribed.

- **Selection by aptitude.** A school selects its pupils on the basis of their aptitude or potential to be good in certain subjects (eg, music). Specialist Secondary Schools are state-funded secondary schools allowed to select up to 10 per cent of students on the basis of their aptitude in some specialist subjects.

- **Selection by faith.** Faith schools may select a proportion of their pupils on the basis of the religious beliefs and commitment or their parents.

✔✗ Evaluation of selection policies

Those in favour of selection by ability (regardless of the type of school):

✗ **Selection by ability in state-funded schools.** Critics point out that a form of selection by ability is also practised in non-selective comprehensive schools as pupils are very often put into streams or sets according to their ability.

✗ **High-ability pupils are held back.** Those in favour of selection by ability (regardless of the type of school) argue that brighter children are held back by the less able in a classroom containing pupils of all abilities. They claim that teaching high-ability children together streams or sets within a school would allow them to be academically 'stretched', rather than being held back by slower leaners who are unable to cope with the work.

✗ **Aptitude tests are misused.** Secondary schools which specialise in a subject can select up to 10 per cent of pupils by tests which show aptitude for that subject. However, tests in specialisms like business or economics are 'absurd' because pupils will not have studied the subjects in primary school, so the tests are used to assess ability.

Those not in favour of selection by ability (regardless of the type of school):

✗ **Reduced risk of being labelled a failure.** There is the risk that failing selection by ability may have a negative effect on children's self-esteem (how they feel about themselves and their ability) which can affect their education. Therefore, by removing selection by ability, children are less likely to be labelled as failures at an early age, and thus avoid the damaging effects of low self-esteem.

✗ **Benefits for pupils of all abilities.** It is argued that that when all pupils of the same age, regardless of their ability, are taught in the same type of school and in the same classroom (mixed-ability teaching), the more intelligent pupils can have a stimulating influence on the less able. Recent research by Smyth et al (2006) has shown that mixed-ability teaching can have beneficial effects on the less able students.

✗ **Criticism of the School Admission Code.** The aim of the School Admission Code is to operate in a fair way: not to discriminate against pupils because of their social, economic, religious or ethnic background. However, popular over-subscribed schools tend to be found in wealthy middle-class neighbourhoods. These schools generally produce good results because they contain children from middle-class homes who do better in education (see exam notes 5 on *Social class and education*) for reasons. This means middle-class parents have a better chance of securing a place at an over-subscribed school than working-class parents (eg, because they are able to afford to move into and live in catchment area of a good school). This means working-class parents lose out on getting places in the popular school because they live in the wrong catchment area and in the poorest areas. This contributes to the cycle of social class inequality in education.

✗ **The use of covert selection.** Some schools use covert (hidden) selection policies in an attempt to pick higher-ability children of those from a higher social class and discourage parents from poorer backgrounds to apply, even though this is forbidden by the School Admission Code. Some of the 'covert methods' are making the school literature difficult to understand for parents with poor literacy; having expensive school uniform or kit; no promotion of the school in poorer areas; asking parents to complete long complicated admission forms, as middle-class parents are more able to complete these than working-class parents.

✗ **Fixing 'banding' tests.** Banding means splitting pupils into, say, five different ability groups and taking in an equal number from each through a test. However, some schools make the ceiling for the lowest-ability band so high that even the pupils in the bottom set can be brighter than average.

Gender and educational policies

• Up until the 19th century (1801–1900), girls were mainly excluded from the education system, although middle- and upper-class girls were largely educated in the home to become good wives, and some working-class girls were taught the basics of reading, writing and domestic skills in schools set up by charities or religious institutions.

• The 1944 Education Act brought free secondary education for both genders but even then girls were discriminated against to some extent. The Act introduced the tripartite system but girls often would have to achieve a higher mark than the boys in the 11+ examination in order to secure a place in a grammar school.

- There have been educational policies to reduce gender differences in subject choices such as GIST (Girls into Science and Technology) and WISE (Women into Science and Engineering), which aim to encourage girls into careers in the sciences and technology.

Ethnicity and educational policies

- Assimilation polices were introduced in the 1960s and 1970s aimed at integrating ethnic groups into mainstream British culture as a way of raising educational achievement. In the late 1990s, compensatory education programmes (eg, Education Action Zones) were offered in areas of deprivation, where a high number of ethnic groups were living, in order to boost those under-achieving in school.

Multicultural education

- The 1980s and 1990s saw the introduction of multicultural policies. The aim was to learn about their own and different ethnic cultures and languages as this would raise the self-esteem of ethnic groups and encourage better educational results. Some educational policies in the 1990s to raise educational achievement of ethnic groups included:
  — Monitoring exam results by ethnicity.
  — Amending the Race Relation Act to place a legal duty on schools to promote racial equality.
  — Introducing 'Saturday school' in the black community.
  — Offering additional English language programmes.

✔✗ Evaluation of selection policies on ethnicity

✗ **Institutional racism is the real reason.** Gilborn (2001) argues that institutional racism in the education system is the real cause of under-achievement among ethnic-minority pupils. For example, teaching an ethnocentric curriculum, the negative labelling of ethnic-minority pupils from teachers, and ethnic-minority pupils being consistently placed wrongly in lower-ability sets all continue to disadvantage ethnic minorities. This is supported by Mirza (2005) who argues that educational policies to raise ethnic achievement have had little impact. Such policies have focused on factors such as the home and cultural factors when the real issue is poverty and racism.

✗ **Compensatory education is inadequate.** One criticism of compensatory education programmes is that no amount of educational resources can adequately compensate for a materially and culturally poor family background.

✗ **Some ethnic groups do not speak English as a second language.** Critics argue that some minority groups who are at risk of under-achieving, such as Afro-Caribbean pupils, already speak English and that this proves that the real cause of their under-achievement is institutional racism within what goes on in school.

✗ **Multicultural education policies trivialise ethnic cultures.** Sociologists argue that multicultural education policies trivialise ethnic cultures by picking out stereotypical features (eg, music, dance, religious ceremonies, customs and cuisine). Such a superficial representation does not deal with the deeper issue of why ethnic-minority children underperform, namely, institutional racism.

✗ **Multicultural education produces further racial stereotypes.** Maureen Stone (1981) argues that multicultural education produces further racial stereotypes. For example, a multicultural curriculum encourages Afro-Caribbean pupils to pursue their own cultural awareness by means such as steel bands, rap music and sports pursuits. This confirms the old stereotypical racial views that Afro-Caribbean blacks are good at 'music' and 'sports' and offers no real further advancement.

✗ **A multicultural curriculum produces greater cultural segregation.** The New Right is critical of policies that promote multiculturalism as this is more divisive for society and produces cultural segregation. They hold the view that education should assimilate cultures into one shared national cultural identity (eg, British culture).

Practice exam questions

AS level exam type questions

1. Define the term 'equality of opportunity'. **[2 marks]**

2. Using **one** example briefly explain how compensatory education programmes have helped students from poor home backgrounds. **[2 marks]**

3. Outline **three** educational policies that may have contributed to social class differences in achievement. **[6 marks]**

4. Outline and explain **two** ways in which government educational policies may have affected social class differences in educational achievement. **[10 marks]**

5. Outline and explain **two** policies or reforms aimed at raising educational achievement.

   [10 marks]

6. Outline and explain two effects of marketisation. **[10 marks]**

7. Applying material from **Item (...)** and your knowledge, evaluate the view that the main aim of education policies in the last 25 years has been to create an education market. **[20 marks]**

8. Applying material from **Item (...)** and your knowledge, evaluate the impact of government education policies on inequalities of achievement between social groups. **[20 marks]**

A level exam type questions

1. Outline **two** features of the 'tripartite system' of education. **[4 marks]**

2. Outline **two** criticisms of the comprehensive school system. **[4 marks]**

3. Outline **two** educational reforms which might reduce "class-based differences in educational achievement". **[4 marks]**

4. Outline **three** educational policies that may have contributed to social class differences in achievement. **[6 marks]**

5. Outline **three** policies that may promote the marketisation of education. **[6 marks]**

6. Outline **three** policies that government or educational bodies have introduced to overcome children's cultural deprivation. **[6 marks]**

7. Applying material from **Item (...)** and your knowledge, evaluate the claim that marketisation and privatisation policies have increased educational inequality. **[30 marks]**

Privatisation & Globalisation of Education Policy

The AQA specification: Education

- The significance of educational policies, including policies of selection, marketisation and privatisation, and policies to achieve greater equality of opportunity or outcome, for an understanding of the structure, role, impact and experience of and access to education; the impact of globalisation on educational policy.

The exam requires that you are able to:

▶ Describe and evaluate the educational policies of privatisation.

▶ Describe and evaluate the impact that globalisation has had on educational policies.

Key term

- **Privatisation** refers to the transfer of government assets or responsibilities (eg, schools) to private companies. In recent years there has been an increase towards the privatisation of public services (eg, education and health services), both in the UK and globally.

- **Globalisation** refers to how countries are becoming more interconnected. This has led to the global spread and influence of all aspects of life (eg, ideas, cultures, consumer goods and economic interests).

Educational policies of privatisation

There are two types of privatisation of education:

- Endogenous privatisation is using the ideas and practices of running private businesses and applying them to the education system so schools, colleges and universities behave, and are run, more like private businesses. Some example of endogenous privatisation are:

  — Privatisation of the education system was first introduced by the Conservative government (1979-1997) through the 1988 Education Reform Act, which included educational policies such as 'marketisation' (eg, publication of school performance tables, parental choice, schools being funded according to the number of students they had).

  — Privatisation continued with the Labour government (1997-2010), for example, by performance-related pay whereby teachers were paid according to how well their students did. A programme of new buildings for schools and colleges was partly financed by the Private Finance Initiative (PFI): private companies built schools but in return were given contracts to receive loan repayment, and to provide maintenance for 25-35 years.

  — The Conservative-Liberal coalition government (2010-2015) continued the privatisation of education, introducing academies which are run and managed by private education businesses. Ultimately, the aim of privatising the education system is to raise educational standards.

- **Exogenous privatisation** refers to the private business sector moving into the education system (formerly run by the central or local government) in order to make a profit, by designing, managing or delivering aspects of education. Private firms and consultants are now very active in selling educational services that have often previously been delivered by local and national government. These can include:

— *School services.* Outsourcing services such as buildings maintenance, provision and management of ICT, catering, cleaning, staff training and development, consultancy and the use of supply teachers.

— *The management of academies.* Many academies are managed by private educational businesses such as Academies Enterprise Trust and E-ACT, which run around seventy secondary schools as well as primary and special schools.

— *School inspections.* Private companies such as Tribal Inspections run school inspections on behalf of Ofsted (The Office for Standards in Education, Children's Services and Skills). However, in 2014, Ofsted announced it would stop using private contractors to carry out school inspections, following concerns over the selection, training and quality of the inspectors employed.

— *Building schools.* PFI schemes give private companies contracts to design, build and manage educational services (eg, catering, cleaning and maintenance). The contract between the private investor and the government (local council) lasts for about 25-35 years, during which time the private companies receive repayment at a high rate of interest from the government, giving them a good profit.

— *Branding of schools.* Private companies are selling schools website construction, logo development and school prospectuses, all designed to give schools a distinct identity enabling them to compete in the educational marketplace.

— *Running the examination system.* The UK's largest exam board, Edexcel Pearson Edexcel, is run by the multinational private profit-making company Pearson PLC. Pearson is one of the world's largest educational and book publishing companies and provides academic and vocational qualifications in over seventy countries.

✔✘ Evaluation of selection policies on ethnicity

✔ **Privatisation raises educational standards.** One argument is that in a competitive education market, local education authorities and schools can compare the services offered by private education companies and select the supplier which is most efficient and offers best value for money, which can only mean more children can be educated to a higher standard.

✘ **Private companies are primarily profit driven.** Private companies may not reinvest profits in education which may lead to a lower quality of education and opportunity for some children.

✘ **Private companies ignore challenging schools.** Schools that are managed by private companies (eg, academies and free schools) need to remain competitive in the education market and will be judged on how well the school performs. This means they are more likely to avoid schools with students who are challenging or of low academic ability, and pick schools which can easily be improved. This suggests that the privatisation of education would allow certain companies to put profit over the needs of the children, and thus reduce the educational opportunities of the children who need them most.

The impact of globalisation on educational policy

- One of the main impacts of globalisation on UK education policy is the greater shift towards treating education more like a business. The two main ways in which globalisation has had an impact are:

Greater privatisation of the education system

- The Conservative government (1979-1997) introduced the 1988 Education Reform Act which introduced marketisation and privatisation policies into the education system. Anthony Kelly (2009) argues that globalisation has increased the trend towards the privatisation of the education system. Many educational organisations and services are now owned by private foreign companies in the UK. For example, some of the PFIs in the UK are financed by overseas companies (eg, Skanska and Kajima). The main leading educational software companies are all owned by global multinational companies (eg, Disney, Mattel and Hambro). The UK's exam board, Edexcel, is owned by one of the largest US educational publishing companies, Pearson.

- Some UK educational companies and organisations also operate internationally. Private schools and colleges have become increasingly reliant upon overseas pupils, particularly from China and Hong Kong. In this process, students can be viewed as commodities to be bought and sold to different educational institutions for profit. Capita, Edison Bright Horizons and Kaplan, to name but a few, all provide different forms of educational services abroad (eg, schools, nurseries, courses, teacher recruitment).

- **Forming educational policy.** Private companies are providing consultancy work by exporting UK educational policies, such as Ofsted-type inspections, to other countries, and then providing the services to deliver such policies.

- **Global economic competitiveness.** UK workers now need to compete with others in a global economy which requires them to have skills that will be valuable in a global market. Globalisation has meant that the British government (like other national governments) has tailored its educational policy to meet the needs of a global economy.

- **Commercialisation.** Private companies (Tesco, Walker's Crisps, Cadburys) are promoting their product or brand by targeting youth consumers through schools, for example, by selling to schoolchildren through vending machines, sponsorships and equipment promotions. This process has been called the cola-isation of schools (especially in the USA). Molnar (2005) suggests that a school's very nature helps the brand be seen as legitimate and acceptable: 'it must be OK' if the school endorses it.

International comparison of education systems

- Globalisation has meant that we can compare the educational performance of students in different countries. OECD's PISA (Programme for International Student Assessment) conducts tests on 15-year-old students from around 70 countries every 3 to 5 years in mathematics, science and reading. The data are then ranked in the form of league tables to show the performance of different countries. By comparing the educational performance of other countries, national governments can reassess existing policies or import educational policies (eg, curriculum reform, teaching and learning) of those countries that are doing well into their own education systems, hoping to raise standards. Ofsted often uses such educational performance comparisons (PISA, 2012) to explain the generally poor performance of British students and has identified possible solutions by copying other the educational systems of countries' (eg, those of Central Europe and Asia) that came top in the international league tables. Alexander (2012) identifies the following specific examples of policies implemented as a result of international comparisons:

— *The national literacy and numeracy strategies* introduced by the Labour government which ran from 1998/9 to 2010. These imposed on every primary school in England a requirement to teach two hours of literacy and numeracy every day.

— *Slimming down the national curriculum.* The 2010-15 Conservative-Liberal Democrat coalition government slimmed down England's national curriculum (from 2014) to 'essential knowledge' in English, mathematics and science and some other subjects, which was defined by the then Secretary of State Michael Gove as 'the essential core knowledge which other nations pass on to their pupils'.

— *Raising the academic entry requirements for trainee teachers* from 2012. This was generally derived from comparisons with Finland, which has, for years, been a world leader in international education assessments.

— *Master teachers.* In 2014, the Labour Party announced plans, if it won the 2015 elections, to create a new elite grade of 'master teachers' in all state schools, specifically citing a similar policy in Singapore (which came 3rd in PISA in 2012).

✔✘ Evaluation of the globalisation of educational policy

✔ **International comparison.** International comparisons provide 'factual evidence' for governments wanting to amend or introduce new policies that may not be welcomed by those in the education system (eg, teachers' unions) or politicians.

✔ **Helps to see which policies work best.** International comparison allows governments to improve their own education system by seeing which policies work best and which do not.

✘ **PISA tests are not comparable.** Those countries that consistently do well in the international PISA tests provide evidence for a very narrow aspect of education (literacy, numeracy and science) and may not provide their children with a wider education. If this were taken into account, the top-performing countries might not maintain their international high rankings.

✘ **PISA is not a valid test.** Alexander (2012) argues the international comparison of test results does not necessarily indicate that education systems are better or worse in different countries, as quality of education could depend on outside-school factors. For example, comparing high-performing countries such as Hong Kong or Singapore with the UK is meaningless because the cultures are so different and the education systems are not comparable (England has approx. 24,000 schools and Singapore has just 350). Alexander argues that the relatively low results of the UK's PISA tests have led to an exaggerated 'PISA panic' in Britain, suggesting the state of British education is in a poor shape, whereas the PISA test may not be valid form of measurement.

✘ **Globalisation may lead to a marginalised education.** According to Stephen Ball, the impact of globalisation on all nations has meant that most changes in educational policies have been geared towards preparing the young for work in a competing economic global market, that is, the development of work-based skills. This may mean that many national governments will place less emphasis on the wider role of education, such as passing on important knowledge (eg, the social, cultural, moral and personal development of the child) which turns individuals into good citizens.

Practice exam questions

AS level exam type questions

1. Define the term 'privatisation'. [2 marks]

2. Define the term 'globalisation'. [2 marks]

3. Using **one** example briefly explain how privatisation may have affected social class differences in educational achievement. [2 marks]

4. Outline **three** educational policies of privatisation that aimed to helped raise educational achievement. [6 marks]

5. Applying material from **Item (...)** and your knowledge, evaluate the impact globalisation has had on UK educational policies. [20 marks]

A level exam type questions

1. Outline **two** ways globalisation has had an impact on the UK's education system. [4 marks]

2. Outline **two** criticisms of the privatisation of education. [4 marks]

3. Outline **three** educational policies that may have contributed to social class differences in achievement. [6 marks]

4. Applying material from **Item (...)** and your knowledge, evaluate the impact globalisation has had on UK educational policies. [30 marks]

Section 2

Research Methods
(including Methods in Context)

AQA Specification

Research methods	AQA
Students must examine the following areas:	• quantitative and qualitative methods of research; research design • sources of data, including questionnaires, interviews, participant and non-participant observation, experiments, documents and official statistics • the distinction between primary and secondary data, and between quantitative and qualitative data • the relationship between positivism, interpretivism and sociological methods; the nature of 'social facts'. • the theoretical, practical and ethical considerations influencing choice of topic, choice of method(s) and the conduct of research

Research methods and key concepts

The exam requires that you are able to:

▶ Understand what is meant by primary and secondary data, and quantitative and qualitative data.

▶ Understand the different ways of evaluating research methods.

Research methods

What is the point of doing sociological research?

The purpose of any sociological research study is to collect information (often referred to as 'data') in order get a better understanding of people's social behaviour and the social world they live in. Sociologists do this by carrying out investigations called 'research studies' to collect evidence. Collecting information helps us to build up or challenge existing sociological knowledge (eg, theories and explanations) about our social behaviour/world. Governments, sociologists and the like can use this information to help improve society.

The different research methods sociologists use

Below are the different research methods that sociologists can use when carrying out an investigation:

- **Experiments** (field and laboratory experiments).
- **Questionnaires** (open-ended or close-ended).
- **Interviews** (structured or unstructured).
- **Observations** (structured or unstructured).
- **Official statistics** (produced by governments, eg, marriage, divorce, birth, death and crime).
- **Documents** (eg, diaries, letters, magazines, photographs, newspapers and television programmes).

Primary and secondary sources of data

When deciding on their research method (as listed above), sociologists have a choice of using either **primary** or **secondary** sources of data. *Primary data* is information that has been collected by the sociologists themselves for their own purpose. *Secondary data* is information that already exists and has been collected, usually by non-sociologists, with quite different purposes in mind to those of sociological researchers. This type of data may then be re-interpreted and re-analysed by sociologists for their own objectives. The table below shows which research methods use primary and secondary sources of data:.

Primary sources of data

- **Experiments**
- **Interviews**
- **Questionnaires**
- **Observations**

Secondary sources of data

- **Official statistics** (eg, government statistics)
- **Documents** (eg, diaries, letters, newspapers and magazines)

✔/✗ Evaluation

Advantages and disadvantages of using primary data

✔ **Control over the research.** The sociologist has complete control of their investigation, which means they can collect the information they want rather than using existing information that may not be completely relevant.

✔ **Original data.** Often no secondary data exist on a particular issue, which means that the sociologist has no choice but to undertake their own research study.

✗ **Cost and time.** Sociologists may not be able to carry out their own research investigation because doing so can be time-consuming and costly.

Advantages and disadvantages of using secondary data

✔ **Quick and cheap.** Using secondary data is much cheaper and less time-consuming then carrying out your own research: the researcher does not have to spend money or time collecting their own information as it already exists.

✔ **Only source available.** Existing secondary sources may be the only option available for sociologists. This is especially true if they are investigating something that has happened in the past, for example, what type of education girls used to have.

✗ **Different purposes.** Secondary information is collected by non-sociologists for very different purposes than those which sociologists have in mind. This means that a sociologist may find some of the information unsuitable for what they are trying to find out.

Qualitative and quantitative data

Sociologists may collect or use two types of data while carrying out a research study. We call these quantitative and qualitative data.

- **Quantitative data.** This refers to information collected in numerical form, that is, in numbers, often in statistics (eg, percentages, averages, tally scores, etc). Some research methods allow the findings gathered by the study to be easily quantified and expressed numerically, for example, carrying out a questionnaire in your school to see how many students think school uniform should be abolished. Research methods that collect quantitative data are referred to as **quantitative research methods.**

- **Qualitative data.** This refers to information that is collected in written words (and/or audio and video) rather than numerically. The purpose of gathering qualitative data is to provide a rich and detailed account of the participants' meanings, thoughts and experiences, allowing a deeper understanding of what they mean. Research methods that collect quantitative data are referred to as **qualitative research methods.**

Research methods that collect quantitative data

Primary sources

- Experiments
- Structured interviews
- Closed questionnaires
- Controlled observations

Secondary sources

- Official statistics

Research methods that collect qualitative data

Primary sources

- Unstructured interviews
- Open questionnaires
- Unstructured observations

Secondary sources

- Diaries, letters, newspapers, magazines

✔✗ Evaluation

Advantages and disadvantages of using quantitative data

✔ **Easy to analyse and interpret.** An advantage of research methods that collect the information as quantitative data is that they allow the numbers to be quantified and summarised, which makes it easy to analyse and interpret the data to see if they identify patterns or causal links. This allows us to make generalisations about cause and effect in human behaviour, for example, that the amount of time young children spend playing violent video games leads to an increase in aggressive physical behaviour at school.

✗ **Time-consuming.** A disadvantage of quantitative data is that it reduces thoughts and feelings to numbers, which limits a deeper understanding of human behaviour and experiences. Quantitative data cannot explain why people do things, just identify trends or relationships. For example, sociologists may find a relationship between middle-age men and high levels of suicide but fails to explain why middle-age men are more likely to commit suicide than other age groups.

Advantages and disadvantages of qualitative data

✔ **Deeper understanding.** One advantage of research methods that collect qualitative data is that they provide a deeper understanding of human behaviour, such as experiences, values, attitudes and beliefs, that cannot be achieved by quantitative methods.

✗ **Time-consuming.** One disadvantage of research methods that collect qualitative data is that information gathered is most often in written form, which is difficult to code, analyse and interpret. Therefore, it is less easy to form conclusions than when using quantitative data.

Evaluating research methods

To determine (evaluate) how useful a research method is (ie, its strengths and weaknesses), we need to consider three key terms: **validity, reliability** and **representativeness.** The perfect research method will strive for all three; unfortunately, however, no research method incorporates all three when gathering data. All research methods have a weakness in regard to one or two of the key terms, and this should always be pointed out when assessing their weaknesses and strengths. When evaluating any research method, you should always ask the questions:

— How **valid** is the study?
— How **reliable** is the study?
— How **representative** is the study?

Reliability

- **Replication of method.** Reliability refers to the replicability of a research method to check if the findings are consistent. If the method used in a study can be easily repeated to check the results, we say it is a reliable method. Methods viewed as being easily replicable are:

  — **close-ended questionnaires**
  — **structured interviews**
  — **controlled observations**
  — **experiments**

The above methods are viewed as reliable because they are conducted and collect data in a structured way, that is, instructions, procedures, questions are all carried out in standardised and/or controlled conditions with little interpretation or involvement on the part of the researcher. This means another researcher can repeat the same standardised format as the original study to see whether similar results are found. The 'unstructured' methods such as open-ended questionnaires, unstructured interviews and participant observations are less reliable research methods. It is very hard to replicate studies using these techniques with the same questions, procedures and conditions as in the original study, given that these conditions are often unique, and therefore difficult to see whether they yield similar results.

- **Reliability of data.** Reliability also refers to how **consistent the findings (data)** are in the study. If the chosen method is easily replicable, we can also check the reliability of the findings. That is, if the study were to be carried out again by other sociologists on a similar or identical group of people and similar results were found, the findings would be said to be reliable. As noted, the 'structured' methods are easier to replicate, to see if the findings are reliable, than 'unstructured' methods.

It is important that the findings are reliable in order for the study to be trusted, so sociologists can make generalisations from them.

Exam advice

Please note: in exams, do not make absolute statements, for example, 'questionnaires are reliable' or 'observations are unreliable', as no research is 100% reliable or unreliable. Instead, write 'high' or 'low'. So, for example, you should say, 'It has been argued that questionnaires are high in reliability'. This is more of an evaluative comment.

Validity

- Another important aspect of evaluating any sociological research is validity. **Validity** refers to how accurate and true the findings of the study are. A study that is valid is one that produces a true picture of what it is aiming to investigate. If the research lacks validity, the researcher cannot ensure that their findings, on the whole, reflect the truth of what the aim of their study was.

Exam advice

Please note: in exams, do not make absolute statements, for example, 'questionnaires are reliable' or 'observations are unreliable', as no research is 100% reliable or unreliable. Instead, write 'high' or 'low'. So, for example, you should say, 'It has been argued that questionnaires are high in reliability'. This is more of an evaluative comment.

Representativeness

- A sample of participants is selected to participate in the study (eg, a few A Level students). The purpose of a sample is that the findings from it reflect or 'represent' the group of people that the researcher is interested in (eg, all A Level students in the country), which is known as the target population. The aim of a sample is to allow the findings collected from a study to be representative (ie, typical) of the target population. Therefore, when we say the findings are 'representative' this means they reflect the views/behaviour of the target population. A study that is representative allows the researcher to make **generalisations** (draw conclusions) from it about the target population.

- If the study is not representative, it is not possible to make generalisations to the larger group in society (target population), which means the findings have no significance and limited use. The larger the sample of people used in the study, the greater the chance that the findings from study will be representative.

The relationship between validity and reliability

- The findings of research can be *reliable* but not *valid*. A study that consistently produces the same results when repeated does not necessarily reflect an accurate picture of what it *set out* to investigate. For example, a group of students used a questionnaire to investigate the drinking behaviour of their teachers on weekdays. The results showed that 1 out of 50 teachers said that they drank during the week. Is this likely to be a true reflection of their drinking behaviour? It is possible that the teachers lied on the questionnaire because they were afraid that the students would disapprove of their drinking habits. The students might administer the questionnaire on other occasions and the teachers might continue to lie, thus producing the same false results consistently. Such findings are *reliable,* but they lack validity because the study failed to find out about the teachers' real drinking habits.

Practice exam questions

AS level exam questions

Paper 2

1. Outline **two** problems of using qualitative data in sociological research. **[4 marks]**

2. Outline **two** problems of using quantitative data in sociological research. **[4 marks]**

3. Evaluate the uses of different kinds of secondary data in sociological research. **[16 marks]**

4. Evaluate the reasons that some sociologists prefer to collect and use quantitative data in their research. **[16 marks]**

5. Evaluate the reasons that some sociologists prefer to collect and use qualitative data in their research. **[16 marks]**

A level exam questions

Paper 1 and 3

1. Outline and explain what is meant by 'validity' and 'reliability' in sociological research. **[10 marks]**

2. Outline and explain **two** reasons that positivists prefer quantitative research methods. **[10 marks]**

3. Outline and explain **two** problems with using quantitative research methods. **[10 marks]**

4. Outline and explain **two** reasons that interpretivists prefer qualitative research methods. **[10 marks]**

5. Outline and explain **two** problems with using quantitative research methods. **[16 marks]**

6. Outline and explain **two** advantages of using secondary data in sociological research. **[10 marks]**

7. Outline and explain **two** reasons that some sociologists prefer to collect and use primary data in their research. **[10 marks]**

Paper 3

8. Applying material from **Item (...)** and your knowledge, evaluate the claim that quantitative research methods may have many advantages, but they tell us little about what people really think and do. **[20 marks]**

The exam requires that you are able to:

▶ Understand the theoretical, practical and ethical factors that influence the choice of research methods.

▶ Understand how sociologists assesses their relative importance when choosing a research method.

Factors influencing choice of research methods

A sociologist needs to decide which research method to use to collect data about people. This is not a straightforward process. There are certain factors involved, which we classify into the three broad categories 'theoretical', 'practical' and 'ethical', and which can influence the sociologist's choice of method and topic of research. The sociologist will have to look at all these aspects before they can decide which is the most appropriate method to use.

— **Theoretical factors.** What type of methodological research does the sociologist prefer: a 'positivist' or an 'interpretivist' approach?

— **Practical factors.** This includes issues such as topic of research, how much time is available, funding, accessibility and personal characteristics.

— **Ethical factors.** The sociologist needs to deal with and resolve any ethical problems that can occur in their research. They may need to modify their design or choose a different research method.

Theoretical factors: positivism or interpretivism

The research method chosen will be influenced by the sociologist's own methodological perspective, that is, whether they are a positivist or an *interpretivist*. When we talk about 'methodological perspective', we are referring to how human behaviour should be studied, that is, what type of data we want to collect. If you are a positivist, you will prefer methods that collect quantitative data whereas if you are an interpretivist, you will choose a research method that collects qualitative data. Therefore, the sociologist's position affects their choice of research method, the kind of questions they ask, the type of data collected, and whether they attribute more importance to reliability and representativeness of data, or validity.

Positivism

● **What is positivism?** Positivists believe the social world is made up of 'social facts' (or objective reality) that exist 'out there' outside our mind, and that are real, just like the physical world. Social facts are often 'abstract concepts' such as 'religion', 'marriage', 'values', 'social control' and 'social integration'. According to positivists, these external abstract social facts can influence the way we think, feel and behave. Sociologists who use positivist research suggest that 'social facts' can be studied using methods that collect quantitative data (see below).

Positivist research is seen as scientific and is used by natural scientists for gathering information about the natural world. This is because data are collected in a systematic and objective manner.

● **Why do positivists prefer quantitative data?** Positivists prefer collecting quantitative data because they can analyse them to see if there are patterns in the information, such as seeing if a causal relationship (cause-and-effect link) exists between two factors, for example, whether parents' income has an effect on a child's GCSE results. This allows positivists to construct laws or theories of social behaviour that can be generalised to the wider population based on the data collected from the sample.

- **Preference of method.** If the sociologist has a preference for positivist research, this means they prefer collecting quantitative data and therefore prefer structured methods of data collection, such as:
  - close-ended questionnaires
  - structured interviews
  - official statistics
  - controlled observations
  - experiments
  - content analysis

  Positivists claim that 'structured' methods of collecting quantitative data are more objective, reliable and representative (as a larger sample is often possible), which they see as being more important characteristics than validity.

Interpretivists

- **What is interpretivism?** Sociologists who use interpretivist research are interested in achieving a deeper insight into human behaviour; they want to get a better understanding of the meanings and reasons we give to situations that influence our behaviour. Therefore, they reject the positivist view that there exists an objective social reality (social facts) that shapes and influences our behaviour, and believe instead that we construct our reality through our daily interaction with other people.

- **Why do they prefer qualitative data?** Interpretivists prefer collecting qualitative data because this allows them to achieve a deeper insight into and understanding of the meanings and motives that govern people's behaviour and attitudes. Interpretivists claim that 'unstructured' methods of collecting qualitative data produce a more valid account of human behaviour, and regard validity as more important than reliability or representativeness, or whether the data allow generalisations to be made to the wider population.

- **Preference of method.** If the sociologist has a preference for interpretivist research, this means they prefer collecting qualitative data and, therefore, unstructured methods of data collection such as:
  - open-ended questionnaires
  - unstructured interviews
  - participant observations
  - documents (life history, novels, letters, diaries, autobiographical mass media reports, etc).

Functionalism, Marxism and Interactionism: Positivists and Interpretivists

Functionalism and Marxism see society as being made up of large social structures/institutions (eg, the judicial system, family, religion and education). These external social structures exist 'outside' us individuals and shape our social behaviour. They therefore take a positivist approach to studying society.

Interactionism believes small-scale face-to-face or small group interactions influence our behaviour, and therefore favours an interpretivist approach to get a better understanding of the society we live in.

Practical factors

Practical and ethical issues are not choices the sociologist makes, like whether to take a positivist or an interpretivist approach, but are factors that may limit their choice of research methods. This means the researcher may need to compromise their own theoretical (positivist or interpretivist) perspective at times because of practical or ethical constraints, which thus influence the methods chosen.

- **Research topic.** The topic to be studied can clearly influence the type of research method used. If the sociologist wants to examine sensitive issues such as domestic violence, an unstructured interview would be more appropriate than a standardised close-ended questionnaire. When investigating deviant or secretive groups such as extreme political parties or criminal gangs, it would also be inappropriate to use structured methods (eg, questionnaires). If, however, the sociologist wants to investigate how many hours students spend doing homework, or what type of families exist in London, for example, then they may take a positivist approach, and use questionnaires.

- **Time.** Different methods vary in the amount of time and cost needed to carry out the investigation – these two are inevitably linked, which can restrict the sociologist's choice of method.

  — *Quantitative methods.* If the sociologist has limited time and funding, they will adopt a quantitative method (questionnaires) as being cheaper and quicker than qualitative methods. For example, the cost of mail questionnaires, in which postal charges take the place of the interviewers' expenses and salaries, is often a fraction of the cost of carrying out a social survey, because interviewers do not need to be paid to conduct the study. Sometimes the population to be covered may be so widely and thinly spread, and the funds available so limited, that the mail questionnaire is the only feasible approach.

  — *Qualitative methods* require much more time and are often more expensive, especially if methods such as covert observation are used, in which the researcher will need to spend much of their time trying to access the group and then building a rapport with it, all of which takes a lot of time and money. The money factor is further explained in the next section.

- **Funding.** Most organisations (eg, universities, governments and private organisations) often fund research information for their own particular purpose. Money is limited; research can be very expensive and can only be carried out if funding is secured. If funding is limited, the researcher cannot explore in as much depth as they may wish, and may have to terminate the research once the funding has stopped. This will often affect the hypothesis put forward for the research. Furthermore, if the research has little commercial value, funding will be hard to secure and it is therefore less likely to be carried out.

- **Accessibility.** There is also the issue of accessibility. Can the sociologist gain access to the people or social situation that they would like to study? Some people may simply refuse to take part, for various reasons. Children, schools and secretive/deviant groups can often make it difficult to gain access, which means researchers will have to find another way of getting the information, or choose another topic to investigate.

- **Personal characteristics.** Some types of research may not be feasible because of the sociologist's own social characteristics, such as sex, age, class and ethnicity. For example, it is unlikely that female teenagers will feel comfortable in answering questions relating to sex and adolescence posed by an older male researcher. The means the personal characteristics of the sociologists can compromise the validity of the research, which must be taken into account when embarking on a topic of interest.

Ethical factors

- **Ethics** refers to morals, that is, what is right and wrong. When carrying out a study, researchers need to think carefully about how the experience may affect the participants. Sociologists need to ensure that taking part in the study will not harm participants in any way, either socially or physically. The **British Sociological Association (BSA)** sets out **ethical guidelines,** which are 'rules' that sociologists must consider when designing and carrying out a study to ensure the wellbeing of the participants. Some of the main guidelines deal with:

  — **Professional integrity**

  — **Informed consent**

  — **Ensuring there is no deception**

  — **Preventing harm and distress**

  — **Confidentiality and privacy**

- **Ethics issues** refer to the moral concerns/problems that can crop up in a study. Will the study have negative effects on the participants, such as psychological damage or mistrust? Different research methods have different ethical problems, although all research studies tend to have some form of ethical issue that the sociologist needs to address. They will need to think about ethical issues during the design stage, when carrying out the study and after it has finished, for example, in the publication of results.

- **Ethics committees**. Organisations (eg, governments and universities) have their own internal 'ethics committees'. The role of these committees is to assess and advise on ethical issues that may arise for the sociologists who wish to carry out a study. Some ethics committees may not approve some research investigations if they feel the risks (physical, social and psychological, legal, or of financial litigation) outweigh the benefits. If this is the case, sociologists may need to consider a different research method.

The influence of ethical issues on choice of research method

Ethical issues can influence the choice of methods in the following ways:

  — If the ethical problems are too great, research methods will need to be changed or modified.

  — If the sociologist feels the ethical issues are minimal or that their research topic is of such importance to society, it may be considered worth breaking ethical guidelines for the greater good of society.

British Sociological Association (BSA) guidelines.

- **Informed consent.** Before agreeing to take part in a study, the participants will need to be fully informed about its aims and procedure, and how the data will be used. They will also need to be informed about their rights, that is, that their confidentiality and anonymity will be respected, and that they have the **right to withdraw** from the study at any time. Children under the age of 16 need the consent of a parent or guardian.

  Ethical issues that occur with informed consent. There can be problems with obtaining informed consent that the sociologist will need to consider (eg, by changing or revising method, or ignoring the issue).

  — *Information withheld.* The participants may have consented to take part, although they may not have been fully informed about the true purpose of the study. This means deception has been used (see below under 'deception').

  — *Field studies.* In field studies such as observational research and field experiments, the participants may be unaware that they are being investigated. Therefore, informed consent is difficult or impossible to obtain.

  — *Young children.* Young children or people with disabilities or impairments may have limited understanding and therefore may not fully understand the research investigation, even if they have given informed consent.

  — *Publication of results.* The researcher may use the results when consent has been withdrawn from the participants.

- **Deception.** The use of deception in a study means the participants were deliberately misled or lied to, or that vital information was withheld about the true purpose of the study. BSA guidelines state that lying to the participants should be avoided. However, some sociologists argue that the use of deception is unavoidable at times, because explaining the true aims of the study can affect participants' behaviour/responses and thus reduces the validity of the research. For example, if it was not for covert methods, we would not have a vital understanding of some secretive groups; for this reason, it is justified.

  Ethical issues that occur with deception. The sociologist will need to consider whether the use of deception is justified, and depending on their conclusion will need to change or revise method, or decide to proceed nonetheless.

  — *Morally wrong to lie.* This is the main ethical issue for covert observational research because the researcher's identity and aim are not known to the participants and therefore they are being deceived. Deception is also often used in experiments, with the participants not being told the true aim of the study.

  — *Lack of informed consent.* If participants have been deceived, they cannot have been fully informed and therefore were unable to consent because they did not know the true purpose of the study.

- **Confidentiality and privacy.** Participants must be guaranteed confidentiality, that is, that all information (data) collected during the study will be kept private. Anonymity must also be guaranteed, that is, the person's identity must be hidden.

Ethical issues that occur with confidentiality and privacy. Confidentiality/anonymity can be an issue if they cannot be guaranteed by the researcher. The participant must be told in advance if this is the case.

— *Confidentiality breached.* An ethical issue may arise when the sociologist needs to decide if information reported cannot be kept confidential for legal, safety or health reasons. The sociologist may uncover unexpected information from the participant such as illegal, abusive or dangerous activities. Does the sociologist report to the appropriate authorities (eg, police, family or head teacher) which may lead to action against the participant? Or would not reporting the findings put others at risk?

- **No harm and distress.** The sociologists have the responsibility to protect participants from any physical and psychological harm (eg, being anxious or distressed, or having feelings of low-esteem or embarrassment) during the research study. Normally, the risk of harm must be no greater than in ordinary life. Equally, the sociologist should avoid any potential risks to their own safety.

Ethical issues that occur with harm and distress. The sociologist will need to revise or change the method if they anticipate possible harm to the participants.

— *Harm/distress.* An ethical issue may arise if an observation, questionnaire or interview provokes negative feelings (eg, low-esteem or worthlessness) or undesirable feelings (eg, embarrassment or stress). The sociologist needs to consider the effect their research may have, although this is difficult to measure as the sociologist cannot always predict the level of harm caused.

- **Professional integrity.** Sociologists need to show professional integrity, which means they need to conduct and report their research in a professional and truthful manner that: [1] does not undermine the reputation of sociology as a discipline; [2] falls within a legal framework (does not break the law).

Ethical issues that occur with professional integrity. Ethical issues as well as illegality may arise if sociologists are drawn into carrying out illegal or immoral activities simply to protect their identity (as in covert participant observation). Most sociologists consider it wrong to take part in or condone illegal or bad behaviour. For this reason, some may refuse to carry out secretive (covert) research, while others may argue the benefits (knowledge and insight) outweigh the cost/risk.

- **Covert research.** Covert research (eg, covert participant observation) is when the identity of the researcher and the purpose of the study are kept hidden (undisclosed) from the group being observed.

Ethical issues that occur with covert research. If the sociologist is considering covert observation, they may choose to break the ethical guidelines concerning deception as opposed to informed consent.

— *Deception/consent/privacy.* There are serious ethical issues in the use of covert research, such as deception, lack of consent and invasion of privacy. In covert research, participants are not told the truth with regards to the researcher's identity and the purpose of the research aim; they are deceived and their privacy is invaded. If the participants are deceived, they cannot have given informed consent.

— *Covert observational research justified.* Some sociologists argue that the use of covert methods may be justified in certain circumstances. For example, it may be justified on the grounds that the participants will change their behaviour if they know they are being studied, which will affect the validity of the findings. It may also be justified when the sociologist faces difficulty in accessing powerful, dangerous or secretive groups.

Which of the three factors is more important?

- Many sociologists would argue that the greatest 'factor' influencing the choice of research method is their theoretical standpoint (positivism or interpretivism); and what kind of data they feel is most useful, quantitative or qualitative. The theoretical standpoint of a researcher is a positive influence on their choice of method, determining the type of data the sociologist wants to use. However, practical and ethical factors can be seen as acting as a constraint on methodological choice. For example, what a researcher would like to do may be restricted by practical issues (time, funding, choice of topic or personal characteristics), and ethical issues (deception, confidentiality, etc), which can limit or cut off their chosen methods. This shows that all three factors are interrelated and all are important.

Triangulation

- Sociologists are not limited to making a choice between quantitative or qualitative methods but combine both methods, which is known as triangulation. The idea of triangulation is that the strength of one method counters the weakness of the other, for example, the findings of a questionnaire can be compared with the findings of an unstructured interview, each thus countering the flaws of the other to 'gain the best of both worlds'. Some researchers 'triangulate' in order to increase the validity (which is favoured by interpretivists), or the reliability and representativeness of the findings (which is favoured by positivists).

PERVERT - Bringing it all together

We can evaluate the strengths and weakness of a research method (a standalone 'research methods' question or a 'methods in context' question) by using the acronym 'pervert' to help you answer any question on research methods more effectively. **PERVERT** stands for:

- **Practical** issues that may restrict the choice of method (time, finances, personal factors, etc).
- **Ethical** issues that may influence choice of method or the effect it may have on people.
- **Reliability** of the information collected – could the study be replicated by others to check the findings?
- **Validity** of the information obtained – will the study provide authentic and true information?
- **Examples** from research studies or application of real-life examples to demonstrate the point you're making.
- **Representativeness** of the information – can the findings be generalised beyond the research sample?
- **Theoretical** issues – will the sociologist's choice of method be based on their methodological preference, that is, positivism or interpretivism?

In the exam notes, we have classified 'pervert' under three main categories:

Theoretical issues	Practical issues	Ethical issues
• Positivism	• Research topic	• Informed consent
• Interpretivism	• Time	• Deception
• Validity	• Funding	• Confidentiality and privacy
• Reliability	• Accessibility	• No harm and distress
• Representatives	• Personal characteristics	• Professional integrity
		• Covert Research

Practice exam questions

AS level exam questions

Paper 2

1. Outline **two** practical factors affecting sociologists' choice of research topic.   **[4 marks]**

2. Outline **two** 'ethical issues' that sociologists might take into account when choosing a research method.   **[4 marks]**

3. Outline **two** factors that influence a researcher's choice of method.   **[4 marks]**

4. Outline **two** problems with the types of research methods that might be used by interpretivist sociologists.   **[4 marks]**

5. Outline **two** problems with the types of research methods that might be used by positivist sociologists.   **[4 marks]**

6. Evaluate the ethical problems that sociologists may face in conducting their research. **[16 marks]**

7. Evaluate how far different factors may affect sociologists' choice of research methods. **[16 marks]**

8. Evaluate the view that theoretical issues are the most important influences when choosing a research topic and the research method to investigate it.   **[16 marks]**

A level exam questions

Paper 1 and 3

9. Outline and explain **two** ethical issues that may affect sociologists' choice of research methods.   **[10 marks]**

10. Outline and explain **two** practical issues that may affect sociologists' choice of research methods.   **[10 marks]**

11. Applying material from **Item (...)** and your knowledge, evaluate the view that different factors affect sociologists' choice of research methods.   **[20 marks]**

12. Applying material from **Item (...)** and your knowledge, evaluate the view that a sociologist's choice of research method is based mainly on practical and ethical factors.   **[20 marks]**

Carrying out a study

The exam requires that you are able to:

▶ Understand the research process: the steps the sociologists will need to go through when designing and conducting a study.

How research is conducted

Below is an overview of the research process. It is a basic step-by-step guide as to how research is conducted in sociology. We have presented it like this to give you a clearer picture and understanding of how everything fits in together, rather than learning 'standalone' aspects of research methods/design.

What is the difference between research methods and research design?

- **Research methods.** This refers to the different ways of carrying out research to collect data, such as experiments, questionnaires, interviews, observations and so on.

- **Research design.** This refers to the overall plan of the research investigation, such as formulating a research question/hypothesis, operationalising your variables, selecting participants (sampling), controlling the variables, apparatus and material to be used, and identifying ethical issues. The researcher will need to design a sound study that should provide the most valid information as poorly-designed research may not give a true picture of what the researcher is intending to find out.

Research design and process

Once the researcher has identified an issue and a research method to investigate it, the next step is to design the study, which involves them making some planning decisions. Below are some of the issues which the researcher will need to think about when designing a study.

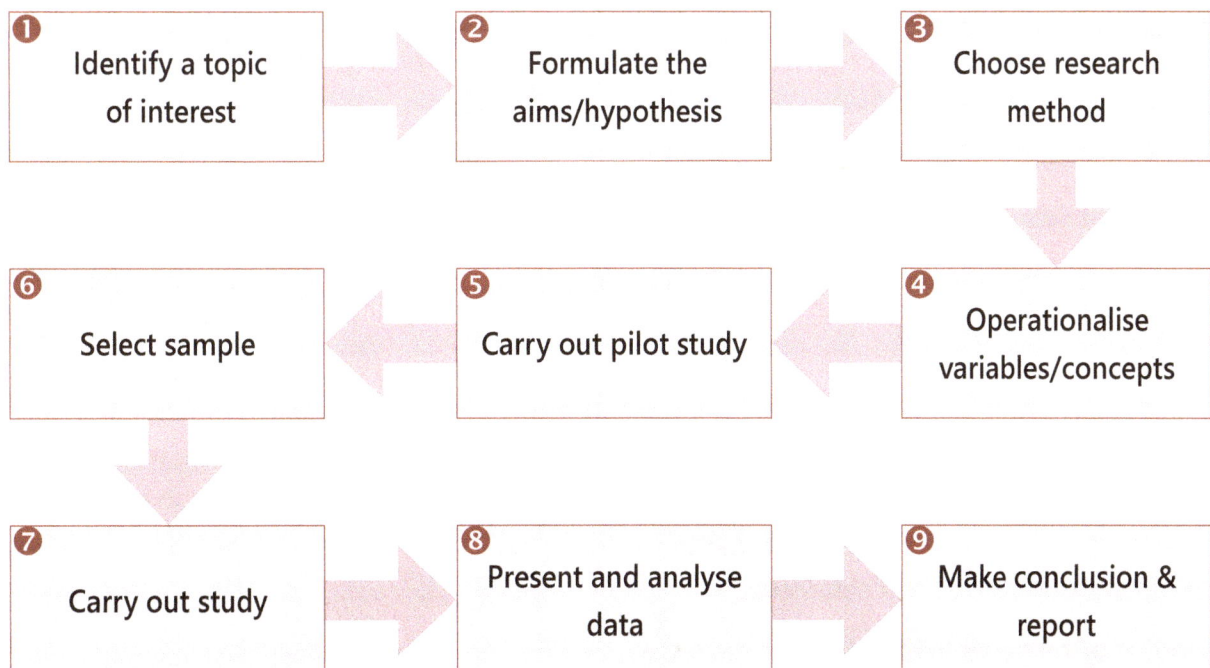

❶ Identify a topic of interest	❷ Formulate the aims/hypothesis	❸ Choose research method
❻ Select sample	❺ Carry out pilot study	❹ Operationalise variables/concepts
❼ Carry out study	❽ Present and analyse data	❾ Make conclusion & report

1. Topic of interest

A topic of interest may derive from an observation made, curiosity, personal interest, previous research or an existing theory.

2. Formulating an aim & hypothesis

- **Aims.** Once you have an idea of what to research, the next stage is to develop a research aim. An aim is a general statement that describes the purpose of the study, so people have a general idea of what the research is about (often having the words 'investigate', 'examine' or 'aim' in the sentence). So, for example, an aim could be:

  — *To carry out an investigation of the relationship between watching violent videos and aggressive behaviour in children.*

  — *To investigate deviant behavior in adolescent teenagers.*

- **Hypothesis.** Once the general aim of the research project has been established, some studies, depending on the type of research, narrow this down to a *hypothesis* (or *research question*, see below). A hypothesis is a precise *testable* statement that involves making a *prediction* of the expected findings of the research to be carried out. A hypothesis involves seeing if one variable has an effect on, or changes, another variable with the aim of discovering a link between the two (cause-effect relationship). Examples of hypotheses are:

  — *Male students between the ages of 16-18 are more deviant than females of the same age.*

  — *Students who study A Level sociology read more newspapers than students who do not study A Level sociology.*

  — *Watching violent videos leads to physically aggressive behaviour in young children.*

  — *Middle-class children are less likely to experience stress than working-class children.*

Every study has an aim, but not every study has a hypothesis; it depends on the type of research you are doing. Some researchers carry out descriptive/explorative research, which means they do not usually start with a hypothesis, but have a research question that has prompted them to find out more information; however, they do not make a prediction although they may develop a hypothesis at a later stage, as they learn more about what they are studying. Generally speaking:

  — Positivists favour quantitative methods as these tend to generate a hypothesis. Studies that collect the results in numbers (eg, questionnaires, official statistics and experiments) are favoured by positivists. This is because they can analyse the data to see if there are links between two variables/factors (cause-effect relationship).

  — Interpretivists favour qualitative methods as these tend to generate a research question or aim, not a hypothesis. Studies that collect the results in descriptive form (eg, written, audio and video) are favoured by interpretivists. This is because they can get a deeper understanding of the meanings that people attach to their behaviour, rather than make predictions about possible explanations of human behaviour.

3. Choice of research methods.
Next, the researcher will need to choose an appropriate research method to address their hypothesis. The choice of research method for collecting the data will depend

on a number of factors, such as what is being investigated; theoretical, practical and ethical issues; the sociologist's position (positivist/interpretivist); and the type of data to be collected (quantitative or qualitative). *See Exam Notes 2 "Factors influencing choice of research method."*

4. Operationalisation of variables. Once the hypothesis has been established, the researcher needs to put the variables/concepts into operational definitions. This is operationalisation: the process of converting the variables in such a way that they can be tested and measured in practical terms. This means that the researcher will need to define exactly how the variables/concepts will be tested and measured. Look at the following two example hypotheses:

— **Watching violent videos leads to physically aggressive behaviour in young children.**

Violent videos can be operationalised by exposure to a set of three violent twenty-minute children's cartoons, one after the other. Aggressive behaviour could be measured by the number of 'kicks' or 'punches' the child subsequently carries out during playtime at school.

— **Middle-class children are less likely to experience stress than working-class children.**

Social class can be operationalised by using questionnaires to assess details of parental occupation, income, housing and so on, as an indicator of the children's social class. Stress could be assessed by a questionnaire using a scoring system.

5. Pilot study. Whatever type of research method is chosen, a pilot study is often carried out. This is a technique whereby the researcher carries out a small-scale practice run on a few participants before the real research begins. The purpose of a pilot study is to reveal any design problems relating to questions, material, procedures, instructions, data handling and so on in the research study itself. It saves a lot of time and money by identifying any design flaws early on, so that they can be amended before the 'real thing' begins. Naturally, this helps to *improve the validity* of the study.

6. Sampling. Next, the researcher will need to consider who are they going carry out the research study on. A small selection of participants is chosen to take part in the study, known as a sample. *See Exam Notes 4 – Sampling*

7. Study. Once the researcher has amended any flaws in research method identified in the pilot study and has selected participants, they can go ahead and execute the real study and collect the results (data).

8. Presentation and analysis of the data. Once the study has been carried out and the data has been collected, the researcher will need to summarise and present the findings collected in a meaningful way. Graphs, tables and bar charts are used to display quantitative data. To summarise qualitative data, one option open to the researcher is thematic analysis, which involves analysing qualitative data (eg, video, audio or written text) for themes, and presenting these in written form. The themes may be grouped together under certain 'headings' and 'subheadings' and discussed, supported by the use of examples and quotations, to arrive at some conclusion.

9. Conclusion and report. The researcher will then conclude whether the findings support the hypothesis. The sociologists may share their findings with others by publishing the study in a sociological journal.

Sampling

Sampling

When conducting any research investigation, the researcher will need to consider who they are going to carry out the research study on. It would be impossible for a researcher to study the entire population (an extremely expensive and time-consuming to try) so a small selection of participants is chosen to take part in the study. This is known as a **sample**.

- **What is meant by target population?** The sample is selected from the *target population*, that is, the group of people the researcher is interested in (eg, A Level students or mothers).

- **What is sampling meant to do?** The aim of sampling is to allow the findings collected from a study to be representative (ie, typical) of the target population. This means it is possible for the researcher to be able to make *generalisations* or draw *conclusions* about the target population.

Key terms

Target population	The group of people that the sociologist is interested in researching in order to draw conclusions about their views or behaviour (eg, single mothers or teenagers.) For example, if a researcher wants to find out female teenagers' views on Michael Jackson, the target population will be females between the ages of 13 and 19. Do not confuse this with the whole population of the country in the UK, for example.
Sampling frame	A list of names taken from the target population from which the sample will be selected. A sampling frame could be the *Register of Electors* (a list of everyone over the age of 18 who can vote in elections), the *telephone directory*, the *Royal Mail Postcode Address File*, *doctors' records* (if permission is given) or a *school roll*. For a sampling frame to be accurate, it must include all the potential members of the target population. If the list is incomplete or inaccurate, the findings from the sample may not reflect the target population which means it may not be representative and generalisations will need to be treated with caution.
Sampling	The process of selecting participants to study from the sampling frame. These are often referred to as *sampling units* (ie, individuals who make up the sample).
Generalisability	The degree to which the sample 'represents' (ie, is representative of) the larger population, in that conclusions from the research on the sample can be 'generalised' to the wider population.
Bias sample	One which does not represent the target population.

Different types of sampling technique

Sociologists will need to decide the appropriate sampling techniques in order to ensure that the sample is representative (ie, reflects/is typical) of the population so they can make general statements about the population on which the sample was based. Generalising means that you declare that the results are true not only of the sample but also among the target population.

Sampling techniques fall into two main categories: **random sampling** and **non-random sampling.**

Random sampling techniques

Random sampling

Random sampling is when *every* person in the sampling frame has an equal chance (50:50) of being randomly selected for the sample. If the population size is small (eg, just the sociology students in a sixth-form college) the names could be written on a piece of paper, placed in a box or hat, shuffled and then picked out until the required sample size is reached. For a larger population, a computer programme can be used to generate a list of random numbers, which are then matched up with the names and addresses on the researcher's population list.

✔✗ Evaluation

✔ **Everyone has an equal chance.** Random sampling reduces the possibility of sample bias as the researcher has no control over who is, or is not, selected. This means that everyone has a genuine and fair chance of being selected, making the sample more representative of the target population.

✗ **Can lead to bias sample.** A weakness of using random sampling is that there is still a small probability that you can end up with a bias sample (eg, in terms of age, gender, ethnicity or social class). For example, in terms of age, you may end up with too many students in the sample than non-students (eg, working adults). This will make the sample unrepresentative of the target population that you are studying and it will therefore be hard to make generalisations from the research findings.

Systematic sampling

Systematic sampling is when the sample of people is selected by choosing every nth name from the sampling frame. So, for example, if you want a 10% sample from 800 students, you may choose a random number such as every 4th, or 7th or 10th person from the sampling frame until you get the desired sample number. Technically speaking, this is not really random sampling since not everyone has an equal chance of being chosen!

✔✗ Evaluation

✔ **More evenly spread.** A strength of systematic sampling is that it is more precise than random sampling, if the sampling frame list is large, as it allows a more even spread of participants.

✗ **Can lead to bias sample.** A weakness of systematic sampling is that it is not totally random: the list in the sampling frame may be arranged in a particular order or systematic way, which may bias the results, and thus not give an accurate representation of the target population. For example, if we take our sample from a list of house addresses in Britain and select every 4thth house, this would generate even numbers, which would give you a sample of houses one side of the road. It is possible that this may be the side that are wealthier, for example middle-class, than those on the other side of the street, which could be working-class.

Stratified sampling

One way to overcome the probability that the sample of people selected may not be very representative (such as those selected in random and systematic sampling) is to use stratified random sampling. This is when the sampling frame is 'divided' into strata (sub-categories) that the researcher is interested in, such as gender, age, class and ethnicity, and then a certain number of people are randomly selected from each of these sub-categories, often in proportion to their representation in the population. For example, if A Level students represent only 20% of all students at a college, then 20% of those A Level students will be chosen randomly from this stratum to be part of the sample.

✔✗ Evaluation

✔ **Reduces sampling bias.** One of the strengths of stratified sampling is that it reduces sampling error (bias). It assures that all subgroups of the population are proportionally represented in the sample.

✗ **Time-consuming to set up.** A weakness of stratified sampling is that it can be time-consuming to organise and calculate the different sampling frames (ie, categories).

Non-representative sampling techniques

There are occasions when studies deliberately have to use a non-representative sample for both practical and theoretical reasons. For example, it may be difficult to obtain a sampling frame because the group may be too small or difficult to obtain (eg, homeless people and illegal migrant workers) or because the group to be studied does not want to be identified for fear of being exposed (eg, deviant or secretive groups).

Quota sampling

Quota sampling, like stratified sampling, divides the target population into subgroups (eg, by sex, age, social class or ethnicity) and the researcher is given a quota (a certain amount needed to sample) that they need to reach. For example, the researcher may need to find 30 women between the ages of 25 and 35 to answer a questionnaire on magazine readership. The first 30 women of the correct age will have filled the quota.

✔✘ Evaluation

✔ **Less time-consuming.** A strength of quota sampling over stratified sampling is that it is less time-consuming and less expensive as no sampling frame is needed.

✘ **Can lead to a biased sample.** A weakness of quota sampling is that there is the possibility that the chosen sample may not be representative, as the researcher's own judgement can lead to bias and thus will result in a distorted quota.

Snowball sampling

Snowball sampling is used when it is difficult or impossible to obtain a sample of people to research on. It is often used when the research is highly sensitive or deals with secretive or deviant groups (eg, criminals, sexual deviants, drug users or religious cults) as individuals may not want to be identified. The researcher will attempt to make contact with a particular existing person or group to be studied. The researcher then asks the participant to recommend another person who fits the sample criteria, and so on until they have built up a number of contacts: hence the name, as the process is like rolling a snowball.

✔✘ Evaluation

✔ **Deep insight.** A strength of snowball sampling is that it provides a valuable insight into social groups that would have been difficult to obtain using a sample frame.

✘ **Unrepresentative.** A weakness of snowball sampling is that it relies on a very small network of people who have come through recommendations. This makes the research findings difficult to evaluate. Participants' information may be biased or incorrect, which makes it difficult to assess, so there is no way of knowing whether the sample is representative of the population or not.

Opportunity sampling

Opportunity sampling (or convenient sampling) is when researchers themselves approach anyone who is available and willing to participate. This can be asking passers-by in the street or a shopping mall, for example, whether they are available and willing to take part in a research study.

✔✗ Evaluation

✔ **Quick and practical.** A strength of opportunity sampling technique is that it is probably the easiest and most practical way of finding a sample of participants, compared to other sampling techniques.

✗ **Prone to bias.** A weakness of opportunity sampling is that the sample may be biased. Choosing who is available to take part means that the sample will be unrepresentative of your target population and it will therefore be hard to make generalisations from the research findings. For example, students are often used because they are convenient to get hold of, but are hardly representative of the population as a whole.

Volunteer sampling

Volunteer sampling (or self-selecting sampling) is when participants have freely self-selected (volunteered) themselves to be part of the study. Volunteer sampling works through advertisements in newspapers, leaflets, posters, television and radio. Potential participants reply to such advertisements.

✔✗ Evaluation

✔ **Quick and practical.** A strength of volunteer sampling is that it is a quick, easy and practical way to find a sample of participants (compared to random sampling).

✗ **Volunteer bias.** A weakness is that the sample could be biased because people who self-select often have certain social or personal characteristics that are different from those who do not. They may be more educated, more enthusiastic or motivated, or more social, all of which may not be typical of the general population. This can make the sample unrepresentative and it would therefore be hard to make generalisations from the research findings. This is known as volunteer bias.

Factors to take into consideration when choosing a sample

The type of sample chosen will be based on factors such as the following:

- The time allocated and funding available for the research study to take place.
  - The size of the sample: generally speaking the larger the sample size, the more likely it is to be representative of the population.
- The methodological perspective:

  Positivists tend to favour research methods that produce quantitative data (eg, questionnaires and official statistics) as these often use a large sample. This makes the findings more representative of the population, which allows for generalisations to be made, with the aim of establishing trends, patterns and relationships.

  Interpretivists, on the other hand, favour research methods that produce qualitative data (eg, in-depth interviews, observations and case studies). They tend to seek a deeper insight into people's motives and the meanings of their actions, as these provide a more valid account. They are not interested in making sweeping generalisations about human behaviour from their results. Therefore, their sample sizes are much smaller and less representative of the wider population.

Practice exam questions

AS level exam questions

Paper 2

1. Outline **two** types of 'sampling procedure' used in sociological research. **[4 marks]**

2. Outline **two** reasons why sociological research is often carried out using "only a small sample of research subjects". **[4 marks]**

3. Outline **two** reasons it may not be possible for sociologists to create a representative sample. **[4 marks]**

4. Evaluate the different methods of sampling in sociological research. **[16 marks]**

A level exam questions

Paper 3

1. Applying material from **Item (...)** and your knowledge, evaluate the usefulness of the different methods of sampling in sociological research. **[20 marks]**

The exam requires that you are able to:

▶ Understand what a laboratory experiment, field experiment and comparative method are.

▶ Evaluate the strengths and limitations associated with each of the types of experimental methods.

▶ Evaluate the strengths and limitations of using experiments when investigating educational issues.

Introduction

Experiments are a method commonly used by natural scientists (eg, in physics and chemistry) when carrying out a research investigation. This method is also employed by social scientists such as psychologists and sociologists. Experiments are used because they allow the researcher a high degree of control over the research in order to test a hypothesis. However, sociologists hardly ever use this method of research investigation. There are two main types of experiments:

— Laboratory experiments

— Field experiments

Laboratory experiments

A laboratory experiment is seen as the most scientific method a researcher can use when investigating human behaviour. It is a **tightly-controlled** research method conducted in an **artificial environment** in order to test a hypothesis. The purpose of conducting a laboratory experiment is to see if one variable, called the independent variable (IV), has an effect on, or changes, another variable, called the dependent variable (DV). The aim is to discover a **cause-and-effect relationship** (or causal relationship) between the two variables, that is, the change that the IV effects on the DV.

Variables are an important feature of experimental research. In a simple experiment, there are usually two variables; the **independent variable** (**IV**) and the **dependent variable** (**DV**). The IV is the one that is *manipulated* and the DV is the one that is *measured* by the researcher. To understand the difference let us take this hypothesis:

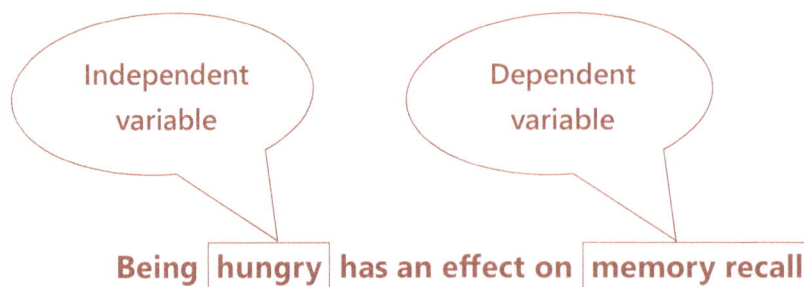

Independent variable

Dependent variable

Being hungry has an effect on memory recall

● **Independent variable (IV).** In the example above, hunger would be our independent variable. In a research experiment, a group of participants went without food for a day (ie, the 'hungry lot'), known as the experimental group. The other group of participants had eaten (ie, the 'not-hungry lot') and were known as the control group. The two groups can be compared to see what effect hunger has on memory recall (eg, remembering words). This is what is meant by manipulating the independent variable (anything that can be varied such as behaviour, items, events, sizes or amounts).

- **Dependent variable (DV).** This is the variable that is measured by data collected (eg, a test score) by the researcher. We measure the effects that the independent variable may have on the dependent variable. In our example above, memory recall would be our DV because we are measuring how good memory recall is (eg, the number of words remembered) when someone is hungry or not hungry.

- **Control.** In order to establish a cause-and-effect relationship between hunger and memory, that is, that the IV was the only thing that had an effect on the DV, the experimenter must deal with other 'interfering variables' that may influence the participant's memory recall (see below for example). The researcher must control these unwanted variables by keeping them constant in both the experimental group and the control group: any changes to the conditions will spoil the results. If any unwanted variable does affect the results, this reduces the validity, which means we can't trust the research findings.

Experiments and cause-and-effect relationships

In order to see if the IV has an effect on the DV, an experiment must have at least two groups (conditions)– one group receives the IV and the other group does not. Then we can compare the results.

— The experimental group is exposed to the IV.

— The control group is not exposed to the IV.

If the results differ between the two groups, and we have assured ourselves that we have controlled any unwanted variables, then we can conclude that any difference in the participants was due to the IV.

Field experiments

Sometimes experiments are not carried out in an artificial laboratory setting, but in a **real-life environment** where people are in engaged in everyday normal behaviour. Experiments might be conducted in schools or shopping malls, or on the streets or in a workplace. Often, the participants do not know they are taking part in a study. Such experiments are called field experiments. In field experiments, the researcher is still able to manipulate the IV in a natural setting, to see the effect it has on the DV.

Two main types of unwanted variables that can affect the validity of an experiment are

Participant variables. These refer to the participants themselves, who could influence the results of the experiment if they are not kept constant in both conditions. Participant variables can be things like age, intelligence and gender.

Situational variables. These relate to the situational setting of the research, which may affect the participants' behaviour, such as noise levels or temperature, light level and time of day.

Example of a field experiment: *Rosenthal and Jacobson, Pygmalion in the classroom (1964)*

Rosenthal and Jacobson (1964) carried out a field experiment to investigate how teachers' expectations of pupils' behaviour can affect their performance. In an elementary school in San Francisco, an IQ test was administered to all children from grade 1 to 6. At the beginning of the school year, teachers were told that in each class, 20% of the children were identified as being more academically able (known as 'spurters'). Unknown to the teachers, these children were just randomly chosen. The way teachers interacted with these 'spurters' had an effect on their intelligence tests: the 'spurters' had made more progress than their classmates a year later. The researchers explained this as a 'self-fulfilling prophecy': the pupils are defined by the teacher in a particular way, predictions are made about their future behaviour (eg, 'bright'); the teacher then applies the label to the student and the student will respond to it, absorb that new identity, and act accordingly.

Field experiments have a greater external validity than laboratory experiments because participants are often not aware that they are part of an experiment and therefore the Hawthorne effect is eliminated (see below). Therefore, the one obvious advantage of the field study is that it can overcome the limitation on research findings from laboratory experiments, that is, that they cannot be generalised to the 'real world'.

The comparative method

- Because of the many practical, ethical and theoretical problems with experiments, such as deception and artificiality, sociologists often use the **comparative method** instead. This technique involves making data comparisons (ie, analysing the data). The aim of comparative methods is to establish a relationship between the variables under investigation. These comparisons can be between two societies, groups or individuals that are identical but for one variable. The two groups are compared across and through time to show if this one difference between them (variable) had an effect. The data used mainly comes from official statistics. Therefore, the sociologist does not actually carry out an experiment on real people – the analysing is in the mind of the sociologists!

- Emile Durkheim (1897) used the comparative method to study suicide. He made a hypothesis that 'suicide' (variable one) was linked to low levels of 'social integration' (variable two). He predicted that unmarried and childless people had a higher suicide rate than married people and those with children (unmarried men would have a lower social interaction with other people). In his comparative research, Durkheim tested his hypothesis by collecting statistical data on the suicide rates of married and unmarried men in various European countries as well as within the same country. He found that his prediction was borne out by the official statistical data on suicide, which showed that married men had a lower suicide rate then unmarried men.

Strengths

- ✔ It enables the similarities and differences between groups to be revealed.
- ✔ Useful for making predictions and creating laws of human behaviour (e.g. Durkheim suicide).
- ✔ If the data sets are large, the information will be deemed as reliable.
- ✔ Avoids the artificiality of lab experiments, and raises no ethical problems (e.g. deception).

What type of data do lab, field and comparative methods produce?

- The results in an experiment tend to be in the form of scores/tally/or some scale of measurements. This means experiments tend to produce quantitative data.

✔✗ Strengths and limitations of experiments

Strengths of experiments

Theoretical issues

✔ **Positivists favour experiments.** Positivists argue that the social world we live in, is made up many external social 'variables' that can influence our behaviour. These social variables can be measured objectively using experiments to gather valid information. This is because experiments, according to positivists, are reliable and objective, producing quantitative data (numerical) which they can analyse the numerical findings to see if they can discover a cause-and-effect relationship between the two variables, with the aim of the findings to be generalised to the wider population.

✔ **Reliability.** Laboratory experiments are easier to replicate than many other research methods. This means that the original experiment can be repeated by other researchers, under the same conditions and following the same procedures, to see whether they obtain similar results. Replicability is important for checking other researchers' work. If the findings are similar, we can be confident that the original results have internal validity and reliability. Field experiments are less reliable than laboratory experiments, because they are carried out in a natural environment where it is difficult to replicate the study under identical conditions to the original. This makes the findings from different field experiments difficult to compare.

Practical issues

✔ **Control of variables.** Laboratory experiments allow a high degree of control over the experimental setting by controlling unwanted variables, allowing the researcher to establish a cause-and-effect-relationship between the IV and the DV. A problem with field experiments is that the researcher has less control over the natural environment. This means that any unwanted variables may be influencing the DV rather than the IV. This reduces the ability to establish a cause-and-effect relationship, which reduces the validity of the research findings.

Limitations of experiments

Theoretical issues

✗ **Artificiality.** Laboratory experiments have been criticised because the experimental setting is artificial: humans often behave differently in artificial laboratory settings than they would in the real world and therefore the results obtained may not be valid. On the other hand, field experiments are conducted in the real world, where the participants are often not aware they are taking part in a study, so the Hawthorne effect is not a problem. This means that the findings of field experiments are often more realistic and true-to-life than those of laboratory experiments, and thus can be generalised to the real world, which is something laboratory experiments cannot do.

✗ **Hawthorne effect.** . If the participants are aware of what the experiment is about then they may change their behaviour and not act as they usually would. This is called 'the Hawthorne effect' and will distort the result of the experiment, and so affect its validity.

Ethical issues

✗ **Deception, lack of consent and psychological harm.** In a laboratory experiment, deception is often used to prevent the people taking part from knowing the real purpose of the experiment (as this would affect their normal behaviour/responses). Informed consent would therefore not have been provided by the people taking part. It is considered wrong to deceive or mislead people as to the true aim of the experiment. In a field experiment, the people are unaware they are taking part in a study; again, this means they have not given informed consent. There is also the possibility that the experiment may cause psychological harm (eg, low-self-esteem, stress or embarrassment).

Methods in context:

Using experiments to investigate educational issues

Experiments have been used to investigate a number of educational issues. Some common issues are:

— Labelling theory/ teachers' expectations (eg, how labelling can affect students' educational performance.

— Classroom interaction (eg, teacher/pupil interaction, examining social variables such as gender, ethnicity and peer-to-peer interaction).

— Pupils' self-concept (eg, how setting and streaming affects pupils' self-esteem).

✔✗ **Strengths and limitations of using experiments to investigate educational issues**

Limitations of experiments

Theoretical issues

✗ **Interpretivists** are opposed to laboratory experiments when studying human behaviour such as teachers and students. This because human behaviour cannot be studied in an artificial setting. Mainly for two reasons; human do not behave as they would in real life in laboratory setting (e.g. to see if labelling occurs by teachers) as this would produces low validity. Also it is virtually impossible to study some aspects of human behaviour using laboratory experiments, for example to see if poverty causes under-achievement in students. Interpretivists argue that even positivist hardly use laboratory experiments to investigated human behaviour. Interpretivist see field experiments ass more 'natural' which produce valid results when studying teachers/students, which avoid the artificially of laboratory experiments (see the study below by Rosenthal and Jacobson, Pygmalion in the classrooms, 1968).

✗ **Use of deception** One way to avoid the Hawthorne effect is not to tell the teachers or students that they are taking part in an experiment (if possible). However, teachers or students may object to taking part, and if deception was used (not telling them they are part of an experiment), this would mean the researcher is not acting ethically.

✗ **Validity issues.** In an educational setting, this means the using made-up artificial setting would tell us very little about what really goes on in a normal real educational setting. Also it is very unlikely that teachers or students for example would behave as they would normally under experimental conditions (see below Hawthorne effect) which means the findings will be low in validity. Field experiments would give more valid information as they avoid the artificiality of a laboratory experiments, and the teachers and students often do not know they are taking part in the experiments—although this raises ethical issues (deception and lack of informed consent, see below).

✗ **Reliability issues.** In an educational setting, it may be difficult to replicate lab and field experiments exactly as the original study because not all schools and children are the same. However, it could be argued that schools and students generally have similar features/behaviours so experiments can to some extent be repeated and yield the same results, e.g. the original 'Pygmalion in the Classroom' has been repeated many times before with similar results.

Practical issues

✗ **Difficult to isolate one variable.** Using experiments in an educational setting such as schools may be practically difficult to isolate the IV (e.g. labelling) and to control all the other unwanted variables to see if the IV (has an effect on the DV (e.g. underachievement). This is because under-achievement are often the result of many range of causes—not just one (e.g. home factors).

✗ **Educational issues not suitable under experimental conditions.** Another practical issue when using experiments in education is that some educational issues do not lend themselves to study in the laboratory. This research method therefore has limited application. For example, you cannot study the consequences of cultural factors on education, study children or teachers for a long period of time, or look at how past events, such as educational policies, have had an impact on education.

✗ **Gaining permission.** A further practical issue when using experiments in education in some schools is that the researcher may not be given permission to carry out experiments. This could be for a number of reasons: the study may be of a sensitive nature and damage the reputation of the school, or the head teacher, teachers and parents may refuse permission for whatever reason (eg, disruption to learning).

Ethical issues

✗ **Young children.** . In an educational context such as schools, an experiment may raise ethical problems. For example, it may be difficult to obtain consent from young children or children with learning difficulties who may not understand the nature of the experiment.

✗ **Psychological harm.** There is also the possibility of psychological harm. For example, if the labelling process is investigated, teachers may experience low-self-esteem or embarrassment if they are deemed to be prejudiced against certain ethnic or social groups. Equally, there is a possibility of disrupting/damaging the student's educational progress, which is unethical *(see the study by Rosenthal and Jacobson, 'Pygmalion in the Classrooms' (1968)).*

✗ **Use of deception.** One way to avoid the Hawthorne effect is not to tell the teachers or students that they are taking part in an experiment (if possible). However, teachers or students may object to taking part, and if deception was used (not telling them they are part of an experiment), this would mean the researcher is not acting ethically.

Practice exam questions

AS level exam questions

Paper 1 – methods in context

Item B – Investigating the effects of streaming

Streaming involves allocating pupils of similar ability to the same class for all or most lessons. This may create a self-fulfilling prophecy, in which the achievement of those placed in higher-ability streams improves, while that of pupils placed in lower streams deteriorates. As a result, those in lower streams may develop a negative self-image, give up trying and even join an anti-school subculture.

Some sociologists may use field experiments to study the effects of streaming. One advantage of this is that the researcher can allocate pupils into high streams and low streams and measure the effect. However, there are ethical objections to the use of field experiments because of the harm they may do to pupils. There are also practical problems in organising such experiments in a school setting.

1. Applying material from **Item B** and your own knowledge of research methods, evaluate the strengths and limitations of using field experiments to investigate the effects of streaming.   **[20 marks]**

Paper 2

1. Outline **two** advantages in using laboratory experiments in sociological research.   **[4 marks]**

2. Outline **two** weaknesses in using laboratory experiments in sociological research.   **[4 marks]**

3. Explain the differences between the 'dependent' variable and the 'independent' variable in sociological experiments.   **[4 marks]**

4. Outline **two** advantages of using the comparative method.   **[4 marks]**

5. Evaluate the practical, ethical and theoretical problems faced by sociologists when using laboratory experiments.   **[4 marks]**

6. Evaluate the problems of using experiments in sociological research.   **[16 marks]**

A level exam questions

Paper 1 – methods in context

1. The 'methods in context' question is set at both AS and A level *(see above AS level exam question, paper 1)*.

2. Outline and explain **two** reasons experiments are often associated with the positivist approach in sociology.   **[10 marks]**

3. Outline and explain **two** reasons "experiments in a laboratory setting are rarely used in sociological research".   **[10 marks]**

Paper 3

1. Applying material from **Item (...)** and your knowledge, evaluate the usefulness of using experiments in sociological research.   **[20 marks]**

The exam requires that you are able to:
▶ Identify the different types of questionnaires.
▶ Evaluate the strengths and limitations of questionnaires.
▶ Evaluate the strengths and limitations of using questionnaires when investigating educational issues.

Questionnaires

A questionnaire can be defined as a list of pre-determined set of written questions, to which the respondents are invited to give their answers. A questionnaire can be handed, posted, emailed to a respondent, or placed in a magazine or on the internet for the respondent to fill in and return to the researchers. This is known as a **self-completion questionnaire.** Alternatively, the person can give the information to the researcher and they can fill in the questionnaire for them. Questionnaires involve asking participants to provide information about themselves on issues such as attitudes, beliefs, opinions and feelings and are used when a researcher wants to gather a large amount of data. Questionnaires and interviews are often referred to as **social surveys.**

Types of questionnaires

Questionnaires use two basic types of question format:

— **Closed questions (close-ended questionnaire).** The questions are already pre-determined, and a range of pre-set possible answers offered, often with the option of circling or ticking the appropriate one. For example: "Do you think mothers should stay at home and look after their children? *Strongly Agree, Agree, Disagree, Strongly Disagree* (please circle answer)."

— **Open questions (open-ended questionnaire).** There are no pre-set answers, so the respondent can express themselves however they choose. For example: "What is your opinion of the latest Harry Potter film?"

Most questionnaires tend to be close-ended, with a pre-determined range of answers.

Type of data produced

— **Quantitative data.** Closed questions are regarded as producing quantitative data since the answer can be put into numbers, which makes the data easier to analyse and draw conclusions from.

— **Qualitative data.** Open questions produce qualitative data because the answers often involve a detailed descriptive account (lots of written information) which offers deeper insight and understanding of what is being investigated.

Design of questionnaire

The researcher needs to ensure that the questions are appropriately worded to eliminate any misunderstandings which may affect the reliability and validity of the data. Some things to consider are shown in the list below.

— **Type of data.** When conducting a questionnaire, the researcher will need to make decisions on design issues such as what type of data they are seeking to gain (qualitative or quantitative), which determines the format of the questions: closed questions or open questions.

— **Wording of the questions.** The researcher needs to ensure that the questions are appropriately worded to eliminate misunderstandings which may affect the reliability and validity of the data. Some things to consider are:

Use plain language	Use plain English as this helps prevent unclear or confusing questions which may be understood differently by respondents, for example, *'How often do you go to the pub?'* This is an ambiguous question because the word 'often' is open to interpretation. This could be replaced with *'How many times do you go to the pub in a week?'*
Avoid leading/ loaded questions	Avoid leading questions which can affect how the respondent answers, for example, *'Don't you think that teachers should be paid more money?'* This type of question leads the respondent to answer 'Yes'. Also avoid loaded questions, which are those containing emotive language which may bias the response of the respondent in a particular way, for example, *'Do you think it is right to kill defenceless animals in laboratories, or should it be stopped?'*
Avoid double-barred questions	Avoid using double-barrelled questions, that is, single questions which have two possible answers such as *'Do you think teachers are tired all the time because they don't get enough sleep or because they drink too much?'* This question should be re-written as two separate questions.
Avoid complex questions	Avoid long difficult sentences that contain jargon (technical words), for example *'Do you think the rise in psychotic illnesses has been due to the pressure of the individualistic lifestyle people lead now, or has the change in legislation towards psychotic illness been the contributory factor for the increase?'*

✓✗ Strengths and limitations of questionnaires

Strengths of questionnaires

On a theoretical level

✔ **Representativeness.** Positivists tend to favour close-ended (especially postal) questionnaires because the data collected from the sample can be very large. This increases the chance of the sample being representative of the target population and means it is possible to make generalisations from the research findings.

✔ **Reliability.** Close–ended questionnaires are seen as being a highly reliable method of gathering data. This is because the questions have been standardised: every participant is asked the same sets of questions to every participant and there is no researcher to influence the person's answers, which makes the results objective. The questionnaire can be easily replicated by other researchers on other groups of people, and data compared. If similar results are found, the reliability and validity of the study increase.

✔ **Hypothesis testing.** Close-ended questionnaires are useful for testing new or existing hypotheses (relationships/links between two variables, eg, educational achievement and the average number of hours of TV watched per week). The data collected can be easily quantified, by being put in numerical form which allows them to be statistically analysed to establish whether a relationship exists between the two variables.

✔ **Before and after comparison.** Questionnaires allow for comparisons to be made. For example, you may want to compare peoples' attitudes to homosexual behaviour in the past and present, and generalisations can be made by comparing the before and after.

On a practical level

✔ **Quick and cheap.** Questionnaires are generally cheap to administer, which makes them cost-effective and more time-efficient than other research methods, especially when funds are limited and a large sample is required. For example, the postal charges of mail or electronic questionnaires are often less than an interviewer's expenses or salary. The lower cost also means that a larger sample of people can be obtained.

✔ **Sensitive nature.** A self-completion questionnaire allows the participants to be more honest with their answers than a face-to-face interview, especially if it addresses sensitive or personal issues. The presence of the interviewer may influence the respondents' answers, which will decrease the validity of the data.

✔ **Researcher bias not a factor.** In postal questionnaires, the researcher has no contact with the participants and therefore research bias is minimal, which increases the validity of the findings.

Limitations of questionnaires

On a theoretical level

✘ **Limited insight.** Interpretivists tend not to use close-ended questionnaires. There is no opportunity to probe deeper, beyond the limited pre-set answers. This prevents them from obtaining an in-depth account of participants' opinions, attitudes, meanings and feelings. Therefore, the information collected from closed questions is likely to be very limited, which reduces the validity of the findings.

✘ **Social desirability effect.** Respondents may answer questions in a particular way that portrays them in a positive light, rather than giving truthful answers. This is known as the 'social desirability effect' which, if it occurs, decreases the validity of the data.

✘ **Possibility of false information.** The respondent may lie or get somebody else to answer the questions, which can also reduce the validity of the findings.

On a practical level

✘ **Low response rate.** Self-completion questionnaires such as postal questionnaires suffer from a low response rate. If the response rate is 25% or less, the failing is so critical as to make the results of very little value as the sample is not very representative of the population group from which the sample was taken. Non-response is also a problem, because the people who do not return questionnaires differ from those who do. Those who do respond often tend to be of a higher class and more educated. This can also reduce the validity and reliability of the findings.

✗ **No flexibility.** The sociological issue under investigation is decided by the researcher in advance, as are the questions and the range of pre-defined answers. In such a situation, there is little opportunity to expand or explore other areas of interest that may open up during the research investigations.

Ethical level

- **Privacy.** The respondent has the right to ensure that any information given is treated as confidential, and, if published, will not be identifiable as theirs. If confidentiality or anonymity cannot be guaranteed, the respondent must be warned of this in advance.

- **Consent.** The researcher will need the consent of the respondent if the data is to be published in the future, and knows that respondents can withdraw all or some of the data is they wish.

- **Risk of harm.** The researcher needs to ensure that the questionnaire and the way the questions are worded do not cause psychological stress, which must not be greater than any caused in ordinary life. If questions are of a personal or sensitive nature that may cause distress, support must be available (eg, counselling) and the assurance given that answers to personal questions not need be given.

Methods in context:

Using questionnaires to investigate educational issues

Questionnaires have been used to investigate a number of educational issues. Some common issues are:

— **Attitudes** (eg, teachers' workload, parents' attitudes)

— **Achievement** (eg, how school factors may contribute to pupils' educational achievement)

— **School experiences** (eg, students' experience of school life)

— **Bullying** (eg, where, when and why it happens, and whether anti-bullying policies are working effectively)

> ✔✗ **In context: strengths and limitations of using questionnaires to investigate educational issues**

Strengths of questionnaires

On a theoretical level

✔ **Valid.** Positivists would argue that questionnaires can produce valid results, especially if the educational issue in question is of a sensitive or personal nature (eg, bullying, or parents' or teachers' views). The use of anonymous questionnaires is more likely to produce more truthful responses than the use of interviews, in which the respondent may feel uncomfortable answering the interviewer truthfully, even though anonymity and confidentiality have been promised.

✔ **Representative.** Generally speaking, questionnaires suffer a low-response rate. However, once consent has been given by the school, especially if the request to complete the questionnaire has come from the head teacher, then pupils, teachers and parents will be more compelled to complete it. If this is the case, the high response rate will make the findings more representative.

On a practical level

✔ **Cheaper and quicker.** Questionnaires are normally quick and easy to administer in an educational setting where basic information is required from teachers, students or parents. This makes them cost-effective and more time-efficient than other research methods, which means that a larger sample of people can be obtained.

✔ **Sampling frame.** Using questionnaires as research methods in schools is relatively easy because the sampling frame already exists (eg, lists of pupils' and staff names), which makes it much easier to draw by either random or opportunity sampling.

Limitations of questionnaires

On a theoretical level

✘ **Validity.** Interpretivists are critical of questionnaires as they give little opportunity for teachers, students or parents to go further than the basic pre-coded answers given. This can result in a lack of insight, meanings and feelings. Furthermore, children may deliberately lie in their answers to the questions 'just for a laugh', whereas parents and teachers may give socially desirable answers, rather than the truth. This reduces the validity of the data collected from the questionnaire.

On a practical level

✘ **Limited use.** A limitation of using questionnaires in schools is that they cannot be used on very young children or those with poor literacy, such as children from ethnic-minority families whose English is not fluent enough to fully understand what the questionnaire is about, and thus may not be willing or able to complete it accurately.

✘ **Response rate may be low.** If the questionnaire is given in class time or within school, the response rate will generally be high. It may be difficult to get the questionnaires back if they have been sent home for parents to fill in. This may make the sample unrepresentative, as it may be that more of a certain type of parent returns them (eg, literate and middle-class parents).

Ethical issues

✘ **Anonymity.** The main ethical problem with questionnaires is in ensuring the anonymity of the respondent or school and that any information given will be treated as confidential and, if published, will not be identifiable as theirs. This is especially true if you are dealing with sensitive topics. Teachers' jobs or health can be at risk, or the school reputation can be damaged, if the results are identifiable to teachers or to the school.

✗ **Consent.** There may also be a problem in getting the fully-informed consent of young children. It may be difficult to explain to young children what the research is about, which means they may not have given meaningful consent as they did not fully understand its nature.

Practice exam questions

AS level exam questions

Paper 1 – methods in context

Item B – Investigating the effects of streaming

Parents play a vital role in pupils' achievement. There may be social class differences in parents' income levels, cultural capital, educational qualifications and attitudes to school, and how they socialise their children, for example by using different speech codes. Similarly, ethnic differences among parents, for example in family structure, discipline styles or home language, may affect pupils' achievement.

Questionnaires may be a good way of investigating the role of parents in pupils' achievement. Pupils can be asked to distribute them to parents at no cost, giving wide coverage. Parents are accustomed to supplying information to the school on a regular basis and this will help to ensure a good response. However, the questions asked may be very personal and some parents may feel that they are being judged.

1. Applying material from **Item B** and your knowledge of research methods, evaluate the strengths and limitations of using questionnaires for investigating the role of parents in pupils' achievement. **[20 marks]**

Paper 2

1. Outline **two** advantages that a sociologist might find in using a postal questionnaire. **[4 marks]**

2. Outline **two** problems associated with using questionnaires distributed through the post or over the internet. **[4 marks]**

3. Outline **two** ways in which a researcher could increase the response rate to a questionnaire posted to potential respondents. **[4 marks]**

4. Outline **two** disadvantages of using questions with fixed response categories in sociological research. **[4 marks]**

5. Evaluate the strengths of using mailed questionnaires. **[16 marks]**

6. Evaluate the problems some sociologists may find when using questionnaires in their research. **[16 marks]**

7. Evaluate the advantages some sociologists may find when using questionnaires in their research. **[16 marks]**

A level exam questions

Paper 1 – methods in context

1. The 'methods in context' question is set at both AS and A level *(see above AS level exam question, paper 1)*.

Paper 1 and 3

1. Outline and explain **two** reasons positivists favour using close-ended questionnaires.   **[10 marks]**

2. Outline and explain **two** reasons interpretivists favour using open-ended questionnaires   .

   [10 marks]

Paper 3

1. Applying material from **Item (...)** and your knowledge, evaluate the claim that what questionnaires gain in reliability and representativeness, they lose in validity.   **[20 marks]**

The exam requires that you are able to:

► Understand the differences between structured interviews, semi-structured interviews and unstructured interviews.

► Evaluate the strengths and limitations of interviews.

► Evaluate the strengths and limitations of using interviews when investigating educational issues.

Types of interviews

Sociologists use three main types of interviews to collect data on participants:

— **Structured interviews** (formal interviews). A structured interview is one in which the questions are read out by the interviewer and decided precisely in advance, with a range of pre-determined answers that the respondent can choose from, for example, Is sociology a difficult A level subject? Yes or No. This type of interview is effectively a questionnaire interview and is particularly useful when obtaining answers to questions of a factual nature.

— **Unstructured interviews** (informal interviews). An unstructured interview is one in which an interviewer introduces a topic in broad terms with a few questions in mind (but no pre-determined answers) to open up a discussion in which the respondent is free to answer in their own words, in greater scope and in any way that they wish. This type of interview is seen to be more appropriate for obtaining opinions and attitudes, producing a large amount of qualitative (written) data, for example, What is your view on extreme religious groups in the UK? A **focus group** interview is a type of unstructured interview in which a 'group' of participants who often share the same experience are interviewed collectively by the researcher.

— **Semi-structured interviews.** One attempt to overcome the limitations of using structured or unstructured interviews is to use a semi-structured interview. This will have some pre-determined questions and a range of possible answers given, whilst some questions will be open-ended. Dobash & Dobash's (1980) study of marital violence is a good example of this.

Structured Interviews

Positivists favour structured interviews because the predetermined answers from the list of close-ended questions mean the answers can be easily 'classified', 'counted' and 'quantified' numerically (ie, they produce quantitative data) which can be displayed graphically using, for example, bar-charts and tables (eg, showing averages and percentages). This allows sociologists to see if there is a pattern or trend in the data, which will enable them to make generalisations or see if there is a link between two variables.

✓✗ Strengths and limitation of using structured interviews

Strengths of structured interviews

On a theoretical level

✔ **Representative.** Structured interviews are relatively quick to administer, which means the sample population reached by this method will be larger than for unstructured interviews. This means it is possible to make generalisations from the research findings to the wider population.

✔ **Reliability.** Structured interviews are seen as being a highly reliable method of gathering data. This is because the questions have been standardised - every participant is asked the same questions - which makes them objective as there is no researcher to influence the person's answers. The questionnaire can be easily replicated by other researchers on other groups of people, and data compared. If similar results are found, this increases the reliability and validity of the study.

On a practical level

✔ **Cheaper.** Structured interviews are generally cheaper to administer than unstructured interviews, as the interviewers require limited training, compared to researchers who carry out unstructured interviews..

✔ **Clarification of questions.** Any confusion over the interpretation of the questions or how to answer them can be cleared up by the interviewer if necessary. This helps to ensure that the survey is completed fully, increasing its validity and reliability.

✔ **Response rate.** The response rates are usually higher than in other survey methods such as postal questionnaires or other self-completion questionnaires. The response rate is normally in the range of 60% to 85%. For example, the British Crime Survey has a response rate of around 75%. This increases the reliability of the findings.

✔ **Easier to analyse.** Pre-coded questions and answers make it easier to analyse as the data collected can be easily quantified, by being put in a numerical form which allows them to be statistically analysed. Researchers can therefore see if patterns or trends exist, or establish whether a relationship exists between the two variables.

✔ **Interviewer effect reduced.** The limited role of the interviewer reduces 'interviewer effect', compared to unstructured interviews, as their involvement with the interviewee is minimal, being confined to asking a list of questions and possible answers.

Limitations of structured interviews

On a theoretical level

✘ **Limited insight.** Interpretivists tend not to use structured interviews. There is no opportunity to probe deeper, beyond the limited pre-set answers. This prevents the researcher from obtaining an in-depth account of participants' opinions, attitudes, meanings and feelings. Therefore, the information collected from closed questions is likely to be very limited, which reduces the validity of the findings.

✘ **No flexibility.** The sociological issues under investigation are decided by the researcher in advance, as are the questions and the range of pre-defined answers. In such a situation there is little opportunity to expand or explore other areas of interest that may open up during the interview.

✘ **Interviewer effect.** The interviewers may unintentionally bias the participants' responses. The wearing of particular clothing or use of certain gestures, as well as the interviewer's tone of voice, ethnicity, age and gender, can all play a part in influencing the answers given by the respondents.

✘ **Sensitive nature.** Structured interviews are not particularly useful when questions of a personal or embarrassing nature are to be asked, as the presence of the researcher may influence how the respondent replies.

On a practical level

✘ **Problems of fixed response questions.** Fixed response questions also suffer from language problems: words may be interpreted differently by different respondents, which reduces the validity and reliability of the findings (if the researcher is not present for clarification).

Strengths of unstructured interviews

On a theoretical level

✔ **Effective of sensitive issues.** An informal conversation between interviewer and interviewee is more likely to generate trust and rapport between them. The interviewee is more likely to open up, especially on sensitive subjects, which increases the chance of their giving true and honest answers, which increases the validity of the findings. A good example of an unstructured interview is given by the sociologists Dobash & Dobash (1980), who carried out an in-depth study of marital violence.

✔ **Deeper insight.** Interpretivists argue that unstructured interviews produce more valid data than structured interviews because they allow for greater exploration and depth of the topic or issue at hand. For example, interviews carried out by Dobash & Dobash were detailed, and lasted for up to 12 hours. Respondents are given the opportunity to express their feelings, reasons and attitudes in ways which are meaningful to them. It is possible to get close to people's actual experiences.

✔ **Clarification is possible.** Compared to structured interviews, unstructured interviews allow meanings, opinions and attitudes to be clarified. For example, you can clarify people's religious views. A skilful interviewer can also probe deeper, expand on ideas and discover what the respondent 'really means', thus ensuring greater validity in the data.

On a practical level

✔ **Less costly and time-consuming.** Although unstructured interviews are more costly and time-consuming than structured interviews, they are still less so than other research methods such as observations.

✔ **Larger sample covered than observations.** Unstructured interviews can cover larger samples than observations, although this is not the case with structured interviews.

✔ **Only research method possible.** An unstructured interview might be the only practical method of gathering information, especially if the group may be deviant and observational research could be too dangerous.

Limitations of unstructured interviews

On a theoretical level

✗ **Difficult to analyse.** Positivists do not favour unstructured interviews because they can produce a vast amount of qualitative (written) data which can be difficult to analyse, making it difficult to generalise from the data.

✗ **Unreliable.** Unstructured interviews have been accused of unreliability because they do not have pre-set questions with pre-determined answers but allow the researcher to freely choose the type of questions to ask. This makes it extremely difficult to compare respondents' answers, which in turn makes it difficult to arrive at a conclusion or generalisation.

✗ **Unrepresentative.** Unstructured interviews take longer to carry out than structured interviews , due to their detailed and time-consuming nature, so the sample tends to be small. For example, Dobash & Dobash only carried out 109 interviews. This makes it more difficult get a representative sample, which in turn makes it difficult to generalise the findings to the wider population.

✗ **Interviewer effect.** The interviewers may unintentionally bias the participants' responses. The wearing of particular clothing or use of certain gestures, as well as the interviewer's tone of voice, ethnicity, age and gender, can all play a part in influencing the answers given by the respondents.

✗ **Social desirability effect.** Since interviewing involves social interaction in which the researcher's status is known, the respondent can give an answer which they believe the interviewer wishes to hear. The respondent may want to present themselves in a positive light and therefore give socially desirable answers, thus affecting the validity of the data.

On a practical level

✗ **Skilled researcher.** The researcher needs to be trained in order to become skilful at questioning techniques to draw out respondents' thoughts and meanings.

✗ **Hired-hand effect.** Interviewing on a large scale involves employing interviewers who may be less committed to the enquiry than the researcher, leading to the 'hired-hand effect'. This includes the failure of adequately recording open answers, deliberately questioning the wrong people out of convenience, and even (occasionally) outright fraudulent completion of schedules by the interviewer (ie, without interviewing). All these possible factors can crucially affect the validity of the data.

On an ethical level (for structured and unstructured interviews)

• **Privacy.** The respondent has the right to ensure that any information given is treated as confidential and, if published, will not be identifiable as theirs. If confidentiality or anonymity cannot be guaranteed, the respondent must be warned of this in advance.

• **Consent.** The researcher will need the consent of the respondent if the data is to be published in the future, and the respondent must know they can withdraw all or some of the data is they wish.

• **Risk of harm.** The researcher needs to ensure that none of the questions are worded in a way which might cause more psychological stress than is normal in ordinary life. If questions are of a personal or sensitive nature that may cause distress, support must be available (eg, counselling) and respondents must be assured that that answers to personal questions not need be given

Methods in context:

Using interviews to investigate educational issues

Structured interviews have been used to investigate a number of educational issues. Some common issues are:

— **Pupil subcultures** (eg, understanding working-class attitudes towards school)

— **Pupils' experience and attitudes in school** (eg, bullying, racism, gender identity and subject choice)

— **Educational achievement** (eg, class, gender and ethnicity)

— **Parents' attitudes** (eg, parents' satisfaction)

✔✗ In context: strengths and limitations of using interviews to investigate educational issues

Strengths of interviews (structured and unstructured)

On a theoretical level

✔ **Replication.** Structured interviews produce more reliable data than unstructured. This means each interview is carried out according to a standardised procedure: the interviewer puts questions in a consistent way (eg, order and tone of voice) and all the respondents answer the same questions. This means the same questions can be repeated by other researchers to see if they obtain similar results. If the findings are similar, we can be confident that the information collected is reliable on certain educational issues being investigated (eg, gender and subject choice at A Level).

✔ **Validity.** Unstructured interviews are more likely than structured interviews to produce valid information. Questions or words that children may not understand can be explained by the interviewer, which will help the children give more accurate answers. This is not possible with a structured interview.

On a practical level

✔ **Cheaper and quicker.** Structured interviews are normally quicker and easier to administer in an educational setting where basic information is required from teachers, students or from parents than unstructured interviews. This makes them cost-effective and more time-efficient than other research methods, which means that a larger sample of people can be obtained.

Limitations of interviews (structured and unstructured)

On a theoretical level

✗ **Validity.** Interviews (structured and unstructured) may not produce valid information. Children may deliberately lie or not give complete or socially desirable answers if questioned by an 'authority figure' whom they view in the same light as a 'teacher'. The responses of parents and teachers may also be questioned: they may also not be totally frank, or more inclined to give socially desirable answers, especially when under scrutiny (eg, school inspection or performance review). This reduces the validity of the data collected from the questionnaire.

On a practical level

✗ **Limited use.** A limitation of using structured interviews in schools is that they cannot be used on very young children, those with poor literacy, or those from ethnic-minority families whose English is not fluent enough to fully understand what the questionnaire is about, and thus may not be willing or able to complete the questionnaire accurately.

✗ **Design of questions.** There is also the practical problem that children's language skills and understanding will not be as developed as those of adults. This means that in a structured interview, the questions may not be fully understood as they may involve concepts of an abstract nature. Children's' responses may therefore be incorrect, or their responses worded incorrectly. For unstructured interviews this may not be so problematic as the researcher can explain things to the children; however, this is not possible with structured interviews.

✗ **Training required.** The interviewer will require more training when conducting unstructured interviews with young children than when conducting an interview with adults. They will need to learn certain questioning techniques (eg, to avoid repetitive, misleading or suggestive questioning) in order for them to really understand the children's thoughts and meanings.

✗ **Interviewer effect.** There is also the practical issue that the researcher will need to consider how the age, sex, and ethnicity of the interviewer can influence the way in which children or parents respond. For example, some children may feel less comfortable with an interviewer of the opposite sex or someone who is younger, whereas some parents or teachers may answer questions differently if the interviewer is of a certain ethnicity or gender, and the questions are of a sensitive nature (eg, to do with religion, sex or racism).

Ethical issues

✗ **Anonymity.** The researcher must ensure the anonymity and confidentiality of those being interviewed, especially if they are dealing with sensitive topics. However, confidentiality may not always be guaranteed. For example, if a child reveals some form of abuse (physical or sexual), the interviewer has a professional duty to report it.

✗ **Requirement for consent.** Permission must be given by the school (eg, head teacher, teachers and parents) to carry out an interview. Any of these may object to interviews and refuse to provide consent, especially if the nature of the study is contentious, (eg, sex-related issues). The school may find conducting interviews too disruptive to children's education, if they are required to come out of lessons.

AS level exam questions

Paper 1 – methods in context

Item B – Investigating anti-school subcultures

Some pupils share sets of values and behaviour patterns that are in opposition to those expected by schools. Sociologists refer to these as 'anti-school subcultures'. Some sociologists use group interviews to investigate anti-school subcultures. These largely unstructured interviews may give younger pupils, in particular, greater confidence when responding to a researcher's questions because they are being interviewed together with their peers.

1. Applying material from **Item B** and your knowledge of research methods, evaluate the strengths and limitations of using group interviews to investigate unauthorised absences from school.

    [20 marks]

Paper 2

1. Outline **two** problems of using unstructured interviews in sociological research.   **[4 marks]**

2. Outline **two** advantages of using unstructured interviews in sociological research.   **[4 marks]**

3. Outline **two** reasons sociologists may choose to use group interviews.   **[4 marks]**

4. Evaluate the reason some sociologists use unstructured interviews.   **[16 marks]**

5. Evaluate the difficulties that sociologists sometimes face in structured interviews.   **[16 marks]**

6. Evaluate the advantages that sociologists may find when using structured interviews.   **[16 marks]**

7. Evaluate the different kinds of interview in sociological research.   **[16 marks]**

A level exam questions

Paper 1 – methods in context

1. The 'methods in context' question is set at both AS and A level *(see above AS level exam question, paper 1)*.

Paper 3

2. Applying material from **Item (...)** and your knowledge, evaluate the usefulness of the different types of interview in sociological research.   **[10 marks]**

The exam requires that you are able to:

► Understand the different types of observational research - participant and non-participant observation.

► Evaluate the strengths and limitations associated with each type of observation.

► Evaluate the strengths and limitations of using observational research when investigating educational issues.

Observation

Different types of observations

Observation is a research method used by sociologists to gather data by watching others in their natural everyday lives. The researcher will need to decide which type of observational method to use from the following:

— **Participant observation (PO).** This is when the researcher joins in and observes the group's everyday activity that is being studied. For example, the researcher may join in the everyday life of 6th form students, interacting in their lessons and non-lesson times. Participant observations are often referred to as **unstructured observations** (see below under 'structured observation') and tend to collect qualitative data.

— **Non-participant observation (NPO).** This is when the researcher observes a group of people or a person, but does not take part in the activity of the group being studied, for example, observing children playing in a school playground from a distance. Non-participant observations are often referred to as **structured observations,** as they tend to collect quantitative data (see below under 'structured observations').

— **Structured observation (SO).** Researchers using participant observations will write everything that they observe or is important to them, probably at a later time when they are alone. This method of recording data freely is often referred to as unstructured ('unstructured observation'). An alternative type of observation is called 'structured observation'. This is when the researcher knows in advance what they are looking for and records the observed behaviour in a systematic and structured manner using an **observational schedule.** A schedule can be seen as a paper with a number of categories or tables labelled with certain behaviours that the researcher will look for and record (eg, using a tally system) as and when they occur. For example, if the researcher is interested in observing aggressive behaviour during playtime in primary-school children, they will record a tally mark in the appropriate category (kicking, slapping, spitting, etc.) every time an aggressive act is carried out. Structured observations are usually non-participant observations and the data collected tend to be quantitative. One example is the Flanders system of Interaction Analysis Category (FIAC).

Covert or overt Observation

The researcher will also need to decide whether their identity is revealed whilst carrying out an observational research. The two types of observation are:

— **Overt observation.** The researcher's identity is revealed to the group of people or person being studied.

— **Covert observation.** The identity of the researcher and the purpose of the study are kept hidden (undisclosed) from the group being observed.

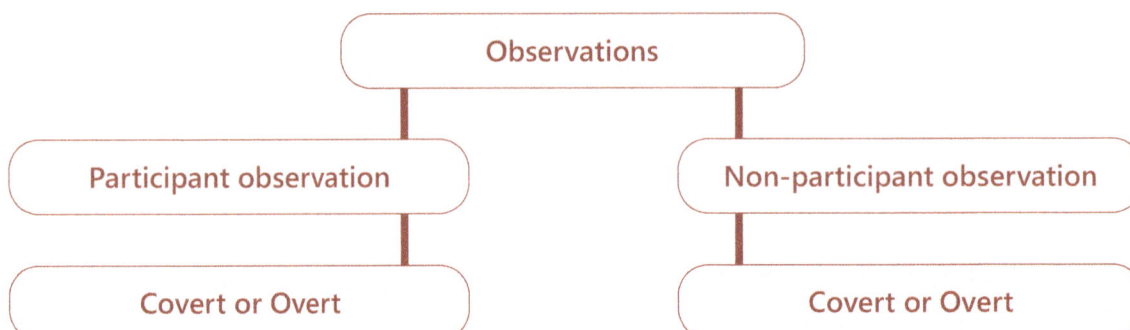

```
                        ┌─────────────────────────┐
                        │      Observations        │
                        └─────────────────────────┘
                ┌────────────────┴────────────────┐
┌──────────────────────────┐      ┌──────────────────────────────┐
│  Participant observation  │      │  Non-participant observation  │
└──────────────────────────┘      └──────────────────────────────┘
┌──────────────────────────┐      ┌──────────────────────────────┐
│      Covert or Overt      │      │       Covert or Overt         │
└──────────────────────────┘      └──────────────────────────────┘
```

✔✖ Strengths and limitations of observations

Strengths of participant observation

Theoretical issues

✔ **High validity.** Interpretivists tend to find PO particularly useful because it produces valid data. This is because it takes place in natural everyday settings, which means those being investigated will often behave as they would normally do, especially if covert PO is used. This allows the researcher to gather a deep insight into behaviour that reflects a true accurate picture of what they are investigating whereas when questionnaires and interviews are used, the respondent can lie or answer inaccurately, making the information incorrect.

✔ **Generating new ideas.** In other research methods, such as social surveys, the questions have already been fixed by the researcher according to what they think is important to the investigation. The limitation of social surveys is that they limit the flexibility for new ideas and information to move research in a new direction. In PO, the researcher enters the study with an open mind and no pre-fixed hypothesis, thus allowing new insights and ideas which they may not initially have considered.

Theoretical issues

✔ **The only investigation possible.** Covert PO may be the only available research method to gain a valid picture of what is going on, especially for deviant social groups such as criminal gangs or religious cults. Such groups may be hostile to, and suspicious of, people from outside so trying to use other sociological methods, such as social surveys, may not be possible.

✔ **Problem of documenting.** It is difficult to document the data. A researcher will struggle to write down everything important while in the act of participating and observing. They researcher must therefore rely on their memory and own personal discipline to write down and expand their observations as soon and as completely as possible: because memory fades quickly, postponing the expansion of notes can lead to loss or inaccurate recording of data. The quality of the data therefore depends on the diligence of the researcher, rather than on technology such as tape recorders.

Ethical issues

✔ **No ethical issues.** The advantage of overt PO is that it does not have any of the ethical problems of covert PO, such as deception, lack of consent and invasion of privacy.

✔ **Dangerous situations avoided.** In overt PO, permission has been granted which prevents the researcher from putting themselves in a dangerous situation or becoming involved in illegal activities.

Limitations of participant observation

Theoretical issues

✗ **Validity.** Positivists have questioned the usefulness of PO for the following reasons:

— **Subjective interpretation.** The validity of results is based on the researcher's own subjective interpretation and understanding of what they are observing. The researcher may have selected the information on what they thought of as important. This will inevitably be based on their own personal values, beliefs and opinions, leading to an imprecise recording of information.

— **Observer bias.** The researcher can slowly be drawn into the group and start seeing themselves as part of the group. This means that the researcher is no longer detached (impartial) and objective in their sociological investigation. They can no longer see things clearly as they have become closer to the social group; this is known as 'going native'.

— **Hawthorne effect.** The presence of a researcher, especially for overt PO, may influence the participants to act differently if they are aware of being watched, making the study pointless. This is known as the 'Hawthorne effect'. If this happens, the findings from the study may not be valid. Covert PO may also be influenced by the Hawthorne effect as the presence of a new member in a group may make others alter their behaviour initially.

✗ **Reliability.** The research findings from PO are viewed as unreliable because they are not carried out according to controlled and standardised procedure, like experiments. Because the observation takes place in the participant's natural setting, it would be extremely difficult to replicate the same study again, under the same test conditions, to see if the research findings are consistent. This means it is difficult to check the validity of observational research.

✗ **Representativeness.** Observational research is carried out on a very small group which may not be representative of any other group in society. This means that it will be difficult to make generalisations and draw conclusions.

Practical issues

✗ **Financial and/or time constraints.** PO can be expensive and time-consuming compared to other research methods, such as questionnaires. Depending on the time and funding available, this will determine whether observation should be used as a research method.

✗ **Access.** It can be difficult or even impossible to access the group you would like to investigate, especially if it is a deviant organisation. At times, access is down to pot luck or whether you know anyone who has access to that particular group (eg, an informant). Access can also be a problem with overt PO, especially if the issue under investigation is of a sensitive nature. Most social organisations, for example schools, will feel uncomfortable having prying sociologists around their premises.

✗ **Staying in.** A real problem of remaining inside the group for covert PO is that it is not as easy as it may seem. You need to be constantly on your guard in order not to expose your true identity, especially over a long period of time, and able to maintain the friendships established. This may require performing an act which may be morally wrong, criminal or even dangerous to secure your hidden identity.

✗ **Getting out.** Leaving the group may also bring its own set of problems. How will the group under observation react if they have found out they have been deceived and lied to if covert PO was used? Will the life of the researcher be in danger afterwards?

✗ **Personal characteristics.** The researcher's gender, ethnicity and age have to be to some extent similar to those of the group under observation if the researcher is to 'blend' in. If this is not possible, access to the group may be unlikely or impossible.

✗ **Recording of data.** Covert PO data can be difficult to document. A researcher needs to find a method of recording data (hidden video/recording device) without arousing suspicion. If not, the researcher must rely on their memory to record the data. Memory fades with time, which opens up the possibility of inaccurate or distorted information.

Ethical issues

✗ **Deception.** Covert PO has been criticised for involving deception in research study. The participants are not told the truth with regards to the researcher's identity and the research aim.

✗ **Lack of informed consent.** Since the participants are deceived, they cannot have given consent to take part in the research study. This raises the issues of lack of informed consent and invasion of privacy. If either of these has occurred, the research should ensure the confidentially of the data (as under the Data Protection Act 1989) and anonymity of the participants.

✗ **Placed in danger.** If the researcher's identity and the purpose of the research (eg, in covert PO) is revealed, the researcher may be put in a position of danger or harm.

✗ **Illegal or immoral behaviour.** If the group engages in illegal or immoral activities, then the researcher may also have to engage in such activities, just to protect their covert identity. This can put them in an ethical dilemma as well as an illegal position.

Strengths of structured observation (non-participant observation)

Theoretical issues

✔ **Behaviour can be quantified.** Positivists tend to prefer SO (NPO) as it tends to produce quantitative data which can be put in numerical form and analysed statistically to assess the existence of a relationship between two variables.

✔ **Data is reliable.** The findings from SO are seen as being reliable because another researcher can repeat the study using the same observational schedule to ascertain if the findings are consistent.

✔ **Unbiased interpretation.** In SO, the researcher will not be involved in the group: they can study in a detached and objective manner without the problem of 'going native', thus increasing the validity of the research findings.

✔ **No Hawthorne effect.** One of the main reasons a researcher may choose non-PO is that it provides a highly valid picture of the social group being investigated. The absence of the researcher eliminates the possibility that participant behaviour will alter in the presence of a new member, be it covert or overt PO.

Limitations of structured observation (non-participant observation)

Theoretical issues

✗ **Reduced validity.** Interpretivists tend not to favour SO as it cannot probe deeper into the participants' behaviour and discover why people behave in certain ways. The validity of the findings will therefore be less than those produced by PO.

✗ **Hawthorne effect.** If the participants are aware of being observed they may change their behaviour, giving rise to the Hawthorne effect.

Ethical issues

✗ **Lack of consent & invasion of privacy.** As SO is usually non-participatory, the participants may be watched without their approval. This raises the issues of lack of consent and invasion of privacy. Ideally, where informed consent has not been obtained prior to the research, it should be obtained afterwards. Also, the researcher should ensure the confidentially of the data and anonymity of the participants they have observed.

Methods in context: Using observations to investigate educational issues

Observational methods have been used to investigate a number of educational issues such as:

— **Pupil subcultures** (eg, the behaviour of pupils in subcultures).

— **Labelling** (eg, teacher/pupil interaction such as racism/stereotyping).

— **Language** (eg, different speech styles of middle-class and working-class pupils used in the classroom).

— **Gender** (eg, seeing how boys and girls behave differently in a classroom setting).

✓✗ Strengths and limitations of using observations to investigate educational issues

Strengths of unstructured observations

Theoretical issues

✔ **Favoured by interpretivists.** Interpretivists favour using unstructured observational research methods. This is because there are no pre-coded behaviour categories, so they do not make assumptions in advance of the issues they would like to observe (as in SO). Instead, the researcher, with an open mind, freely writes down the behaviour they are observing, allowing them to get a better understanding of why teachers and students behave the way they do as well as generating new hypotheses and ideas which they may not have considered before. This cannot be done with a pre-determined SO.

Limitations of unstructured observations

Theoretical issues

✗ **Hawthorne effect.** Positivists would question the validity of unstructured observation because it does not give an accurate and true picture of what is being investigated. Most school observations (such as in a classroom setting) can lead to the Hawthorne effect, whereby the mere presence of an observer may influence those being observed (eg, teachers/students) to behave differently and unnaturally, which can affect the validity of the research findings. For example, teachers may put on a display, an 'image of professionalism', to hide their true behaviour. However, the Hawthorne effect may be a problem initially, but after a period of time, as the teachers and students become more familiar with the researcher, they may eventually start to behave normally, although this is questionable.

✗ **Going native.** Even if the researcher spent months in the classrooms in order to make the teachers and the students feel more at ease, there is the potential problem that over time, due to the nature of the research, the researcher will be drawn into the daily life of a classroom and build up 'friendships' with the teachers and pupils. If this happens, the researcher may no longer be objective in their sociological investigation. This means they will no longer see things clearly, and may become unintentionally biased in their investigation, a problem known as 'going native'.

✗ **Reliability.** Unstructured observations on education are viewed as unreliable because the information is not recorded by a systematic and standardised procedure but in a very flexible way (jotting down on paper) which makes it difficult to replicate results.

✗ **Representativeness.** Observations in educational settings (eg, of teachers or students) often deal with a small sample size. This means the sample is not representative of other educational settings, which reduces the ability to make generalisations from the findings.

Practical issues

✘ **Access.** Permission must be granted by the school (eg, head teacher, teachers or parents) to carry out an observational research study. Some teachers or parents may object to this, depending on the nature of the study.

✘ **Personal characteristics.** The researcher's age, gender, ethnicity or other personal characteristics can be an issue. If the observer is much older or from a particular ethnicity or gender, they may find it difficult to blend in with the group that is being observed. There is also the issue that some teachers or students may act differently or antagonistically towards the observer, which can affect the validity of the study.

✘ **Time-consuming.** Observational issues can be time-consuming as they will need to consider the school timetable, holiday, control over access, and health and safety legislation. This also makes observational research expensive.

Ethical issues

✘ **Overt observation only possible.** Sociologists need to follow ethical guidelines, which means that observing children in a covert manner is not ethically acceptable. The British Sociological Association guidelines for ethical practice state that the consent of the child (under the age of 16) should be obtained as well of that of the parent. This means that CO is ruled out and overt observation only viable option (most observations carried out in schools or with children tend to be overt, which raises the issue of validity). If the observer sees children who have broken school rules, or behaved in a way that will get them into trouble, they are obliged to report it. If this is documented in the report, the researcher must guarantee confidentiality and anonymity due to the sensitive nature of the topic, as the careers and reputations of individual teachers and managers, and of the schools, may otherwise be harmed.

Strengths of structured observations

Theoretical issues

✔ **Reliability.** The findings from SO are seen as being reliable because another researcher can repeat the study using the same observational schedule to ascertain if they are consistent.

Practical issues

✔ **Quicker and cheaper.** SO is quicker and cheaper, and requires less training, than unstructured observational methods. This is because when using SO, the observer uses a pre-defined observational schedule. This can easily be converted into quantitative data form and analysed statistically to see whether there is a relationship between the two variables of interest.

Ethical issues

✔ **No ethical issues.** If SO is used in a school setting, teachers and students would be aware of it and so no real ethical issues involved. As long as the purpose is known and confidentiality is maintained, the research study should be ethical.

Limitations of structured observations

Theoretical issues

✗ **Lacks insight.** Interpretivists are critical of the use of SO in an educational setting, such as a classroom. This is because simply counting classroom behaviour and classifying it into a limited number of pre-defined categories ignores the questions of why pupils and teachers behave the way they do and thus does not give a real insight into and understanding of their behaviour.

Practice exam questions

AS level exam questions

Paper 1 – methods in context

Item B – Investigating ethnic differences in education

Not all ethnic groups do equally well at school. In general, pupils of Chinese and Indian heritage achieve more highly, while pupils from Black Caribbean, Pakistani and Bangladeshi backgrounds do less well. Black pupils are also more likely to be formally excluded from school than those from other ethnic groups. Some White groups, such as Roma/Gypsy children, do particularly badly. These patterns may be due to a variety of home and school factors.

Sociologists may study ethnic differences in education by using overt non-participant observation. This method allows the researcher to witness interaction processes first hand.

1. Applying material from **Item B** and your knowledge of research methods, evaluate the strengths and limitations of using overt non-participant observation for investigating ethnic differences in education. **[20 marks]**

Paper 2

1. Outline **two** differences between overt and covert approaches to research. **[4 marks]**

2. Outline **two** advantages in using covert participant observations in sociological research. **[4 marks]**

3. Outline **two** disadvantages in using covert participant observations in sociological research. **[4 marks]**

4. Outline **two** advantages in using overt participant observations in sociological research. **[4 marks]**

5. Outline **two** disadvantages in using overt participant observations in sociological research. **[4 marks]**

6. Outline **two** problems with joining in the activities of the group under study when carrying out sociological research. **[4 marks]**

7. Evaluate the advantages of using participant observation in sociological research. **[16 marks]**

1. Evaluate the problems of using participant observation in sociological research. **[16 marks]**

2. Evaluate the advantages of using non-participant observation in sociological research.

    [16 marks]

3. Evaluate the view that participant observation is both unscientific and unethical. **[16 marks]**

A level exam questions

Paper 1 – methods in context

1. The 'methods in context' question is set at both AS and A level *(see above AS level exam question, paper 1)*.

Paper 1 and 3

2. Outline and explain **two** ethical problems of covert research. **[10 marks]**

Paper 3

3. Applying material from **Item (...)** and your knowledge, evaluate the usefulness of observational sociological research. **[10 marks]**

4. Applying material from **Item (...)** and your knowledge, evaluate the view that participant observation is both unscientific and unethical. **[10 marks]**

The exam requires that you are able to:

▶ Understand the different types of documents sociologists use in sociological research.

▶ Evaluate the strengths and limitations of documents.

▶ Evaluate the strengths and limitations of using documents when investigating educational issues.

Documents

Sociologists often use document resources in their research investigations. Documents are written, pictorial or audio material produced by government bodies, organisations and individuals. They are referred to as **secondary resources** as they have already been collected, so the researcher is 'borrowing' the existing information which they will need to analyse and interpret the data for their own research purposes. There are different types of documents, which can be broadly classified as:

Personal documents

Personal documents can be letters, diaries, memoirs, autobiographies, suicide notes, photos, videos, etc, which depict the meanings, opinions, feelings and experiences of an individual or small group of people. Some examples:

— **Autobiographies** for example, *Long Walk to Freedom* (1995) by Nelson Mandela, which is an account of his experiences and struggle against apartheid in South Africa.

— **Diaries** for example, *The Diary of Anne Frank* (1947), which provided a rich account of what life as a persecuted Jew was like during the Nazi occupation of Amsterdam in World War II.

Public document

Public documents can derive from many sections of public life, such as government departments (eg, reports and official statistics), businesses, organisations, charities, schools, etc. They also include mass media sources such as television, newspapers, advertisements, magazines and the internet. An example:

— **The Macpherson Report (1999)** – a government report by Sir William Macpherson into the racially-motived murder of Stephen Lawrence and its poor handling by the Metropolitan Police including their failure to convict the 'obvious' suspects, which led to the police force being labelled 'institutionally racist'. The report recommended a number of government initiatives to tackle institutional racism within the police force.

Historical document

Historical documents can either be public or personal, and have been created in the past. They can be very useful to sociologists as they are often the only sources available, especially if they want to examine and compare trends of social changes over a period of time. For example:

— **Geoffrey Pearson's 'Hooligans: A History of Respectable Fears' (1983)** analysed historical documents showing that there have been repeating cycles of moral panic about unprecedented levels of youth crime since the 16th century (1501-1600). His findings suggest that today's perceived alarming rise in youth crime is not a new phenomenon but a misconception, as each generation has feared youth behaviour.

— **Philippe Aries' 'Centuries of Childhood' (1962)** investigates the history of 'childhood' (a stage of life with unique characteristics, eg, behaviour, play and dress), using historical documents such as medieval paintings to support the idea that 'childhood' did not exist in pre-modern European society, but that children were treated like little adults. It argues that it was not until the 18th century (1701-1800) that the notion of 'childhood' was created.

Content analysis

Mass media resources such as TV programmes, advertisements, newspapers, magazines, speeches, songs and transcripts of interviews are often analysed by sociologists using **content analysis.** As the name suggests, this is a technique used to 'analyse' the 'content' of qualitative data. The purpose of content analysis is to summarise a large of amount of qualitative material by converting it into numerical form (quantitative data, ie, numbers).

Sample material. Once the researchers have identified their aims and hypothesis, they will need to select sample material which is representative of the topic of interest to be analysed (eg, which magazine), taking into consideration *quantity* (eg, 20 magazines), *frequency* (eg, every fortnight) and *length of time* (eg, over 6 months).

Creating categories. The researcher will need to analyse the material in a systematic manner. One way to do this is to create a grid sheet with named categories. How the researcher names each category will depend on what they are looking for in the material to be analysed. The information is then extracted from the material and recorded in the appropriate category. Depending on what the researcher wants to investigate, the analysis of the material can be based on words, themes, concepts or images. For example, a sociologist may decide to merely count and record how often instances occur on TV, using a tally score (eg, how many times a negative word is said). Below is an example of a content analysis study which aims to show how often males and females are portrayed in advertisements during week days and evenings, and at weekends.

	Daytime	Evening	Weekends
Adult male	38	62	70
Adult female	69	48	50

Who prefers documents, positivists or interpretivists?

— *Interpretivists* tend to like documents as they are mainly classified as **qualitative data.** They provide a rich and detailed account into people's meanings, thoughts, feelings and experiences, giving a deeper understanding of human behaviour. For this reason, they are preferred by interpretivists as they are high in validity.

— *Positivists* tend to reject documents as being unreliable and unrepresentative sources of information. However, some documents can be **quantitative data,** making them useful to positivists, such as government statistical publications (eg, on population, education and crime) as they are presented mainly as facts and figures. Therefore, they find such documents are useful because they are easier to analyse and interpret than qualitative data, enabling the sociologist to draw conclusions about such issues as trends and relationships.

Positivists can also use qualitative data by converting them into quantitative data by the use of *content analysis.* This type of analysis enables the researcher to 'edit' the vast amount of written data by summarising them into numbers in a meaningful way (eg, tables, graphs and charts).

Can we trust documents?

John Scott (1990) provides guidance on how to assess the usefulness (validity) of all types of documents by suggesting a four-point criteria check:

— **Authenticity.** This refers to authorship. Can we identify and verify that the piece of writing is the genuine work of the author, or is it a copy or a fake?

— **Credibility.** This refers to the accuracy of the document: is it free from error and distortion? Was the author sincere in their written material?

— **Representativeness.** Is the information typical of the same subject matter in that particular era (time/place) or is the information 'out of the ordinary'? If so, can we generalise from the information? If not, we need to treat it with caution.

— **Meaning.** This is concerned with the interpretation and understanding of the documents. What does the information tell us? Is it clear, or is it open to interpretation of the author's actual meaning?

✔✗ Strengths and limitations of using documents

Strengths of using documents

On a theoretical level

✔ **Deeper insight.** Documents that produce qualitative data provide a better insight into people's lives and meanings. Those who adopt an interpretivist approach argue that this is the only way to get a better insight into really understanding people's motives and the reasons behind their behaviour.

On a practical level

✔ **They are readily available.** The use of documents as a research method is much cheaper and less time-consuming than other methods (eg, interviews and observations). This is because the researcher does not have to spend a great deal of money or time collecting their own information, as it already exists. This allows the analysis and interpretation of the data to be carried out relatively quickly.

✔ **Accessibility.** Personal documents may provide information on areas of social life which sociologists cannot readily study with primary research for a number of reasons. For example, Tony Blair's written memoirs, A Journey, (2010) are a personal account of life as a prime minister, and documents written by those engaging in illegal, secretive or deviant activities describe circumstances where it would be unsafe for the researcher to collect data (eg, IRA, BNP or terrorist or extreme religious groups).

Limitations of using documents

On a theoretical level

✗ **Faulty memory.** Documents, especially personal and historical, are heavily dependent on people's memories and can be prone to 'false memory syndrome', that is, information may be distorted, selective or incorrect. This can reduce the validity of the information.

✗ **Bias.** Documents can be biased towards the writer's attitudes and opinions, and are written for a particular audience in mind. Again, this makes the validity difficult to prove.

✗ **Unrepresentativeness.** Documents, especially personal ones, often represent the experiences and events of an individual or a small group of people, and this makes them unrepresentative, so it is difficult to generalise from the findings. However, government statistical data, such as official statistics, are based on very large samples which make them representative of people's general views.

On an ethical level

● **Consent given?** The original author or organisation must be informed and provide consent to use their material, especially if the research is of a sensitive nature. However, there may be practical problems to this as the person may be deceased or untraceable. This raises the ethical issue of whether it is acceptable to use (especially if it will be published) existing material if consent cannot be given.

● **Historical documents.** Informed consent cannot be given with many historical documents, as the author is often no longer alive. This raises the issue of invasion of privacy and confidentiality of data. Moreover, this sort of use is open to abuse as the researcher can alter the material by exploiting or distorting it to support their research purpose.

Strengths of content analysis

✔ **Useful technique.** Content analysis is a very useful research technique for analysing and summarising a large body of qualitative material, allowing the researcher to draw conclusions from the data.

✔ **Reliability.** The data produced from content analysis can be reliable. This is because it can be easily repeated by other researchers using the same grid sheet to see if the same results are found.

✔ **No researcher effect.** Content/thematic analysis does not involve the researcher interacting with the participants because the information has already been gathered. This means that the research cannot influence the participants' behaviour, which makes the results more valid.

Limitations of content analysis

✗ **Loss of insight.** Content analysis means counting up numbers and then describing the pattern or relationship that these numbers seem to suggest. Interactionists claim that this has limited use as it cannot offer explanations as to why such patterns and relationships occur in the first place.

✗ **Reliability and validity issues.** Content analysis relies on the researcher's subjective interpretation. Different researchers may have different interpretations of the material, which may result in the recorded data being placed in incorrect categories. This inconsistency reduces the reliability and validity of the findings.

✗ **Unrepresentativeness.** A weakness of content/thematic analysis is that the few selected sample materials may be unrepresentative (eg, the selection of a few books or an interview transcript), which makes the findings difficult to generalise from.

Methods in context:

Using documents to investigate educational issues

Documents have been used to investigate a number of educational issues. Some common issues are:

— **Public/historical documents** (E.g. Ofsted inspections reports, school policies, prospectuses, governors meeting, educational)

— **Personal documents** (E.g. teachers written reports on pupils, pupils written work, pupil-to-pupil text messages, notes passed in classroom, pupil dairy)

✔✗ Strengths and limitations of using documents to investigate educational issues

Strengths of documents

On a theoretical level

✔ **Validity.** Personal documents can provide information that provides insight and understanding for certain meanings, beliefs and behaviours held by teachers and students. For example, a historical dairy written by student's during the Second World War gives valuable information as to what school life was under those conditions.

On a practical level

✔ **Cheaper and quicker.** Access to public documents is generally quick and easy and relatively cheap to acquire. However, this may not be true of all personal documents. Some personal documents may be more difficult to access if they are produced by pupils or teachers, as they may not want to have their personal information put 'in the spotlight', and thus may not allow the researcher to have access to them.

Limitations of documents

On a theoretical level

✗ **Validity.** Some personal documents are written with an audience in mind, that is, to be read by others, which means they may not provide a completely valid account. There is also the problem of interpretation and understanding. For example, an adult researcher may not accurately interpret correctly what a young pupil meant.

Also, some pubic documents may not provide a valid account. For example, school websites, school prospectuses, school inspection reports and assessment material can be manipulated in a way to present the school in a more desirable light that it really is. This is especially when schools need to attract 'pupils' to attend their school (manipulation of school prospectuses to attract parents) or to maximise funding (manipulation of school documents produced for government), or to increase a better Ofsted inspection report (e.g. unfavourable information/exam performances is suppressed is withheld by the school for inspectors).

✗ **Representativeness.** Information provided in personal documents will often be based on the personal experience of the teacher or pupils that produced it. This means the findings from such a small and unique sample will make it difficult to generalise.

Ethical issues

✔ **Historical documents—no real ethical issues.** There are no ethical issues with public or historical documents because they are already in the public domain, which can be accessed by others.

✗ **Personal documents—issue of consent.** With personal documents, this can raise ethical issues. The researcher needs to seek consent to use it, from those who created the personal document, especially if the research is of a sensitive nature such as pupils or teacher's diary or school report.

✗ **Personal documents—issue of confidentiality.** There is also the issue of confidentiality with personal documents. For example, school or student reports are confidential documents, the researcher needs to guarantee the anonymity of who they refer to (unless there are legal, safety or health obligations).

Practice exam questions

AS level exam questions

Paper 1 – methods in context

Item B – Investigating applications and admissions to secondary schools

Sociologists are interested in the processes by which pupils and their parents apply to, and pupils are admitted to, secondary schools. Much evidence suggests that working-class and minority ethnic group pupils are less likely to apply or to gain admission to higher status schools with good results. Sociologists sometimes study applications and admissions to secondary schools by analysing documents. For example, study of the home/school contracts of high status schools may show that they require parents to make commitments that poorer families cannot make. Similarly, if researchers can obtain application forms and entrance test papers, these can be analysed for cultural bias.

1. Applying material from **Item B** and your knowledge of research methods, evaluate the strengths and limitations of documents to investigate applications and admissions to secondary schools.

[20 marks]

Paper 2

1. Outline **two** differences between public and personal documents. [4 marks]

2. Outline **two** reasons why "the content of newspapers and television programmes is generally treated with caution by researchers". [4 marks]

3. Outline **two** advantages of using personal and historical documents in sociological research.

[4 marks]

4. Outline **two** disadvantages of using personal documents in sociological research. [4 marks]

5. Outline **two** disadvantages of using public documents in sociological research. [4 marks]

6. Outline **two** disadvantages of using media reports in sociological research. [4 marks]

7. Outline **two** practical problems of using historical documents in sociological research. [4 marks]

8. Evaluate the disadvantages sociologists may find when using documents in their research.

[16 marks]

9. Evaluate the advantages sociologists may find when using documents in their research.

[16 marks]

A level exam questions

Paper 1 – methods in context

1. The 'methods in context' question is set at both AS and A level *(see above AS level exam question, paper 1)*.

Paper 1 and 3

2. Outline and explain **two** problems of using secondary data in sociological research. [10 marks]

Paper 3

3. Applying material from **Item (...)** and your knowledge, evaluate the usefulness of different kinds of secondary data in sociological research. [20 marks]

The exam requires that you are able to:

▶ Understand why sociologists use official statistics in sociological research.

▶ Evaluate the strengths and limitations of official statistics.

▶ Evaluate the strengths and limitations of using official statistics when investigating educational issues.

Official statistics

Statistical data collected by or on behalf of local and national government departments are referred to as **official statistics.** Official statistics are **quantitative data** and usually come from social surveys such as questionnaires and interviews. Official statistics examine a wide range of behaviour mainly related to population, social and economic issues. Official statistics are referred to as **secondary data** because the information has already been collected by the government. Sociologists 'borrow' the already collected data for their research purposes.

Examples of official statistics

— Examples of official statistics are facts and figures on birth, death, marriage, education, unemployment, health, migration and crime. One well-known example of a government survey is the **Census** of the whole UK population (every ten years since 1841), by means of a questionnaire provided to every household in the UK which collects information on population, families, education, occupation, transport and leisure. The data builds up socio-economic characteristics of the whole of the UK, which helps governments locate and provide resources more effectively and plan for housing, education, health and transport services for the future.

Accessibility of statistical publications

— Official statistics are available to the public through a range of publications such as **Social Trends** (http://data.gov.uk). This provides a summary of statistical information under specific headings such as Education, Employment or Crime taken from a wide range of government departments. The **Office for National Statistics (ONS)** (http://www.statistics.gov.uk) is the UK government's main office for compiling and publishing all official government statistical data.

✔✗ Strengths and limitation of using official statistics

Strengths of official statistics

On a theoretical level

✔ **Positivists prefer them.** Positivists find official statistics useful because they produce quantitative data. These are easier to analyse and interpret than qualitative data because they enable the sociologist to come to conclusions from information such as patterns, trends and causal relationships (cause-and-effect relationships).

✔ **Reliability.** Positivists argue that official statistics are a generally reliable source of information. For example, crime statistics provide reliable quantitative data on criminal activity and trends. This is because criminal statistics are based on court convictions and crimes recorded by police officers, who all follow a uniform standardised set procedure, with the same categorising or coding used every time a crime is committed.

✔ **Representativeness.** Official statistics are collected by research methods such as standardised questionnaires and interviews. These are generally conducted on very large samples of the population, which makes the information more representative, allowing generalisations to be made upon the population under investigation.

✔ **Useful for governments.** Statistical data are very useful for governments as they can help them formulate social policies and intervention strategies. For example, the analysis of fertility rates has shown a rise in teenage pregnancies in economically deprived areas. This allows the allocation of funds and resources to tackle the problem of teenage pregnancies in such areas. It also allows governments to make predictions as to future behaviour, such as between the relationships of these two variables, teenage pregnancies and deprived areas, and act accordingly.

✔ **Comparisons can be made.** Statistical data are good for making 'before and after' study comparisons. A sociologist can analyse statistical data to examine the effects in the changes that laws can have on human behaviour, for example, the amount of alcohol-related violent behaviour before and after the 24-hour drinking law was introduced. Statistical data can be used to make comparative studies between groups, for example, to compare the types of crimes that the middle class and working class may commit or a cross-cultural study comparing teenage pregnancies and abortion rates in different countries.

✔ **Change over time.** Statistical data allow the sociologist to examine social trends in society and identify how they have changed over a period of time, for example, religious attendance or marriage trends: the average age of first marriage for females and males, or the changing number of marriages over a period of time.

On a practical level

✔ **They are readily available.** The use of official statistics is much cheaper and less time-consuming than other research methods. This is because the researcher does not have to spend money (statistics publications are free to access from government websites) or time collecting their own information. This allows the analysis and interpretations of the data to be carried out relatively quickly.

Ethical issues

✔ **Ethically sound.** Official statistics pose few ethical issues because they are secondary data that have been collected and compiled by official government agencies. The sociologist therefore does not have to worry about dealing with issues such as causing psychological harm, obtaining consent, confidentiality and anonymity as the information is already in the public domain.

Limitations of official statistics

On a theoretical level

✗ **Validity is an issue.** Interpretivists argue that official statistics are not a valid source of information and do not give a true picture of human behaviour. Statistics are the product of human processes (interpretation and decision-making) which are prone to errors, manipulation and mistakes which make them less valid than positivists claim. For example, crime statistics do not reflect a true picture of the level and nature of crimes in the UK. They only include crimes known to the police and ignore those which go unreported for reasons such as triviality, embarrassment, fear of reprisals or difficulties of detection (eg, tax evasion) or a police officer's decision not to record them, which can be based on a number of factors (see criticism below under 'unreliable').

✗ **Lacks depth.** Interpretivists argue that statistics lack insight into human behaviour. They do not explain the 'why questions'- why people act the way they do. For example, crime statistical patterns show that the most likely offenders are often young, working-class and male with a high proportion being black and poorly-educated. However, they fail to explain why (the cause) this group commits such crimes in the first place.

✗ **Official statistics can be manipulated.** Official statistics are compiled and published by the government, which makes them prone to **political bias.** A controversial example is the official 'total unemployment' statistics. It was noted that Conservative governments made more than 30 changes to the way unemployment was defined in the 1980s and 1990s. All these resulted in lower statistical figures (which made the government appear to be doing something about it). For example, during the 1980s, the definition of unemployment changed from those just registered as unemployed (but not claiming) to only those who claimed unemployment benefits (eg, income support and job seekers allowance). This excluded those who were unemployed but on government work-related training schemes, married women seeking work as their husbands' incomes make them ineligible for income support, the under-18s and those 'not actively seeking work' (eg, single parents and disabled adults).

✗ **Unreliability.** Official statistics can be an unreliable as a source of data. For example, it will depend on the court of law and the discretion of the police officer as to whether individuals accused of committing crimes are cautioned, arrested, charged and convicted, all which can affect the criminal statistics recorded.

On a practical level

✗ **Unavailable information.** Depending on the aims and hypothesis of the sociological researcher, the required information may not be obtained from official statistics, which renders them useless as a research method.

Ethical issues

✗ **Problem of interpretation.** Published sociological research findings may reveal socially sensitive information (eg, ethnicity and crime). This could be misinterpreted by the public, which could lead to the group being negatively stigmatised.

Methods in context:

Using official statistics to investigate educational issues

Official statistics have been used to investigate a number of educational issues, including:

— **Educational achievement** (eg, class, gender and ethnicity).

— **School performance** (eg, league tables).

— **School attendance** (eg, truancy and school exclusions).

✔✗ In context: strengths and limitations of using official statistics to investigate educational issues

Strengths of official statistics

On a theoretical level

✔ **Reliability.** Official statistics on education are generally reliable. This is because the government follows standardised procedures, definitions and categories when collecting educational statistical data. This standardised method can be replicated every year, and this allows comparisons to be made (eg, on truancy levels).

✔ **Representativeness.** Educational statistics are funded and collected by government organisations. This means that large funds make it possible to collect information on every pupil in the country. For example, all schools must complete a school census three times a year. it would not be feasible for sociologists to collect such a large quantity of data, let alone sift and analyse the information! This makes educational statistics highly representative and allows generalisations to be made.

On a practical level

✔ **Easy to analyse.** Positivists tend to favour the use of educational statistics because they can be easily analysed for changes over time and between groups, and to see if patterns, trends and correlations exist (eg, analysing exam performance by gender, class or ethnic group).

✔ **Cheaper and quicker.** Official educational statistics are easy to obtain as they have already been collected by the government and are accessible to everyone by downloading the relevant file from a government website. This means a sociological researcher can use the information freely without having to spend a large amount of money or time, unlike many other research methods such as observations or unstructured interviews.

Limitations of official statistics

On a theoretical level

✗ **Validity.** Interpretivists are critical of educational statistical data. This is because they are created by people, which means they can be deliberately manipulated in order to be presented in a more positive light. For example, schools may manipulate records of absences or truancy. They may also refrain from entering some pupils in GCSE exams (asking some pupils to drop a subject) in order to improve their position in the league table.

✗ **Cannot explain the 'why' question.** Educational statistics are useful to show patterns, trends and comparisons, such as between gender and educational achievement. However, they cannot explain, for example why boys underachieve at GCSE level, but only give a frequency or percentage of how many fall short of the 5 A*-C. Therefore, the researcher cannot identify if home background or school life are among the reasons for boys' under-achievement..

✗ **Official statistics have limited use.** Educational statistics have limited use in investigating certain educational issues. For example, a sociologist cannot use statistical data to find out about labelling, gender and classroom behaviour, pupil subcultures, hidden curriculum, etc. For such educational issues, observations and interviews are better research methods.

Practical issues

✗ **Official statistics have limited use.** Educational statistics have limited use in investigating certain educational issues. For example, a sociologist cannot use statistical data to find out about labelling, gender and classroom behaviour, pupil subcultures, hidden curriculum, etc. For such educational issues, observations and interviews are better research methods.

✗ **Collected for non-sociological reasons.** Educational statistics are collected for government purposes rather than sociological research. Even when educational statistics may be of interest to the sociologist (such as those regarding social class and education), the concepts and definitions applied by government may be different to those applied by sociologists. For example, the government's official definition of 'social class' is based on those students who are eligible for free school meals whereas sociologists may define itin terms of cultural values, property ownership, etc. This means that the sociologist may find the definition unsuitable or use the government's definition with reluctance.

Ethical issues

✗ **Problem of interpretation.** There are no real ethical issues. However, information on a particular ethnic group or class on educational matters such as exam performance or truancy could be misinterpreted by the public, which could lead to the group or class being negatively stigmatised.

Practice exam questions

AS level exam questions

Paper 1 – methods in context

Item B – Investigating truancy from school

Truancy – unauthorised absence from school – is closely linked to educational under-achievement. Pupils doing badly at school are more likely to truant, and persistent truants tend to leave school with few qualifications. Truancy is also linked to juvenile delinquency.

Some sociologists may use official statistics to study truancy. The government collects statistics from every school, and these show national trends and patterns, such as that truancy peaks in year 11 and is more common among pupils receiving free school meals. Truancy statistics can also be used to discover the effect on pupils of factors such as changes in educational policies.

1. Applying material from **Item B** and your knowledge of research methods, evaluate the strengths and limitations of using official statistics for investigating truancy from school. **[20 marks]**

Paper 2

1. Outline **two** advantages of using statistics in sociological research. **[4 marks]**

2. Outline **two** disadvantages of using statistics in sociological research. **[4 marks]**

3. Evaluate the practical and theoretical issues involved in using statistics in studying society. **[16 marks]**

4. Evaluate the use and limitations of official statistics in sociological research. **[16 marks]**

5. Evaluate the advantages of using official statistics in sociological research. **[16 marks]**

6. Evaluate the disadvantages of using official statistics in sociological research. **[16 marks]**

A level exam questions

Paper 1 – methods in context

1. The 'methods in context' question is set at both AS and A level *(see above AS level exam question, paper 1)*.

Paper 1 and 3

2. Outline and explain **two** advantages of using official statistics in sociological research. **[10 marks]**

Paper 3

3. Applying material from **Item (...)** and your knowledge, evaluate the usefulness of using official statistics in sociological research. **[20 marks]**

Section 3

Families and Households

AQA Specification

Families and Households	AQA
Students are expected to be familiar with sociological explanations of the following content:	• the relationship of the family to the social structure and social change, with particular reference to the economy and to state policies

• changing patterns of marriage, cohabitation, separation, divorce, childbearing and the life course, including the sociology of personal life, and the diversity of contemporary family and household structures

• gender roles, domestic labour and power relationships within the family in contemporary society

• the nature of childhood, and changes in the status of children in the family and society

• demographic trends in the United Kingdom since 1900: birth rates, death rates, family size, life expectancy, ageing population, and migration and globalisation |

The AQA specification: Families and Households

- The relationship of the family to the social structure and social change, with particular reference to the economy and to state policies.

The exam requires that you are able to:

▶ Understand and evaluate the functionalist perspective of the family.

Introduction

In general, the functionalist perspective is seen as a **structural theory** because it claims that the social structures in society (eg, religion, family, education, media and the law) perform a number of 'functions' which shape and influence our behaviour. We will now examine the functionalist view of the role that the family performs in society, and with regard to its own members.

Functionalist perspective on the family

Positive function. Functionalists argue that for society to be stable and function effectively (eg, without disorder, conflict and tension) individuals must share the same norms and values (**value consensus**) and that this is achieved with the help of the **family**. The family helps perform certain functions such as **socialisation,** for example by teaching its members to share the norms and values that are accepted by society. This brings **social order** and thus creates a society in which people can exist harmoniously, instead of one of with conflicting values and norms which can lead to disorder and instability. Therefore, functionalists view the family as playing a **positive** role in society.

Murdock: the four functions of the nuclear family

George Murdock (1949), a functionalist, carried out a cross-cultural survey which examined a total of 250 societies of various kinds, from hunters and gatherers to large-scale industrial societies. He concluded that the nuclear family is so important that it is universal: it exists in all societies and therefore must serve essential functions for society and the individual. He claims the family performs four important functions, which are:

Economic. The family as a collective resource is able to satisfy the economic needs (eg, security, food, home and money) of its members more effectively than a single individual living alone.

Sexual. The family allows the adults to fulfil their sexual needs, thus preventing deviant sexual behaviour (eg, rape). The family (husband and wife) also socialises its members (ie, children) in the accepted template for appropriate sexual relationships (eg, loving, marital and heterosexual rather than homosexual or promiscuous).

Reproduction. The family provides a stable environment for producing and looking after children, which is essential for society to exist.

Educational. The family teaches children the values and norms of acceptable behaviour in society.

Parsons' 'fit theory'

Talcott Parsons (1955) studied American families in the 1950s and developed a 'fit theory' of the family. This theory claims that the structure of the family changes over time to suit ('fit') the type of society that exists at that time. He argues that the extended family was normal in pre-industrialisation times, as it ideally suited this type of society, whereas the nuclear family is more suited to industrial society. His 'fit' theory is expanded in more detail below:

The family in pre-industrial society

- In pre-industrial society, the extended family was the norm and was a multi-functional unit: it carried out many functions, such as caring for elderly grandparents, educating children and farming the land to provide food for its members.

The family in industrial society

- The demands of industrial society brought about changes to the family structure, with the extended family becoming a smaller nuclear family. This was ideally suited to an industrial society because:
  - A nuclear family is geographically mobile. Industrialisation emerged in many different places and brought new opportunities for work. It was easier for the nuclear family to move for work than for the whole of the extended family to be uprooted (eg, think how difficult moving elderly grandparents would be).
  - A nuclear family allows for social mobility. Industrial society allowed social mobility - an opportunity for a person's social status to rise through their merit (ability and hard work) - whereas in a pre-industrial society, where the extended family was the norm, the status of the son would have been ascribed (fixed) by his father. For example, the son would continue to work in the family cattle-farming business. The change from extended to nuclear family prevented conflict between parents and their upwardly mobile children, which could threaten the stability of the family.
- Industrialisation also meant that the modern nuclear family lost some of it functions (to other specialist institutions such as schools and health services) and now performs two essential functions which Parsons refers to as two basic and irreducible functions. They are:
  - Primary socialisation of children – the process that takes place during the early years of childhood when children are taught society's values and norms.
  - Stabilisation of adult personalities – the pressures of living and working in a modern industrial society to achieve success (wealth and social status) can threaten to destabilise the personalities of both husband and wife (mental health). Parsons suggests the family helps to stabilise their personalities when there is a sexual division of labour in the family. He proposed that the female is ideally suited to perform the expressive role – providing for the caring, nurturing and emotional needs of the children and husband – while the man is more is suited to play an instrumental role – being the breadwinner who provides for the economic needs for the family.
- Functionalists see the nuclear family as the 'ideal' and most 'natural' type for society. They see divorce, the decline of marriage and alternative family types as threatening the stability of society.

✓✗ Evaluation

✔ **Traditional nuclear family plays an important role in socialisation.** There is research evidence to support the functionalist theory that the nuclear family is the ideal type for society. Research evidence suggests that the traditional nuclear family plays an essential role in the healthy social development of children and that other forms of family, such as single-parent families, do not do so well in socialising their children into the accepted norms and values of society.

✗ **Feminists critique.** The functionalist theory of the family has been criticised by feminists as they see family life as being unequal, with the man benefiting more than the woman. The role of the woman is mainly responsibility for the domestic duties of housework, child-care and looking after the husband's needs, while the husband enjoys more time for leisure pursuits. This suggests the role of woman in the family is one of oppression and exploitation, which feminists find unacceptable.

✗ **Dark side of the family.** The functionalist theory tends to 'idealise' the family and ignore the 'darker side' of family life. For example, domestic violence and mental illness such as depression, eating disorders, schizophrenia and child abuse, can all be due to the family, as suggested by feminists and clinicians such as psychologists and psychiatrists.

✗ **Postmodernist critique.** Postmodernists argue that functionalist views, such as those of Parsons and Murdock, are outdated and no longer valid. This is because their theory was based on an American middle-class society of the 1950s and therefore not applicable to a modern multicultural society, which has a diversity of family and household types (eg, single-parent, homosexual and cohabitig). Therefore, postmodernists claim that it does not make sense to talk about the traditional nuclear family as being the normal or best family type, or the only family type that performs essential functions in society.

✗ **Parson's expressive and instrumental roles are outdated.** Some sociologists argue that Parsons' traditional gender roles performed by men and women (instrumental and expressive) in the family are outdated, since Parsons' theory was based on circumstances in the 1950s. The result of feminisation in the 1970s has been a change in social attitudes towards, and trends in, family arrangements. For example, in many families, the woman is also now a wage-earner and often prioritises her career over the role of a housewife. This has meant that both men and women interchangeably play expressive and instrumental roles and suggests that Parsons' view of the traditional gender roles within the family is no longer valid.

✗ **Family has lost its importance.** Some sociologists have questioned the importance of the function the family plays in today's society. This is because some of the functions that the family performs are now being taken over by other institutions. For example, many working parents send their pre-school children to day-care centres such as nurseries and playgroups, which play an important role in helping young children to acquire the correct social skills, values and behaviours for society (ie, socialisation).

Practice exam questions

AS level exam questions

1. Define the term 'primary socialisation'. [2 marks]

2. Define the term 'expressive role'. [2 marks]

3. Define the term 'instrumental role'. [2 marks]

4. Define the term 'nuclear' family. [2 marks]

5. Define the term 'ascribed status'. [2 marks]

6. Using **one** example, briefly explain how the family is losing its functions. [2 marks]

7. Outline **three** functions that functionalists see the family performing. [6 marks]

8. Outline **three** criticisms of the functionalist view of the family. [6 marks]

AS & A level exam questions

1. Outline and explain **two** reasons for the rise of the nuclear family. [10 marks]

2. Applying material from **Item (...)** and your knowledge, evaluate the contribution of functionalist views to our understanding of the family. [20 marks]

A level exam questions

3. Applying material from **Item (...)**, analyse **two** reasons for the rise of the nuclear family. [10 marks]

The Marxist Perspective on the Family

The AQA specification: Families and Households

- The relationship of the family to the social structure and social change, with particular reference to the economy and state policies.

The exam requires that you are able to:

▶ Understand and evaluate the Marxist perspective of the family.

Introduction

Marxism is known as a conflict theory because it sees capitalist society as consisting of two main social classes. The two social classes in society are:

- **Ruling class (or bourgeoisie):** people who own the means of production, (eg, factories, shops and land) whose aim is making money. This group of people is often referred to as the capitalist class.

- **Working class (or proletariat):** people who work for the ruling class in return for a wage. Members of the working class are often paid far less than they deserve and are therefore seen as being exploited by the ruling class in order to maximise the latter's profit.

Marxism suggests that in a capitalist society the relationship between the two classes is unfair. The working class demands to be paid more for their labour, the ruling class wants to keep wages to a minimum to maximise its profit and thus a conflict of interest occurs between the classes.

Marxist perspective on the family

Marxists reject the view that the nuclear family performs an important function for all of society, as functionalists suggest. They see the family as benefiting the capitalist class (ie, capitalism), which helps contribute to the inequality between the classes. The family does this by:

- **Allowing wealth to be passed on.** Friedrich Engels (1884) analysed the family historically to see how it had evolved over time, tracing it from the times of our earliest human ancestors, when humans were promiscuous and the family did not exist, to its present form, that is, a monogamous nuclear family. Engels argues that the monogamous nuclear family developed at the same time as ownership of private property (when men could buy and own their own property) and the emergence of inheritance. Upon his death, a man had to ensure that his property was inherited by (passed on to) his own children. The only way he could be certain that he was the 'father of his children' was by making the woman his property (ie, marriage) and restricting her sexual freedom (to ensure paternity). The monogamous nuclear family appeared as the most appropriate solution for this. This ensured that the rich could pass on their wealth to their family members and in this way the social class system was reproduced from one generation to the next.

- **False class consciousness.** Eli Zaretsky (1976) sees family life as a distraction from the exploitation of capitalism. The expressive role of the wife, that is, providing emotional support, security and comfort, helps distract the man from the oppression and exploitation of his work environment. Therefore, the working-class family helps maintain a 'false class consciousness' since the man is not aware that he is being exploited.

- **Ideological function.** David Cooper (1972) sees the family as serving an ideological function (or as an ideological conditioning device) because it teaches values that are ideal for capitalism. The family teaches children to accept certain attitudes, such as respect for and obedience to authority, punctuality and hard work. Such values help to lay the foundation for the obedient and submissive workforce required by capitalism.

- **Consuming goods.** The family serves the interest of capitalism by being one of the largest consumers of the products it produces, often through the power of the media. For example, advertisers encourage families to be in competition with each other ('keeping up with the Joneses'), and exert pressure to keep up with the latest consumer trends (eg, in mobile phones, trainers, televisions and cars). Children are also heavily targeted by advertisers to use their 'pester power', which refers to children's ability to persuade their parents to purchase items they might not otherwise buy. This ensures the continuation of the production of goods, enabling the capitalists continue to make a profit.

✔✘ Evaluation

✘ **Too much emphasis on the negative side of the family.** Marxism tends to focus on the negative aspects of the family and ignores the happiness that family life can bring. The fact that the family can bring satisfaction (intimacy, security and emotional support) to both males and females is made clear by the fact that the family remains popular in many contemporary societies.

✘ **Nuclear families are still the best option.** Marxist theory has yet to establish a viable alternative family type that would benefit society. It could be argued that that the nuclear family is presently the best type of family for the child's social and cognitive development.

✘ **Nuclear families are less common now.** Marxist theory may no longer be valid because it is based on the traditional nuclear family. In contemporary society, there is diversity and variation in family structures and living arrangements depending on ethnicity , social class and sexuality. For example, Marxism assumes that the breadwinner in the family is the man and that the housewife is the woman. This arrangement is now less common, so it is hard to see how the expressive role of the female helps distract the man from exploitation (the ideological function) by capitalism.

✘ **Marxist ideas are difficult to test.** Some Marxist concepts are hard to investigate by means of a research study to check their validity. For example, Marxists claim that the family helps maintain a 'false consciousness'. This concept would be very hard to operationalise (in a way that can be tested and measured). How would a researcher investigate this to discover if false consciousness is occurring in the family?

Practice exam questions

AS exam questions

1. Using **one** example, briefly explain how the family benefits capitalism. **[2 marks]**

2. Outline **three** ways in which Marxists say that the family benefits capitalism. **[6 marks]**

3. Outline **three** criticisms of the Marxist view of the family. **[6 marks]**

AS & A level exam questions

4. Applying material from **Item (...)** and your knowledge, evaluate the view that the main role of the family is to serve the interests of capitalism. **[20 marks]**

A level exam questions

5. Applying material from **Item (...)**, analyse **two** functions that the family performs for capitalism, according to Marxists. **[10 marks]**

The AQA specification: Families and Households

- The relationship of the family to the social structure and social change, with particular reference to the economy and state policies.

The exam requires that you are able to:

▶ Understand and evaluate the feminist perspective of the family.

Introduction

Feminists view the family as serving the needs of a patriarchal (male-dominated) society. Their research has focused mainly on housework arrangements, domestic violence and the power relationship within the family. Feminism also examines how women's role in the family has contributed to the economy of society. There are different branches of feminism, all with a slightly different viewpoint. However, they all agree that the family is oppressive towards and exploitative of women. There are different branches of feminism, which hold different views:

— Liberal feminism

— Marxist feminism

— Radical feminism

Liberal feminism

- **Practical solutions.** Liberal feminists hold the view that women have been discriminated against and exploited in the family. This is because there is inequality in the arrangements regarding household chores, roles and power (eg, decision-making over issues such as how to spend money) between the husband and the wife. Liberal feminists aim to address such inequalities by moving towards a more egalitarian relationship. They offer practical and realistic solutions (compared to radical feminists, see below); for example, liberal feminists played a part in changing legislation on rape in the family (eg, rape within marriage was made illegal in 1991). They were also influential in changing attitudes towards family life in relation to domestic arrangements (eg, housework and childcare).

- **Outside the family.** Liberal feminists also played a role in changing policies regarding gender inequality. For example, laws were introduced in the 1970s, such as the Equal Pay Act, the Sex Discrimination Act and the Employment Protection Act.

Marxist feminism

- **Capitalism is the real cause of exploitation.** Marxist feminists emphasise that capitalism is the main cause of exploitation and oppression of women in the family, not necessarily the family itself. According to Marxist feminists, the family is another institution (like religion) that serves the needs of the capitalist economy. The reason for this is that the wife's subordinate domestic role in the family serves the needs (emotional, social and physical) of the husband, who is the 'wage-slave', thus enabling him to perform his job more effectively to the benefit of the capitalist economy (ie, the ruling class).

- **The family produces cheap labour.** Benston (1972) argues that the wife's unpaid domestic 'labour' (ie, housework) in the house is crucial for a healthy capitalist society. In Marxist language, the wife produces and rears (cares for) future exploited workers (her children) at no cost to the ruling class. She also keeps the adult worker (her husband) in 'good running order' by caring for his needs, which allows him to be an effective wage labourer, thus maximising profits for capitalists, again at no cost to them.

- **Safety valve.** Ansley (1972) agrees with Parsons (a functionalist sociologist) that the family environment helps the husband and wife maintain their psychological well-being (providing emotional and social support for each other) which Parsons refers to as the *stabilisation of the adult personality.* However, Ansley disagrees with the functionalist view that this benefits the family, believing instead that it really benefits capitalism. This is because family life and the emotional support provided by the wife for the husband act as a safety-valve (emotional release), enabling him to escape the mundane nature, stress and frustration that work produces. Family life prevents the husband from dealing with the real cause of his frustration, that is, the exploitative workplace environment.

Radical feminism

Radical feminists generally agree with liberal and Marxist feminists' view on the role of women in the family, although they see the family as an institution that exploits and oppresses women in all aspects: emotionally, economically and physically. More notably, they take a 'harder line' in dealing with exploitation and oppression than the other feminist approaches. Some of the issues radical feminists discuss in regard to the family are:

- **The abolition of the family.** Kate Millet (1970) views the family as male-dominated, with men using their physical power to assert their control, which can often lead to domestic violence. For example, research studies carried out by Dobash & Dobash (1979) found that 25% of all assaults reported to police in Scotland were by husbands on their wives, and argue that this may be a gross underestimation. Millet argues that husbands' violence towards their wives is accepted by certain ethnic cultures and that some, eg Asian cultures, view it as the norm. A possible solution, according to the radical feminist Firestone, is to create separate community units in which women live independently from men. This would result in the abolition of the family and its exploitation and oppression of women. Furthermore, it would stop the family acting as a factory that produces traditional gender roles in their children, and thus stop gender inequality in society as a whole.

- **Lesbian relationships.** Radical feminists argue that heterosexual relationships can often be a place in which women have to endure physical abuse. For example, Calhoun (1997) claimed that battery, rape and child abuse is common in heterosexual relationships. Unfortunately, most women and children are dependent on their husband financially, which means they are unlikely to leave an abusive situation. Calhoun advocates other types of family arrangements, such as lesbianism, rather than the traditional family arrangement. A lesbian arrangement prevents the physical and mental abuse as both partners are female and therefore more likely to develop an egalitarian domestic relationship.

- **Economic arrangements.** Radical feminists see the family as an economic system that primarily benefits the man. They argue that domestic arrangements are left to the wife, whereas husbands control the finances and decision-making. Research studies have found that women are more likely to be passive in a heterosexual relationship, with the wife more likely to agree with her partner's financial decisions than the other way round (Delphy & Leonard, 1992).

- **Pregnancy and child-rearing are the cause of inequality.** Radical feminists claim that it is unfair that married women have to give up work to bring up their children and take on domestic responsibilities because this makes women vulnerable, and dependent on their husbands for financial support. Some radical feminists, such as Firestone (1979), claim that gender inequality in the family (and society) is due to the women's biological sexual reproduction system (ie, pregnancy and child-rearing). She argues that conception should be accomplished artificially, taking place outside the body in an artificial womb so that women are freed from financial dependence on men.

Post-feminism

The increase in different family types (single-parent, gay and lesbian, co-habiting) in society has meant the nuclear family is generally no longer the dominant family type in the UK. The domestic arrangements are so varied that a feminist approach may no longer be applicable. Therefore, post-feminists argue that family life does not always produce inequality and exploitation, as men and women have many choices open to them and so can choose what family type best suits their needs.

✔✗ Evaluation

✗ **Postmodernist theory.** The increase in different family types (single-parent, gay and lesbian, co-habiting) in society has meant the nuclear family is generally no longer the dominant family type in the UK. Domestic arrangements are so varied that a feminist approach may no longer be applicable. Therefore, postmodernists argue that family life does not always produce inequality and exploitation, as men and women have many choices open to them and so can choose what family type best suits their needs.

✗ **The nuclear family is becoming less common.** Morgan (1975) is critical of the Marxist feminist view because he sees the traditional nuclear family structure in modern capitalist society as becoming less common, and alternative family structures (as suggested by postmodernists) as rising. For example, when both partners work, or are gay or lesbian, it is more difficult to see how the 'wife' can be seen as an instrument for capitalism to 'rear cheap labour' or act as a 'safety valve'. This would suggest that the arguments proposed by feminists are, to some extent, no longer applicable to today's society.

✗ **Women can negotiate their domestic role.** Women now have more career opportunities and are more financially independent than ever before. This means they are not merely passive victims of exploitation but can negotiate their domestic role (eg, by using child-care support).

✗ **Feminist theory ignores the positive side of the family.** Feminists focus too much on the negative side and ignore the positive side of family life. For example, some women enjoy running a home and raising children while the husband goes to work. This is supported by some ethnic groups such as Asians (eg, Pakistani, Indian), in which women claim that it is important for the wife to stay at home.

✘ **New Right sociologists** have criticised the feminist approach as tending to ignore the harm that other family structures (eg, single-parent, gay or lesbian) can cause. For example, New Right sociologists argue that single-parent families can be dysfunctional for society as well as for the individual. Research evidence suggests that social problems such as the rise of anti-social behaviour, the formation of the underclass, educational under-achievement and the decline of moral values, are due to the erosion of the nuclear family and the rise of single-parent families.

Practice exam questions

AS exam questions

1. Define the term 'patriarchy'. **[2 marks]**

2. Using **one** example, briefly explain how liberal feminists see gender inequality in the family might be overcome. **[2 marks]**

3. Using **one** example, briefly explain how family life may benefit men more than women. **[2 marks]**

4. Using **one** example, briefly explain how men may be 'able to exploit and oppress women within the family'. **[2 marks]**

5. Outline **three** criticisms of the feminist view of the family. **[6 marks]**

AS & A level exam questions

6. Outline and explain **two** ways in which family life may have a harmful effect on women. **[10 marks]**

7. Applying material from **Item (…)** and your knowledge, evaluate the contribution of feminist views to our understanding of the family. **[20 marks]**

A level exam questions

8. Applying material from **Item (…)**, analyse **two** views of the radical feminist view of the family. **[10 marks]**

The New Right theory of the family

The AQA specification: Families and Households

- The relationship of the family to the social structure and social change, with particular reference to the economy and state policies.

The exam requires that you are able to:

▶ Understand and evaluate the New Right theory of the family.

New Right theory

- The New Right theory really began in the early 1980s and was formulated by thinkers who share conservative values and ideas about the family (favoured by the Conservative government of the time). Like the functionalists, the New Right accepts the view that the nuclear family is natural, and the most desirable type of family for a stable society. It supports the traditional family type, that is, a heterosexual married couple with one or two children, with the male as breadwinner and the wife being economically dependent on the husband (ie, the division of labour).

- The New Right argues that in the last 30-40 years, traditional beliefs about marriage and family have declined in popularity. This is because they have been eroded by social changes such as the influence of feminism, changes in divorce laws (which led to a rise in divorce rates), decline of religious beliefs, increase in homosexual relationships and sexual permissiveness. The consequence has been a rise in delinquent behaviour, the growth of an underclass, and the weakening of moral values due to the lack of suitable role models and family values.

The solution of New Right thinkers

The New Right's concern to preserve the traditional family led it to develop a 'pro-family' pressure-group in the 80s. Their ideas influenced both Conservative and Labour government ideologies towards the family. Their solutions to preserve the family from erosion are:

- **Discourage welfare dependency.** People should become self-reliant instead of depending on welfare. The New Right argues that the welfare system has to be changed since it encourages a dependency culture which leads to deviant life styles. For example, many young teenagers are becoming single mothers as an alternative to having a career, as the state provides them with a home and an income. The New Right believes this ever-growing class of young single mothers, and all the social problems associated with them, are partly responsible for the breaking-down of society.

- **Provide tax relief for nuclear families.** Tax allowances should be offered to married couples (ie, they should pay less tax) in order to strengthen the traditional family in society.

- **Change social policies.** Social policies and initiatives that encourage mothers with young children to return to work have been criticised by the New Right as this can cause maternal deprivation. (Separation of mother and infant during an early stage of the child's life can have a negative effect on the child's social and emotional development later in life). Supporting research studies have found that early maternal deprivation can cause emotional problems and anti-social behaviour amongst adolescents (Bowlby (1944), 'Juvenile Thieves' study).

- **Change divorce legislation.** The changes in divorce legislation since the 1960s (eg, the Divorce Reform Act of 1971) have made it easier to obtain a divorce. Such reforms have weakened the commitment of couples to remaining in a marriage. The New Right would like to see a change in divorce laws which would make it harder for couples to separate.

✔✗ Evaluation

✔ **Importance of socialisation of young children.** It is an increasingly accepted view that the nuclear structure of a family is important to the healthy socialisation of children, and that the breakdown of this has been the cause of anti-social behaviour.

✔ **Has had an impact on government policies.** The New Right theory has been influential in changing government social policies that favour the concept of the traditional nuclear family type. For example, the Child Support Agency (CSA) was set up in 1993 in response to New Right theory. The aim of the CSA was to make the non-resident or absent parent (usually the man) play a more responsive role by forcing him to pay financial maintenance. The New Right also had an influence on the recent introduction of mediation therapy (a form of marriage counselling) prior to divorce.

✗ **Blaming the victim.** One criticism of the New Right perspective is that it tends to blame victims rather than the structure of society. Many social problems may be due to economic factors, such as a lack of jobs or low wages.

✗ **Too idealistic.** The nuclear family to which New Right theorists aspire only fits a minority of households in a modern multicultural society, and may be seen as idealistic. Furthermore, idealising the nuclear family also suggests that other family types, such as single-parent or homosexual families, are inferior.

✗ **Moral panic.** Politicians, along with the media, have been criticised for creating a moral panic (exaggeration) about the decline of the nuclear family. They have exaggerated fear of breakdown which has led to a moral panic in relation to absent fathers, homosexual families, single-parent families, anti-social behaviour, etc.

Practice exam questions

AS & A level exam questions

1. Applying material from **Item (...)** and your knowledge, evaluate the contribution of New Right views to our understanding of the family.   **[20 marks]**

The AQA specification: Families and Households

- Changing patterns of marriage, cohabitation, separation, divorce, child-bearing and the life-course, and the diversity of contemporary family and household structures.

The exam requires that you are able to:

▶ Describe the main changing patterns of marriage that have occurred in the last 50 years (ie, decline.)

▶ Offer reasons for the causes and consequences of the decline of marriage.

▶ Describe the views of the different sociological perspectives towards the changing patterns of marriage.

Introduction

Statistical evidence clearly shows that fewer people are getting married. Evidence for this is due to a number of factors such as:

— changing attitudes towards marriage

— the declining stigma of divorce

— the increase in 'singleness'

— changes in the divorce laws

Some theoretical perspectives welcome this change (eg, feminists and, to some extent, postmodernists), whilst others have been highly critical (eg, the New Right), claiming that the decline of marriage is destroying the very fabric of society, as well as the institution of family life.

Changing patterns of marriage

- **First-time marriages.** Much of the 20th century (1900-1999) saw an increase in the popularity of marriage, which peaked in 1971. However, there has been a steady decline, especially in first-time marriages, over the last 40 years. In 1972, there were 426,000 first marriages but by 2013 this had declined to 247,890.

- **Re-marriages.** Re-marriages increased from 57,000 in 1961 to 82,000 in 2013 (for one or both of the partners in that year).

- **Average age of marriage.** The average age in 1971 was 24 for men and 22 for women. By 2013, the age had increased to 30/31 for men and 28/29 for women.

- **Religious marriages.** Approximately 33% of marriages involved a religious ceremony in 2013, compared with about 50% in 1991.

Reasons for the decline of marriage

- **Cohabitation.** The statistics above show that fewer people are getting married than at any time in the last century, and more people are choosing to cohabit (live together as couples without being married). The Social Attitude Survey that has measured public opinion every year since 1983 suggested in 2013 that people's perception of marriage is less important, and people are choosing cohabitation as an acceptable long-term alternative to it. However, some people see cohabitation not as an alternative to marriage but rather as a prelude (testing compatibility before marriage itself).

- **Declining stigma.** The stigma attached to alternative types of marriage has declined. Attitudes towards cohabitation have changed: people who cohabit are no longer seen as 'living in sin'. It has become quite the norm to cohabit or live alone in modern Britain; however, this may still seem unacceptable to some ethnic minorities, such as Asian families.

- **Singlehood.** An increasing number of people choose not to get married and would rather live alone. In England in 1971, 6% of people between the ages of 25 and 29 who held a professional occupation lived alone, whereas by 2013 this had increased significantly, to 25%. A negative stigma was often attached to living alone , particularly for women; in a modern society, however, it is often seen as a positive and fashionable lifestyle option.

- **Changing female attitudes.** Women's attitudes towards marriage and family life have changed drastically in the last 40 years. Wilkinson (1994) refers to this as genderquake, claiming that young females no longer prioritise marriage and children, and see having a career and economic independence as coming first. Even attitudes towards divorce have changed; it is viewed as less of a cause for scandal and gossip and more as a routine aspect of life which happens in most families.

- **Changes in the divorce law.** Divorce rates have increased rapidly over the last 50 years. The changes to divorce laws have meant much quicker and easier divorces, especially as a 'no blame' policy has been introduced. The rise in divorce also means that the positive view of marriage has weakened, and many people see cohabitation as a viable alternative to marriage.

- **Teenage pregnancies.** The UK has the highest rate of teenage pregnancy in Europe in the 16-18 age group. The majority of these teenage mothers are unmarried and supported by state housing and benefits. Thanks to the support of the state, women feel more able to survive independently as lone mothers or divorcees.

  Delay in marriage. Chester argues that the decline in marriage rates is partly because many are delaying the age at which they marry, rather than not marrying at all. The average age at first-time marriages in 2001 was 28.4 years for the bride and 30.6 for the groom. Women delay marriages because they want to develop their career and enjoy a period of independence.

Theoretical views of the decline of marriage

- **Feminist approach.** Feminists claim that cohabitation is a positive development, opening up greater choices and freedom for women (Gittins 1993). This not only benefits women but also benefits men, as new choices are also available to them. For example, men now have the choice of playing a less traditional masculine role.

- **The New Right.** The New Right is critical of any family type other than the traditional nuclear family. Therefore, they see cohabitation and diverse family types as fundamentally wrong. The New Right argues that cohabitation provides a less stable and secure basis than marriage for the partners, and for any children they might have. This view is supported by a survey carried out in 2000 by the Institute for the Study of Civil Society which found that cohabiting couples are less happy and less fulfilled than married couples, and are more likely to be abusive, unfaithful and stressed. They also claim that the traditional family provides for the growth of healthy moral children and that the decline in traditional nuclear families can lead to the increase of educational failure and delinquent behaviour among young children. The New Right solution to the rise of cohabitation is to cut the over-generous benefits to single parents, enforcing responsibility on parents in an attempt to strengthen the position of the traditional family.

- **Postmodernist view.** Some sociologists have argued that we live in an era not of modernity but of postmodernity. This is a time of change, when people have realised that there is no 'best' type of family and there are no agreed norms and values directing family. It no longer makes sense to ask what type of family is dominant. Family life and the type of family structure is in a period of uncertainty, heading in an unknown direction. Judith Stacey (1996) welcomes this family diversity as it may bring with it equal domestic arrangements.

Practice exam questions

AS exam questions

1. Define the term 'reconstituted family'. **[2 marks]**

2. Define the term 'serial monogamy'. **[2 marks]**

3. Using **one** example, explain how changes in the position of women have led to changes in the pattern of marriage. **[2 marks]**

4. Outline **three** ways in which marriage and cohabitation are becoming increasingly similar.

   [2 marks]

5. Outline **three** reasons for the decline of marriage in the UK. **[6 marks]**

6. Outline **three** reasons there has been an increase in cohabitation. **[6 marks]**

7. Outline **three** reasons for the increase in the proportion of births taking place outside marriage.

   [6 marks]

8. Outline **three** reasons that the average age at which people first marry has been rising.

   [6 marks]

AS & A level exam questions

9. Applying material from **Item (...)** and your knowledge, evaluate the reasons for the changes in the patterns of marriage and cohabitation in the last 40 years or so. **[20 marks]**

A level exam questions

10. Applying material from **Item (...)**, analyse **two** reasons for changes in the patterns of marriage and cohabitation in the last 40 years or so. **[10 marks]**

The AQA specification: Families and Households

- Changing patterns of marriage, cohabitation, separation, divorce, child-bearing and the life-course, and the diversity of contemporary family and household structures.

The exam requires that you are able to:

▶ Describe the main changing pattern of divorce in the last 50 years (ie, an increase in divorce rates).

▶ Offer reasons for the causes of increased divorce rates.

▶ Describe various sociological reasons for, and perspectives on, the increase in divorce rates.

Key terms

- **Divorce:** The legal termination of a marriage.

- **Separation:** When couples have ended the relationship and live apart but are still legally married.

- **Empty-shell marriage:** When a couple are considered to be living together and still legally married, but the marriage itself has broken down; in most cases, the couple stays together for the children's sake but they no longer care for each other.

Divorce trends

- **Trend.** In 1936, 6,000 divorces were granted in the UK. In the eprly 1960s, the approximate rate of divorce per year was 27,000. This had doubled to approximately 57,000 by the end of the 1960s and, again, to 125,000 by 1972. In 2013, there were approximately 120,000 divorces. If rates continue to rise at the present rate, around 40% of marriages will end in divorce. Britain now has the highest divorce rates in Europe.

- **Interpretation of trend.** The increase in divorce rates suggests the institution of marriage is in real crisis. However, this may only paint part of the picture, since the real extent of marital breakdown is hard to establish as some couples stay together even if the marriage has failed. This is known as an 'empty-shell marriage' and it is difficult to measure (eg, respondents to a survey may not reveal details of or lie about their marriage).

Causes for the increase in divorce

- **Changes in divorce laws.** Changes in the law have made it easier and cheaper to file for a divorce. It was not until the 20th century that divorce became easy to obtain. The 1923 Matrimonial Causes Act gave both men and women equal rights for grounds for divorce (before then it had been difficult for a woman to obtain a divorce), enabling either spouse to get a divorce on the basis of matrimonial offence (ie, adultery). The 1969 Divorce Reform Act brought about the biggest change as it became easier for couples to escape an unhappy marriage as neither had to provide 'fault' with each other (eg, matrimonial offence) as grounds for divorce, allowing them to divorce after they had been separated for two years. The 1984 Matrimonial and Family Proceedings Act made divorce possible after one year.

- **Interpretation of divorce laws.** Changes in divorce laws have made it legally and financially easier to obtain a divorce, so many empty-shell marriages that had been formally maintained were terminated. However, critics argue that legislative changes are regarded as an *enabling factor* in explaining divorce rather than a *causative factor.*

Causes of martial breakdown

- **Declining stigma.** There is less stigma (negative labelling and disapproval from others towards those who are divorced. Divorce is now socially more acceptable and often seen as the 'norm' in modern society. The regularity of divorce and the publicity given to divorce in high places (eg, within the royal family) has helped to normalise it. A possible explanation why divorce has less of a 'stigma' is secularisation. Britain has arguably become a more secular society, which has resulted in marriage becoming less sacred and less of a spiritual union and more of a practical commitment which can easily be abandoned. Fewer than half of all weddings now take place in a religious building, and a new law in the 1990s reinforced this trend: marriage ceremonies can now take place in a wide range of venues (eg, football grounds).

- **Changes in women's roles.** Perhaps this is a key factor behind the rise in divorce levels during the 20th century: the status of women has significantly improved, more women work and are financially independent and thus many are no longer reliant on men for financial security. This has increased women's readiness to start divorce proceedings. Divorced women can also receive a range of government benefits so marriage is less of a financial necessity, which makes it easier for them to escape an unhappy marriage.

- **The growth of the privatised nuclear family.** Functionalists argue that the increased distance of the nuclear family from the extended family means that it is not easy for partners to seek advice or temporary refuge with relatives when there is marital conflict. Isolation from extended family places greater demands and expectations on each partner within marriage, with some not being able to cope.

- **The ideology of romantic love.** Partners in marriages based on romantic love tend to have an idealised view of 'marital life'. This has led couples to have high expectations that marriage (the partner) will provide happiness, emotional fulfilment and a sense of togetherness. Marital conflict may arise when the expectations are not met by the partner, which can lead to misery and dissatisfaction.

- **Role conflict.** Nicky Hart, a Marxist, suggests that in a capitalist society, the demand for material success requires that both spouses work as wage earners. However, 'working wives' are also expected to be responsible for domestic chores and child-care, and thus conflict between the spouses and marital breakdown may result. This is due to a contradiction between the woman's traditional housewife role, and the economic burden of being a wage-earner.

Sociological perspectives on the consequences of the increase in divorce

- **Feminist.** Feminists see divorce as 'the great liberator', because it enables women who are deeply dissatisfied with their marital partner to sever ties with him. If a spouse is violent, then divorce is considered a better option for both the abused partner and for the children.

- **The New Right.** The New Right has emphasised the negative consequences of divorce for both the individual and society. Its main concerns are:

— **Economic consequences.** The rise in single-parent families will mean that they will be among the poorest sections of society, which also has economic consequences for the state: single-parent families often become reliant on welfare benefits.

— **Emotional and behavioural consequences.** Divorce has a negative effect on the child's social and emotional development, especially if the child is of a young age. For example, boys growing up without their father (living with their mother) will not have a male role model to guide them in their development of moral behaviour. The consequences of this will be behavioural problems (deviant or anti-social behaviour) and under-achievement in school, leading to unemployment later in life and dependence on welfare benefits.

Practice exam questions

AS type exam questions

1. Define the term 'divorce rate'. **[2 marks]**

2. Outline **three** reasons for the increase in UK divorce rates since the 1970s. **[6 marks]**

AS & A level exam questions

3. Outline and explain **two** reasons changes such as the increased numbers of divorces, lone-parent families or births outside marriage do not necessarily mean that the family is in decline. **[10 marks]**

4. Applying material from **Item (...)** and your own knowledge, evaluate sociological contributions to our understanding of the trends in divorce in the United Kingdom. **[20 marks]**

5. Applying material from **Item (...)** and your knowledge, evaluate the view that changes in the law are the main cause of increases in the divorce rate. **[20 marks]**

A level exam questions

6. Applying material from **Item (...),** analyse **two** reasons for changes in patterns of divorce since 1970. **[10 marks]**

The AQA specification: Families and Households

- The diversity of contemporary family and household structures.

The exam requires that you are able to:

▶ Describe how family and household structures are becoming more diverse.

▶ Assess whether the nuclear family has been replaced by a wide variety of types of families.

▶ Give reasons for rise in the varieties of family and household types in contemporary UK society.

Key term

Family diversity refers to the different varieties of family and household types that exist. These can be traditional nuclear family, extended family, reconstituted family, single-parent household, cohabitating couples, one-person household, group of friends or gay or lesbian couples.

Introduction to family diversity

It has generally been assumed that the traditional nuclear family has been the dominant family type. The image of the happily-married couple with two children (nuclear family) is prominent in many advertisements and known as the cereal package family: a happy smiling nuclear family consuming cereals or pouring Oxo gravy over their Sunday roast. The assumption has been that this type of family is central to people's experiences, and the norm in the UK. However, recent research has suggested that over the last 40 years in the UK, there has been an increase in the variety of household and family types, and that the idea of a 'typical family' is misleading. Rapoport and Rapoport (1982) argue that the departure from the 'cereal package family' type does not derive purely from negative reasons (eg, marital breakdown) but has become an increasingly personal choice.

Changing pattern of family diversity

Statistics from official social trends (2013) suggest that between 1971 and 2013 (over 40 years) the average British nuclear family not only became smaller, but that there was also a decrease in the number of nuclear families. For example, nuclear families with one or two children fell from approximately 30% to 18% while at the same time cohabitation rose from 3% to 11%, making cohabitation the fastest-growing family type in the UK. There was also a big jump in single-person households, from 17% to 30%.

The decline of the nuclear family

The study by Robert and Rhona Rapoport (1982) was one of the first to bring to our attention the steady decline of the traditional nuclear family, as well as the idea of family diversity. The fact that the 'conventional family' no longer makes up a majority of households or families is only one aspect of the diversity identified by the Rapoports. They identify five distinct elements of family diversity in Britain:

— Organisational diversity. By this, they mean that there are variations in how family types are structured (organised). For example, in some families, both the husband and wife are wage-earners (joint conjugal roles) while in others it may be just the husband (segregated conjugal roles). Types can include reconstituted families, single-parent families, cohabitation and so on.

— Cultural diversity. Different cultural, ethnic and religious groups have different family structures. For example, the extended family is common among the Asian community.

— Social class diversity. There are differences between middle-class and working-class families in terms of relationships between adults and the way in which children are socialised. Rapoport and Rapoport suggest that middle-class families are more child-centred than working class families.

— Life stage diversity. Different family structures often result from the stage people have reached in their 'life-cycle'. For example, newly-married couples without children may have a different family life from those with dependent children or retired couples whose children have achieved adult status, or widows and widowers who are living alone.

— Cohort diversity. Different generations of people will have had different attitudes and life experiences. This can affect the family life-cycle or the type of family that exists. For example, some may view divorce or cohabitation as morally wrong, which will inevitable mean less of that type of family in society.

Regional and family diversity

Eversley and Bonnerjea (1982) have identified distinct family types in different regional areas of Britain. For example, coastal areas attract large numbers of older people. Inner cities tend to experience a higher number of poor families, single-parent families and immigrants. Old declining industrial areas in the North of England (eg, Sheffield) tend to have a high number of extended families; however, as industrial areas decline and there is an increase of poverty, a pattern of varied family types emerges (eg, single-parent families).

Social class and family diversity

There are class variations in families and households in terms of domestic labour, education and parenting. In a traditional working family, the husband and wife are more likely to have segregated conjugal roles, a closer kinship network and patriarchal family arrangements. A middle-class family is more likely to be symmetrical (more likely to have joint conjugal roles with the woman in full-time paid employment) than patriarchal, and more likely to have help with domestic arrangements, such as a cleaner to deal with household chores.

Reay et al (2004) argue that middle-class women invest more emotional time in their children's education than working-class parents (eg, active monitoring of school progress, questioning teachers about their children's school performance and so forth). Middle-class parents are also more likely to employ nannies and au-pairs for their children, whereas working-class families are more likely to use family (grandparents) and friends.

Extended family and family diversity

There has been a shift to a smaller isolated nuclear family with less face-to-face contact with relatives, although many families keep in touch by phone, internet or emails or during special occasions (eg, birthdays and weddings). It may therefore be that the nature of the extended family has changed rather than that the concept has disappeared.

Ethnicity and family diversity

Ethnic groups with different cultural backgrounds have contributed to the proliferation of family forms that differ significantly from those of the indigenous majority. These will often differ in size, type and views on marriage and divorce. Furthermore, there are important differences between the families and households of different ethnic groups (Pakistani and Indian families, for example).

Asian families

- Asian families (eg, Pakistani, Bangladeshi and Indian) tend to have more children and be larger than the typical British household family, and are usually large, multi-generational households (eg, father/ wife, his son/daughter and grandchildren and grandparents — usually the husband's grandparents).

- Nearly all Asian families are patriarchal in nature, with conjugal roles being segregated between the husband and wife. Asian men and women are more likely to marry earlier and have higher rates of marriage and fertility (children), and are less likely to divorce and therefore to form lone-parent families than their white counterparts and other ethnic groups. However, Westwood and Bhachu (1988) suggest that men and women in certain Asian ethnic groups (Indian) are moving away from their extended families and towards a more nuclear family (eg, newly-weds moving out of their parents' home).

Afro-Caribbean families

- Tariq Modood et al (1997) found that in the last 40 years, there has been a substantial increase in lone parenthood from families with Afro-Caribbean origins. In the UK, they now make up the highest proportion of single-parent families or single (never married) mothers. As a consequence, Afro-Caribbean families have a lower marriage rate and higher divorce rate than white or Asian ethnic groups. (Berthoud et al, 1999)

Neo-conventional families

Chester (1985) argues that the nuclear family is still overwhelmingly the dominant form; he refers to the modern nuclear family as the neo-conventional family, made up of two parents and a small number of children. The main change is in the economically active role of the wife (hence the term 'neo-conventional' family). It is true statistically that nuclear families make up a small percentage of households in the UK; nevertheless, more people still live in nuclear families than in any other family form, which shows it is still the most desired type of family structure. Also, the fact is that the great majority of people live in a nuclear family at some time in their lives.

The view that the nuclear family is no longer the norm has been disputed by other sociologists. Somerville (2000) argues that these changes are exaggerated. The apparent diversity of family life is based on a snapshot at any one time and, if a life-cycle approach is taken, many people have a fairly conventional experience of the family.

Modernism, postmodernism and family diversity

- **Modernity.** Giddens argues that we live in an era of late modernity which is a world full of choices. The rise in diversity is due to the increase in choices we have in a modern world. Individuals and families are now more able to exercise choice and make personal decisions as to domestic and family arrangements than previously. Most people feel they do not have to get married before having sex, and being a parent outside of marriage is increasingly accepted as a legitimate option: people can choose to cohabit or live alone, and the type of relationship they prefer. In a modern world, their options are no longer constrained by social convention (eg, attitudes towards marriage or divorce) and/or economic need (eg, women do not rely on men for financial security).

- **Postmodernity.** Some sociologists have argued that we live in an area not of modernity but postmodernity. As society is changing so fast, family life has become uncertain, most people feel they do not have to get married before having sex, and being a parent outside marriage is increasingly accepted as a legitimate option. People have come to understand that there is no 'best' type of family and therefore it no longer makes sense to ask what type of family is dominant in society. Judith Stacey (1996) welcomes this family diversity as it may bring about equal domestic arrangements.

Reasons for the rise in family diversity

Below are some of the reasons that have contributed to family and household diversity:

- **Affluence.** There is a correlation between poverty and family size: poorer families tend to have more children and affluent couples tend to have smaller families.

- **Divorce.** Changes to divorce laws (easier availability and lower cost) have led to an increase in single-parent families and reconstituted families). Similarly, changes in attitudes to divorce and single-parenting have resulted in less stigma (social disapproval) being attached to these statuses.

- **Medicine.** The availability of contraception (enabling planned families) and abortion change how people relate to each other in terms of creating families. Lone-parent households have increased in number, partly due to increased divorce, but also because pregnancy is no longer automatically seen as requiring legitimation through marriage.

- **Sexuality.** Increasing tolerance of 'alternative sexualities' (such as homosexuality, bisexuality or transsexuality) serves to increase household diversity.

- **Religion.** The decline in the power of organised religion can account for:
  — Increases in cohabitation.
  — A decline in the importance of marriage.
  — Increases in divorce.
  — The availability of remarriage after divorce, and so forth.

Conversely, amongst some ethnic groups the reverse may be true - their religion may put great emphasis on marriage and disallow divorce.

Reasons for the rise in singleton families

A singleton is a person who lives by themselves. There has been an increase in the rise of single households; below are some of the reasons why:

- **No longer a stigma.** People do not worry as much about living alone as there is less social stigma attached to it. This is especially true for women, and enables them to pursue a career and not worry about the pressures of not being married.
- **Rise in wealth.** A rise in wealth means that people can afford to live on their own.
- **Divorce.** Increase in divorce rates may mean that one parent lives alone. For example, women tend to get custody of the children so men tend to live by themselves, unless they remarry.
- **Geographical mobility.** Increased geographical mobility (eg, for job reasons) may mean that it is necessary for people to live away from their family.
- **Death.** An increasing number of women live by themselves because of the death of their husband, as women live longer than men.

Conclusion

It seems that in contemporary Britain, a variety of family and household types exist, with the nuclear family still being predominant. However, there is clear evidence that lone-parent families, reconstituted families and homosexual families are increasing. There is little evidence that a large proportion of people are choosing to live on a long-term basis in alternatives to the nuclear family. For example, in 1994, 8% of the population cohabited, usually for only two years or less. This would suggest that the demise of the nuclear family has been exaggerated (as suggested by Somerville). The apparent diversity of family life is based on a snapshot at any one time and, if a life-cycle approach is taken, many people have a fairly conventional experience of the family.

Practice exam questions

AS exam questions

1. Define the term 'beanpole family'. [2 marks]

2. Define the term 'the pure relationship'. [2 marks]

3. Using **one** example, explain how family may vary between ethnic groups. [2 marks]

4. Outline **three** reasons that family and household forms are becoming increasingly diverse. [6 marks]

5. Outline **three** ways in which greater ethnic diversity has contributed to family diversity. [6 marks]

6. Outline **three** types of family structures. [6 marks]

7. Outline **three** ways in which high divorce rates might be a major source of increased family diversity. [6 marks]

8. Outline **three** reasons that the nuclear family, even if in slightly modified form, remains very popular in Britain today. [6 marks]

AS & A level exam questions

1. Outline and explain **two** reasons for family diversity in today's society. **[10 marks]**

2. Applying material from **Item (...)** and your own knowledge, evaluate sociological contributions to our understanding of family diversity. **[20 marks]**

3. Applying material from **Item (...)** and your knowledge, evaluate the view that there is a greater diversity of family types and lifestyles today. **[20 marks]**

4. Applying material from **Item (...)** and your knowledge, evaluate the view that the growth of family diversity has led to the decline of the traditional nuclear family. **[20 marks]**

A level exam questions

5. Applying material from **Item (...)**, analyse **two** criticisms of the individual thesis. **[10 marks]**

6. Applying material from **Item (...)**, analyse **two** reasons for ethnic differences in family and household patterns. **[10 marks]**

The AQA specification: **Families and Households**

- The diversity of contemporary family and household structures.

The exam requires that you are able to:

▶ Describe trends in and reasons for the growth of lone-parent families.

▶ Describe and evaluate the different sociological perspective views on lone-parent families.

Introduction: the rise of lone-parent families

With regards to lone-parent families, the Office for National Statistics (2013) found:

- Lone–parent families increased from 8% in 1971 to 25% in 2013.
- One in four children live in a lone-parent family.
- 91% of women account for lone-parent families, and men the remaining 9%.

The UK has the second-highest rate of lone-parent families in the European Union after Denmark. The growth in the number of lone-parent families in the last 40 years has generated a great deal of controversy. Criticism has mainly come from the New Right whereas feminists and postmodernists have welcomed the rise of family diversity, including that of single-parent families, as bringing freedom and choice, especially to women. The main discussion is over how this has impacted society, with the New Right arguing that lone-parent families have an effect on children's cognitive and social development: children do not do as well at school (under-perform) and are more likely to become anti-social (delinquent) and grow up in poverty than children in a traditional two-parent family.

The causes for the rise in lone-parent families

Lone parenthood can come about through a number of different routes:

People who are married can become single parents through:

— Divorce

— Separation

— Death of a spouse

Lone parents who have never been married:

— May have been living with the other parent when the child was born, but subsequently stopped living together.

— May not have been living with the other parent when the child was born.

Allan and Crow (2001) note that the increase in lone parenthood is mainly due to two factors: an increase in marital breakdown (particularly divorce), and a rise in births to unmarried mothers. Below we give the main reasons:

- **Divorce.** The 1969 Divorce Reform Act made it easier and cheaper for couples to escape an unhappy marriage as neither had to provide 'fault' with each other (eg, matrimonial offence) as grounds for divorce, allowing couples to divorce after they had been separated for two years. The 1984 Matrimonial and Family Proceedings Act made divorce possible after one year. Therefore, divorce is considered as the main cause of the rise in lone-parent families.

- **Economic independence.** More young women are entering professional or other careers, which gives them greater economic independence (therefore they are less dependent on financial support from a husband) which means they are living alone for a longer period than did earlier generations before settling into marriage and motherhood.

- Women now have greater economic opportunities and choices. The rise of economic independence means they are less dependent on financial support or security.

- **Changing attitudes.** There has been a growing tolerance of lone-parent families and births outside marriage. The stigma attached to children of unmarried mothers has reduced considerably over the years. There is also less pressure on mothers to remarry, and lone-parenting has now become to an extent the norm, although some still see it as not the correct type of family in which to raise children. A possible explanation why divorce has less 'stigma' is secularisation. Britain has arguably become a more secular society in which religion has little control over people's lives, especially their views on marriage (fewer than half of all weddings now take place in a religious building), cohabitation and divorce.

- **Welfare system.** The New Right argues that over-generous welfare payments have been the major cause of the increase in lone-parent families. Women no longer rely on a man or marriage to support them.

Why are lone-parent families normally headed by women?

— Women are more likely to be given custody of the children by the courts than men.

— Men have better-paid jobs so may be reluctant to give up their jobs to look after their children.

— The father may have abandoned the mother before the birth.

— Men will view the idea of giving up work to look after children as a threat to their masculinity and fear being ridiculed.

— Women are seen as being better suited to nurturing and raising children then men, so being a single-parent mother is more socially acceptable than being a single-parent father.

Functionalists & the New Right: critical view of lone-parent families (and family diversity)

- Functionalists and the New Right are critical of lone-parent families, seeing them as a threat to society. Their main argument is that lone-parent families are less able to provide proper socialisation and moral education for children than traditional two-parent families. As a consequence, children do not do as well at school (under-perform), and are more likely to engage in anti-social behaviour (delinquency) and grow up in poverty. Children will also grow up with little understanding of the responsibilities and duties of a father. Below are some of the reasons:

Social/emotional issues:

- **Emotional problems.** Studies have shown that children from lone-parent families are more likely than those from nuclear families to be emotionally disturbed, delinquent, educationally under-achieving or engaging in drug abuse. Reasons for this could include tension before and after divorce, unhappiness caused by feelings of rejection by the absent parent, dominant media images of happy two-parent families, and a lack of adult breadwinners.

- **Low IQ and poor physical health.** This concern has been reinforced by Dennis & Erdos. In 'Families without Fatherhood' (1992), they studied 1,000 children in Newcastle and found poor physical health, low IQ scores and criminal records to be positively related to the lack of a father, especially amongst boys. They argue that poverty and unemployment are marginal factors behind criminality and anti-social behaviour.

- **Correlation between Afro-Caribbean families and delinquent behaviour.** Other studies have suggested that the fact that the highest proportion of lone-parent families is found among Afro-Caribbean people is linked to why Afro-Caribbean children are under-achieving in school, and criminal behaviour is high amongst Afro-Caribbean males. However, others have criticised this, arguing that anti-social behaviour is not purely the result of lone-parenting, but that there could be other explanations such as racism or poverty.

Ecomomic issues

- **Financial burden on society.** Lone-parent families are more likely to become dependent on the welfare state than find work. As a consequence, lone parents who are reliant upon benefits tend to live in poor housing and have low standards of living. Government statistics published in 2014 show that social security and benefits cost the taxpayer £110 billion, which is double what the government spent on education (£54 billion) and health services (£65 billion). The argument is that a huge amount of taxpayers' money is spent unnecessarily funding lone-parent families.

- **Underclass.** Charles Murray (New Right) has suggested that lone-parent families (mainly unmarried young mothers) are a contributory factor to the creation of a new social class called the 'underclass'. Murray argues that the welfare system encourages a culture of dependence: young mothers have children without providing for them and assume that the welfare state will support them and their children. The New Right would like to abolish or drastically cut welfare benefits, which would reduce dependency culture and births outside marriage, in an attempt to reinforce the position of the traditional family structure.

Positive view of lone-parent families (and family diversity)

- **Feminists.** Feminists are supportive of lone-parent families (and family diversity) because they give women independence. They see lone-parent families as a viable alternative form, in which women are free from male domination and exploitation. They argue that there are times when a one-parent family may be the best option for both the mother and the children if, for example, the father is violent.

- **Postmodernists.** Postmodernists claim that family diversity is the result of a society that offers a greater level of freedom and more lifestyle choices to both men and women than ever before. As a result, different family types should not be seen as either right or wrong, since there is no correct family type in a plural and fragmented society. Judith Stacey (1996) claims that different family forms give people the opportunity to develop according to their own particular needs and situations.

- **Criticism of the New Right.** A number of sociologists do not support the New Right view that the welfare state is responsible for the increase in lone-parent families. Some of the reasons are:
    - There is little incentive to become a lone parent. that is, to be reliant upon state benefits, with poor housing conditions and poor living standards. This is not something people aspire to.
    - There is evidence that a large majority of lone parents do not wish to be reliant on state benefits. They would prefer to work for a living but find it impractical to do so (The Green Paper, *Supporting Families*, 1998).
    - Lone parenthood is often a temporary and relatively short-lived family situation. Lone parents may cohabit with a new partner, get married, or be reconciled with their previous partner to form a new two-parent household.
    - Feminists reject the view that lone-parent families are inadequate in socialising children, claiming that such a claim is really a way for governments to reduce public spending on lone-parent families.

Conclusion

It is easier to identify the reasons that lone-parent families have increased than to ascertain whether single parents have a negative effect on society. Although there may be a link between lone-parent families and children engaging in anti-social behaviour and performing poorly at school, the evidence remains inconclusive. Other facts may account for anti-social behaviour and educational failure in children so it could be unfair to suggest that having a single parent is the only cause. In terms of economic issues, there are concerns that single parents can be a financial burden for the economy because providing support for them through government benefits is very expensive.

Practice exam questions

AS exam type questions

1. Define the term 'the pure relationship'.   **[2 marks]**

2. Outline **three** reasons that lone-parent families are generally headed by women.   **[6 marks]**

3. Outline **three** reasons for differences in the proportion of lone-parent families among different social groups.   **[6 marks]**

4. Outline **three** reasons for the increase in single-person households.   **[6 marks]**

A level exam type question

5. Outline and explain **two** changes in society which have contributed to the increase in single-person households.   **[10 marks]**

|

The AQA specification: Families and Households

- The nature and extent of changes within the family, with reference to gender roles, domestic labour and power relationships.

The exam requires that you are able to:

▶ Describe the changes that have occurred in marital roles in terms of domestic labour and relationships.

▶ Assess the view that marital roles have changed in contemporary society.

▶ Give reasons for the rise in the symmetrical family.

Key terms

- **Conjugal roles (or gender roles).** This refers to the marriage roles (eg, duties and responsibilities) played by the husband and wife, or those cohabiting.

- **Segregated conjugal roles.** This refers to the role of the husband and wife within the family being clearly separated: the husband is usually the breadwinner and the wife usually deals with domestic duties and child-care.

- **Congregated conjugal roles.** This refers to the roles of the husband and wife within a family being shared between them (eg, housework and child-care).

- **Domestic labour.** This refers to the work performed in the home (eg, cooking, cleaning and child-care).

- **Power relationship.** This refers to who controls the finances and decision-making, (ie, husband or wife).

Introduction: Gender roles, domestic labour and power relationships

When we talk about gender roles, we are referring to the marital roles the husband and wife perform within the family, two of which are domestic labour and power relationships. Domestic labour refers to housework duties and child-care. Power relationships refer to who controls the finances and decision-making, husband or wife.

The debate. Sociological research suggests that in the contemporary UK, traditional marital roles are breaking down and changing toward more egalitarian (equal) relationships. Since the 1970s, there has been a change in terms of husband's and wife's roles and responsibilities: from the husband as the primary breadwinner and the wife in charge of household duties and child-care towards a more equal division of domestic roles and responsibilities. This implies that most marriages are becoming egalitarian. In other words, there has been a shift from segregated conjugal roles to joint conjugal roles. However, feminists disagree and are much more cautious about drawing such a conclusion. They point to inequalities in domestic labour, power and control that persist in modern family relationships.

Domestic labour

Theoretical views

From a theoretical point of view, functionalists argue that a move away from the traditional family model is damaging to society, whereas feminists welcome moves towards greater equality.

- **Functionalist.** Functionalists, such as Talcott Parsons (1965), identified two marital roles performed by the husband and wife. The husband plays the instrumental role, that is, the breadwinner (providing money and resources), whilst the woman plays an expressive role, that is, providing care and emotional support for her husband and children. Parsons believes the domestic division of labour between the husband and wife is natural, as it is based on biological difference: women are more naturally suited to the expressive role and men the instrumental role. Therefore, according to Parsons, this domestic arrangement is best for the family and society. This is supported by Goldberg (1977) who argues that all known societies have a patriarchal structure, and that male dominance in the family is biologically rooted, based on the physical strength of men (a socio-biological explanation). Such a view is also supported by the Conservative Party (politicians) and the New Right (conservative thinkers).

- **Feminists.** Ann Oakley (1974) rejects the claim that the division of labour is 'natural' and found in all societies, and argues that the traditional family set-up benefits men more than women. She sees the unfair division of labour as having its origins in industrialisation. Industrialisation locked women into the mother-wife role due to a series of Factory Acts restricting child employment, which forced women to supervise and care for the children, especially after 1941, when male workers demanded a withdrawal of female labour from factories. In 1942, the Mines Act banned women from working in the mines. These changes in the workforce allowed the gradual development of domesticity, which required women to take a subordinate household role. According to Oakley, this shows that the housewife role is socially constructed rather than biologically natural.

Research evidence for greater conjugal role equality

- **The symmetrical family.** Young & Willmott (1973) carried out a research study (questionnaire and observations) of families based in London. They found that by the 1970s, there had been a shift from segregated conjugal roles towards what they termed 'the symmetrical family'. This meant the roles of husband and wife were similar: they equally shared housework duties and looking after the children, and both had paid jobs and spent their leisure time together. An egalitarian relationship was therefore more evident, especially in middle-class families.

Research evidence against conjugal role equality

- Feminists such as Ann Oakley (1974) have questioned the validity of Young & Willmott's findings that the family is becoming more symmetrical. Some of the criticisms are with regards to:

  - Methodological flaws. One of the questions asked whether the husband carried out household chores. They found that 72% of husbands 'helped around the house' during the week (eg, washing the dishes). This does not amount to equality as the husband could have performed the chores only once or twice a week. This shows the questionnaire was poorly constructed as it did not take into account the daily volume of domestic chores the husband would perform.

— **Over-exaggeration of equality.** Young and Willmott's research study did not fully explain what they meant by 'equality'. Oakley suggests that answering 'yes' to one of the questions about doing at least one chore per week was not a sign of equality, and that therefore Wilmott and Young exaggerated their findings.

- **Housework.** Oakley (1975) in 'The Sociology of Housework' carried out interviews on a sample of 40 women between 20 and 30 years of age with one or more children under the age of five. She found a clear division of labour: the wives still doing most household work and childcare, with little help from the husband, showing that domestic duties were still predominantly the responsibility of the woman. She also found a class difference in terms of domestic labour: there was evidence of males carrying out more domestic chores in middle-class than in working-class families.

Allan and Crow (2001) suggest that the increase in the contribution of the husband is not significant and that, in fact, women being in paid work has not led to greater equality. Now most women have greater pressure upon them as they have the dual burden of paid work and responsibility for domestic work in the home.

- **Parenting.** Ferri and Smith (1996) in 'Parenting in the 1990s' used data from a large survey aimed at childcare. They found that regardless of whether the woman was employed or not, it was still her responsibility to look after the children. They also found that roughly 75% of women were still responsible for cooking, cleaning and laundry, which would suggest that segregated roles still exist, even when women are in full- or part-time employment. This is supported by Boulton (1983) who found that men may help out with aspects of childcare (eg, nappy changing) but that women still undertake most of the work and have the main responsibility for children.

- **British Attitudes Survey.** The view that household work and childcare are not equally shared between the husband and wife is supported by large-scale surveys known as the *British Social Attitudes Survey* (1997) and the British Household Panel Survey (2009). Both surveys found that there still exists a clear division of labour in most British households. For example, washing and ironing is still largely done by women (79% in 1997) supporting the view that household work and childcare is still mainly carried out by women. However, they did find some more evidence of equality: more tasks done by men or more sharing between partners (about 10%, 1997).

- **Ethnic families.** Research into ethnic-minority groups and gender roles found that women are still primarily responsible for domestic duties and childcare. Asian families (eg, Pakistani and Bangladeshi) both expressed a clear preference for segregated conjugal roles and felt that it was a woman's role to care for the family and the children, even suggesting that female employment was prohibited (Beishon, Modood and Virdee, 1988).

Power relationships

Husbands tend to control money and decide how it is spent in the family, regardless of whether the wife is in employment or not. One of the reasons men take a greater share of the resources and demand more control over decisions is that they tend to earn more, and women will often be economically dependent (especially during the stages of child-birth and child-care).

- **Decision-making.** Edgell's (1980) 'Middle Class Couples' suggests that power in decision-making is heavily biased towards the husband, even in middle-class families (as women tend to work in middle-class families). His studies found that the wife makes trivial decisions (eg, interior decoration, children's clothes and food shopping) whereas the husband makes really important decisions such as finance, moving home and buying a car. This would suggest that men have the control and power over issues that are seen as important.

Leighton (1992), in a more recent study, found that the power to make decisions changed when the male became unemployed. Her study of professional couples showed that working wives took responsibility for utility bills and often decided how money should be spent. This would suggest that those who are in full employment often hold the power to make the more important decisions.

- **Finances.** Pahl and Vogler's (1993) 'Money and Marriage' interviewed 102 couples with children on how they managed their money. They found men had two types of control over family income:
  - The allowance system: in which men work and give their non-working wives an allowance from which they budget to meet the family's needs.
  - The pooling system: in which both partners are equally responsible for managing their finances (joint bank account). There has been an increase in the pooling system in recent years (due to the rise in women's employment).

The pooling system would suggest a trend towards greater equality of access to and control over finances for women; however, Vogler (1994) found that most men had control over the pooling system and often made the decisions about how the money was spent.

- **Emotional care.** Duncombe and Marsden (1993) interviewed 40 couples and found that women often need to work at keeping the family happy, holding relationships together and making everything go smoothly. They found that men had problems expressing intimate emotions with their partners. In addition, men were not aware that there was an 'emotional issue' requiring attention in order to make the relationship work. They saw women doing a triple shift: housework and childcare, paid work and emotional work.

- **Control and domestic violence.** Radical feminists welcome a move to a more symmetrical family, but in their view, such a move is far from good enough. They see society, including the family, as patriarchal (ie, male-dominated) and so believe that real equality will not occur until the family is abolished and patriarchy removed from society. Kate Millet (1970) sees the family as male-dominated, with men benefitting from women's unpaid domestic labour and sexual services and using physical power or domestic violence (or the threat of it) to assert their control; at times this can lead to actual violence and abuse.

There is supporting evidence for the radical feminist view. Dobash and Dobash (1992) carried out research in Scotland based on police court records and interviews with women who were living in a women's refuge and had been physically assaulted by their husbands. They found that violence was triggered when husbands felt their authority was being challenged. They concluded that marriage legitimises violence against women by giving power and authority to men and dependency to wives.

Reasons for the change from segregated to joint conjugal roles

Below are some of the reasons there has been shift from segregated to joint conjugal roles (or the rise of the symmetrical family, (ie, division of labour becoming equal).

- **The increase in women working.** The increase in the number of women working has led to women having more independence and authority in the family. This is because the female partner has her own income, is less dependent on her male partner and therefore has more power and authority when it comes to decision-making and financial matters.

- **Women's rights have improved in society.** The improvement of women's rights in society (eg, the Equal Pay Act (1970) and the Sex Discrimination Act (1975)) has forced men to accept women as equals and not simply as housewives and mothers.

- **The importance of female financial contributions in the home.** The importance of female partners' earning in maintaining the family's standard of living may have encouraged men to help more with housework in a recognition that the women cannot be expected to do two jobs at once.

- **Improved living standards.** Improved living standards in the home, such as central heating, TV, games and 'all the mod cons' have encouraged men to spend more time at home, and share home-centred leisure with their female partner.

- **Less reliance on the extended family.** The decline of the extended family, coupled with greater geographical mobility in society, has meant there is less pressure from the extended family on newly-married or cohabiting couples to retain traditional roles in the family, making it easier to adopt new ones. As the nuclear family is geographically more mobile (eg, relocating to find work) and thus away from the extended family and quite isolated, husband and wife's dependence upon each other can be increased, and they are therefore more likely to share their friends than have separate ones.

Practice exam questions

AS Level type exam questions

1. Define the term 'joint conjugal role'. **[2 marks]**

2. Define the term 'segregated conjugal role'. **[2 marks]**

3. Define the term 'division of labour' in the family. **[2 marks]**

4. Define the term 'dual burden'. **[2 marks]**

5. Define the term 'domestic division of labour'. **[2 marks]**

6. Using **one** example, briefly explain how greater gender inequality may lead to family instability. **[2 marks]**

7. Using **one** example, briefly explain why the 'pooling system' of managing household finances may not always show equality between spouses. **[2 marks]**

8. Using **one** example, briefly explain how family life may disadvantage women's careers. **[2 marks]**

9. Outline **three** reasons for social class differences in child-rearing practices. **[6 marks]**

10. Outline **three** characteristics of the symmetrical family. **[6 marks]**

11. Outline **three** reasons that domestic labour is often not regarded as real work compared to paid employment. **[6 marks]**

12. Outline **three** characteristics of the 'privatised' family. **[6 marks]**

13. Outline **three** reasons for continuing inequality between men and women in contemporary families. **[6 marks]**

14. Outline **three** reasons that husbands may be more likely to take the more important decisions. **[6 marks]**

AS Level and A Level exam questions

1. Outline and explain **two** changes in society which have contributed to women's changing roles within families. **[10 marks]**

2. Outline and explain **two** possible reasons for the rise of the 'symmetrical family'. **[10 marks]**

3. Applying material from **Item (...)** and your knowledge, evaluate the view that the division of labour and power relationships in couples are equal in modern family life. **[20 marks]**

4. Applying material from **Item (...)** and your knowledge, evaluate the view that it no longer makes sense to talk about the 'patriarchal family'. **[20 marks]**

A Level type question

5. Applying material from **Item (...),** analyse two reasons for patterns of domestic violence. **[10 marks]**

The AQA specification: **Families and Households**

- The relationship of the family to state policies.

The exam requires that you are able to:

▶ Describe how state policies affect family life.

▶ Describe the main sociological perspectives on social policies on the family and how they differ.

Key term

Social policy refers to guidelines or laws created by governments (or governmental departments) with the intention of bringing about change in people's behaviour for the greater good for society. Social polices regulate many aspects of our social life, such as the family, education, marriage and work, to name but a few. 'No-smoking' and 'anti-racist' policies are examples.

Introduction: social policy and the family

- **Direct effects.** Social policies that are specifically directed towards the family can have an influence on family life. For example, in Britain, you can only be legally married to one person at a time (ie, serial monogamy) and cannot be married to more than one person (ie, polygamy or polyandry). In China, the government introduced a one-child policy because of overpopulation.

- **Indirect effects.** Social policies directed to areas of social life (eg, the economy or education) can still have an impact on the family. For example, raising the school-leaving age has had the effect of making young people dependent on their families for longer and, as they cannot work, may restrict the families' income.

Perspectives on policy and the family

Different theorists have different views on the relationship between social policies and the family. Feminists and Marxists are critics of government policies on the family because they see them as biased. They argue that they tend to favour the traditional nuclear family in which there are two parents. Functionalists and the New Right view the traditional family as a crucial 'building block' of a stable society and therefore favour social policies that reinforce the nuclear family.

Functionalism

Functionalists believe that the state (government) acts in the interest of the whole society and therefore take a positive view of social polices because they believe they will benefit everyone. For example, the welfare state takes a lot of pressure off the family with regards to education and health, which allows the family to perform the essential functions of socialising children and caring for the family members.

The New Right

The New Right takes a negative view of some current government policies because it believes they undermine the traditional nuclear family. They see the family as being under threat from liberal social policies that encourage deviant lifestyles and family diversity, especially lone-parent families, as this is damaging to the stability of society, as well as to the child's moral, social and cognitive development. The New Right criticises many welfare policies because they have been the major cause of the increase in lone-parent families. The generous benefits to lone parents mean women no longer rely on a man or marriage to support them. This is turn creates a dependency culture, in which individuals depend on the state to support their families.

They argue that policies that help with child benefits or child support encourage mothers to go back to paid work (thus failing to put the needs of their children first), that divorce laws made it easier to end marriage, and that abortion laws and the relaxation of laws against homosexuality undermined traditional morality. The New Right argues that such liberal social polices played a major role in causing social problems such as crime, delinquency and drug abuse in the young. To the New Right, the family operates properly when it remains stable and the wife is responsible for socialising children so that they conform to society's norms and values. The husband, as principal breadwinner, is disciplined by the need to provide for his family.

Feminists

Many feminists are critical of family social policy because it tends to support the traditional patriarchal family type, that is, two parents and their children. They argue that government polices reinforce the ideology that women's place is in the home and the men's role is as the breadwinner. For example, maternity leave is much longer than paternity leave, reinforcing the belief that women's primary role is child-carer.

Marxists

Marxist are also critical of social polices because they really benefit the rich and powerful minority class of people called the bourgeoisie (ie, the ruling class - owners of factories and businesses, and the government) at the cost of everyone else (ie, the working class— known as the 'proletariat'). They argue that inequalities exist in society between the bourgeoisie and the working class, whose labour is exploited by the bourgeoisie for a profit. Marxists argue that social policies which appear to be making improvement to people's lives such as free education, health care and the welfare system, or solving problems (eg, anti-social behaviour, poverty and educational under-achievement) are just 'smokescreens' which maintain the status quo by preventing conflict and possible revolutionary action (eg, strikes and riots) by the working class that may threaten the privileged position of the bourgeoisie.

New Labour and Conservative governments

In recent years, the government has become increasingly concerned about families. The question is whether government policies should support the nuclear family as the ideal type, or rather recognise and support the other family structures.

Both Labour and Conservative government policies have tended to support the traditional nuclear family, ie, the belief that marriage is the ideal state and is best for children. They have both introduced policies to strengthen this view. For example, the current Conservative Party government (2010-present) has introduced a 'Married Couple's Allowance' for married couples, suggesting that marriage is better (and more financially advantageous) than any other kind of relationship. The previous Labour government policies (1997-2010) towards the family were more liberal and tended to support a wider range of families and living arrangements. For example, low-income families, especially lone-parent families, received tax benefits such as the Working Families Tax Credit. These top up the wages of a parent or parents to help with childcare costs, as these can put parents off returning to work. This was to encourage single mothers to return to work, which shows Labour moved away from the idea that families should have a single earner and that women should stay at home to look after children.

Policies which do not support conventional families (or have encouraged more wives to work):

- Equal Pay Act (1970), Sex Discrimination Act (1975) and Employment Protection Act (1975).
- Divorce Reform Act (1969), which made divorce easier and increased the number of people who obtained one divorce, leading to more lone-parent and reconstituted families, and also to more people living alone.
- Working Families and Child Tax Credit: Introduced in 2003, Working Tax Credit is given to those on low working incomes (often lone-parent families) to top up their income. Child Tax Credit is a payment to support families with children with childcare costs (as the cost of childcare can put parents off returning to work). This was to encourage single mothers to return to work rather than claim benefits.
- Welfare state benefits for lone-parent families.
- Same Sex couple (Act 2013). Allows same-sex couples to obtain essentially the same rights and responsibilities through civil marriage.
- Child-care vouchers. The Labour government introduced 'Childcare Vouchers' in 2005 to help with childcare costs (eg, childminders, nannies and au pairs, nursery schools, play schools and crèches). These might make it easier for women to break away from the expressive role and return to work with their children are being cared for.

Policies which do support conventional families (or have encouraged wives to stay at home):

- The Child Support Agency (CSA) was set up 1993 and made it a legal requirement for any individual (usually the father) who had deserted their partner to raise their child 'alone' to contribute towards the maintenance of the child. This made it difficult to escape financial responsibility for their children and absentee parents were thus forced to fulfil part of their instrumental role even when not physically present.
- Maternity leave. Regulations relating to maternity leave and pay reinforce traditional gender roles. In Britain, fathers have very limited rights to leave work on the birth of a child, compared with women. Furthermore, 'benefits for pregnancy and the period after childbirth are inadequate, reflecting the assumption that women have the support of a male partner.'
- Marriage Tax relief. The State encourages a couple to marry through such means as the married couple's tax allowance policy, introduced in 2015, under which married couples pay less income tax.

(This does not apply to unmarried people cohabiting).

- **School opening times.** It could be argued that schools are organised in such a way that it is difficult for lone-parent and dual-worker families to combine work with domestic responsibilities.

Below are some of social policies that have a direct and indirect influence on the family

Direct influences	Indirect influences
- **Marriage laws:** whom we marry, what age we can marry, how many people we can marry. - **Abortion Act (1967):** legalisation of abortion - **Divorce Reform Act (1969):** made it easier for married couples to be separated – no longer had to prove 'fault'. - **Other laws:** marital rape is illegal, children are protected against violence and neglect from abusive parents. - **Custody laws:** in the event of separation and divorce, there are laws which govern parents' contact and financial responsibility. - **Maternity/paternity:** laws which determine the period of absence from work granted to a mother/father before and after the birth of a child. - **Tax and child benefits:** the married couple's tax allowance and child benefits all affect family income. - **Child support agency:** absent parent must now contribute towards the maintenance of the child. - **Same-sex couple:** same-sex couples can obtain essentially the same rights and responsibilities as civil marriage partners.	- **Housing:** government policies towards housing will affect low-income families. - **Education:** raising the school-leaving age has had the effect of making young people dependent on their families for longer which, as they cannot work, may restrict families' income. - **Health:** laws will affect the right to obtain in-vitro fertilisation and the use of reproductive technology. - **Contraception pill:** In 1961, the contraceptive pill was made widely available on the NHS - **Transport:** the provision of public transport affects job opportunity and therefore family incomes. - **Employment:** people are affected by rules about maternity leave and the hours young people can work. Financial income can also have an impact and may determine the size of your family - **Equal Pay Act (1970):** requires employers to pay men and women equal pay for equal work. - **Immigration polices:** laws that restrict immigration may prevent a husband, wife or partner moving to Britain

Conclusion

It is clear that the different sociological perspectives hold different views on social policies and the effects they have on the family and whether they are desirable. Equally, governments have become more explicitly concerned with family over the last two decades than at any previous time due to the changing nature of the family. Although most policies and politicians are in favour of the traditional nuclear family, they realise that it seems to be in decline. For this reason, government has increasingly recognised that it is not possible to follow policies that pretend that most people continue to live in conventional families; therefore social policies now tend to reflect alternative family forms.

✓✗ Evaluation of social policies

✗ Functionalist view of social policies criticised. Functionalists assume that all social policies will benefit everyone in society but this may not be the case. For example, there have been policies introduced over the years, such as freezing Child Benefit, cuts in education spending and the introduction of student loans, which have an impact on poor families.

✗ Feminist views on social policies have been criticised. Feminist views have been criticised because not all social policies are there to maintain the traditional patriarchal family. For example, there are now laws on marital rape and domestic violence and men can now be prosecuted for such acts. Furthermore, the easy divorce laws and the introduction of Same Sex Couple Act are not only policies that favour different family structures but also show that women now have much more independence and freedom within a family.

✗ New Right. Some of the government policies that the New Right helped set up, such as the Child Support Agency, have been criticised. Many argue that the main aim of the CSA is not to help children but rather to save the Treasury money, since maintenance payments usually reduce the benefits paid to single parents. Indeed, in its first year the agency saved £530 million of taxpayers' money.

✗ Government policies are incoherent. It is difficult to determine the extent to which government policies support and maintain the traditional nuclear family. Some policies seem to suggest that they do (eg, the CSA) while others are less clear-cut. For example, childcare benefits and provision seem to send out a mixed message. Does helping with child care reduce the incentive for mothers to seek paid employment or does it encourage them to go back to work? Equally, many governments have gradually made divorce easier to obtain and this, it is sometimes argued, has undermined the traditional centrality of the conjugal relationship by producing large numbers of lone-parent and reconstituted families.

Practice exam questions

AS Level type questions

1. Define the term 'gender regime' in relation to social policies on the family. **[2 marks]**

2. Using **one** example, briefly explain how laws or government policies may affect roles and relationships within the family. **[2 marks]**

3. Using **one** example, briefly explain how functionalists see the role of social policies. **[2 marks]**

4. Outline **three** social policies or laws that may affect the family size. **[6 marks]**

5. Outline **three** social policies or laws that may affect the family.   **[6 marks]**

6. Outline **three** government policies and/or laws that may shape the experiences of children today.   **[6 marks]**

AS Level and A Level exam questions

1. Outline and explain **two** social policies or laws that have affected the position of children in the family.   **[10 marks]**

2. Outline and explain **two** ways in which changes in society may have weakened the traditional nuclear family unit.   **[10 marks]**

3. Applying material from **Item (...)** and your knowledge, evaluate the view that the main function of laws and policies on families and households is to reproduce patriarchy.   **[20 marks]**

4. Applying material from **Item (...)** and your knowledge, evaluate the impact of government policies and laws on family life.   **[20 marks]**

5. Applying material from **Item (...)** and your knowledge, evaluate the ways that government policies and laws may affect the nature and extent of family diversity.   **[20 marks]**

The AQA specification: Families and Households

- Demographic trends in the UK since 1900; reasons for changes in birth rates, death rates and family size.

The exam requires that you are able to:

▶ Describe the demographic trends in the UK (ie, birth rates, death rates, ageing population and migration) and reasons for the changes in them since 1900.

▶ Describe the consequences of these demographic changes, especially to family size.

Key term

- **Demography** is the term used to study the size and growth of the human population by looking at statistical data such as birth rates and death rates. Identifying 'demographic trends' involves analysing how the population size has changed over the years.

- **Birth rate** refers to the number of live births per every 1,000 of the population per year.

- **Fertility rate** refers to the average number of children a woman will have during child-bearing age (eg, 15-44). This is often known as total fertility rate (TFR).

- **Infant mortality rates (IMR)** refers to the number of deaths of infants under one year old per 1,000 live births.

- **Death rates** refers to the number of deaths per 1,000 of the population per year.

- **Migration** refers to population movement. People leaving the country (ie, the UK) to live in another country is called emigration. People coming to live in the country (ie, the UK) from another country is called immigration. The term net migration refers to the number of people immigrating minus the number of people emigrating.

Demographic trends in the UK since 1900

Population growth

Demography is the study of population size and growth over time. At the beginning of the 20th century, in 1901, the population of the UK was around 38 million. In 2014, there were approximately 64 million people living in the UK. There are now more people living in the UK than at any time in the past. Population projections suggest that the population will continue to increase, and that by 2031 an estimated 71 million people will be living in the UK. This shows that the population of the UK has grown throughout the century (100 years). Natural causes (there are more births than deaths) as well as net migration (more people coming in to than leaving the UK) are the main reasons for the increase in the population.

Factors that affect the population growth

The four main factors that lead to changes in population size are:

— Number of births

— Number of deaths

— Immigration

— Emigration

Birth and immigration will lead to an increase in population, whereas death and emigration will lead to a decrease in population.

Demographic changes:

There have been a number of demographic changes in terms of birth rate, fertility rate, death rate and immigration. Such demographic change has had effects on society, one of these being an impact on the size and type of the family. Trends, reasons and effects each brings to society and the family are summarised below.

Births

- **Trends in birth rates.** Birth can be measured by birth rates and total fertility rates. Overall, the number of births in the UK has gradually declined throughout the last century. In 1900, there were 29 live births per1000 women and in 2014, the number had fallen to approximately 12. However, there have been periods where there have been significant increases in live births, often referred to as baby booms. Baby booms occurred just after World Wars 1 and 2 (1914-1918 and 1939-1945) and in the 1960s, as the post-war baby boom worked its way through the general population.

- **Trends in Total Fertility Rates.** The TFR has fallen throughout the century. In 1900, the TFR averaged 3.5 children per woman. By the 1930s, this had fallen to 2.4 and declined further, to 1.9, in the 1960s. By the 1990s, it was down to 1.7. This decline briefly continued into the 21st century reaching the lowest point in 2001, with an average of 1.6 children per woman. However, interestingly, the birth rate since then has increased slightly. In 2005, it rose to 1.8 and remains at approximately this figure today, suggesting a 21st century baby boom; however, this remains low in comparison to the turn of the century.

Reasons for the decrease in birth rates – why are women having fewer children?

Sociologists have identified four main reasons for the decline in the birth rate during the 1900s:

- **The availability of birth control.** The increase in the availability and reliability of birth control in the 1960s (eg, oral contraception such as the 'pill' and the intrauterine device known as the 'coil') has been one of the main reasons for the decline in birth rates. In 1974, contraceptives became free on the National Health Services (NHS) to all women, whether married or single. Secondly, the legalisation of abortion (free under the NHS) in 1967 also contributed to the falling birth rates, especially among the younger female age-groups. Although birth control techniques are significant reasons for the declining birth rate they do not, of course, explain why people want to limit the size of their family in the first place.

- **Fall in infant mortality rate (IMR).** Until 1945, children were at greater risk of early death through infections and diseases (eg, measles, mumps, polio, diphtheria and TB). In 1900, the IMR for the UK was 154 per every 1,000 live births. In 1945, this fell to 49, in 2007 to around 5.5 and to just 4 in 2013.

Previously, families would attempt to have more children to compensate for the risk that a child might not survive into adulthood. However, with the falling IMR and more and more children surviving into adulthood, women need to have fewer children now.

- **Women prioritise careers.** Women are now more career-oriented, which has meant that they may delay having (which means fewer children), or choose not to have, children.

- **Child-centred families.** Families are now more child-centred (putting the child's needs above anything else) than before. This means families are now having fewer children than before, believing that they should concentrate on giving them a better quality of life in terms of opportunities and resources.

- **Economic reasons.** Until the late 19th century, children were largely seen as an economic asset as they were a source of income to the family. For example, ten-year-old children would be able to start work. This meant the more children a family had, the greater its income (children required no schooling) and so they were seen as an investment. In the 20th century, with laws banning child labour and education made compulsory, children became an economic liability. This is because they have to be supported for longer periods in education, for example, compulsory education is longer than before, and they often go to college and university. The financial burden of raising children has meant that parents are more inclined to have fewer children than before.

Evaluation: consequences of birth rate and fertility rate

- **Family size.** The TFR obviously affects family and household size: the more children a woman has, the bigger the family. For example, family size in the UK has reduced from around 6 children in 1870, to 4 children in 1900, 2.7 in the 1960s and 1.6 in 2001, although it rose to 1.9 in 2014. However, the increase since 2001 may not be due to increased birth fertility rates but to immigration. Mothers from the Asian continent are more likely to have a high fertility rate (ie, more children) than those born in the UK. However, future birth rate projections suggest that this may not play a major factor and that birth rates will remain constant at approximately 1.8 children per woman.

Deaths

- **Trends in death rates.** In the UK, the mortality rate (death rate) in 1900 was 19 per 1,000 people, which fell to 15 in the 1950s. By 2014, it had fallen to 9 per 1,000. This clearly shows that death rates have fallen in the UK, although there have been noticeable fluctuations, for example during the two World Wars (1914-1918 and 1935-45) and during times of influenza epidemics and cold winters, which tended to see an increase in death rates.

Reasons for the decline in death rates

Sociologists have identified four main reasons for the decline in death rates since the 1900s:

- **Public environmental health improvement.** During the 20th century, drastic improvements in environmental health services led to a rise in life expectancy. Purer drinking water supplies, better sewage, disposal and drainage systems and better housing meant that fewer people died from contagious, waterborne diseases.

- **Improved medicine.** Until the 1950s, medical improvements did not play a part in reducing death from infections. Since then, improvements in medical care such as preventative and combative measures against infections and diseases (eg, penicillin, antibiotics, vaccines and immunisations) have played a major part in reducing death rates. There has also been drastic improvement in diagnostic and surgical techniques (eg, detection of and screening for cancers, and open-heart surgery). The continuous improvement of our medical knowledge means people have a greater chance than ever before of living longer.

- **Improved health awareness and education.** Improved diets and nutrition over the last 25 years may account for the reduction in death rates. People are taking more heed of medical advice from health organisations on eating behaviours. Not only has this reduced the chance of developing diseases such as cardiovascular disorders, it has also meant better body resistance to infections and diseases, which increases the survival rates of those who did succumb to these.

- **Improved welfare state provisions.** Prior to the development of welfare services, ill-health was due to poor housing conditions. With the establishment of the welfare system during the Second World War (1944), living standards improved considerably for people as they had access to better and damp-free housing, making them less prone to illness. Equally, free personal health care was introduced in 1948 through the National Health Service (NHS), which meant better medical provisions and support for the elderly.

Life expectancy

Life expectancy refers to the average period that a person may expect to live. Life expectancy has increased in the UK. In 1900, a new-born baby boy could expect to live on average 50 years and a new-born baby girl 57 years, whereas in 2014, a new-born baby boy could expect to live on average 80 years and a new-born baby girl 83 years. Better medical care and knowledge, better welfare provisions for the elderly and awareness of the importance of diet and exercise are all reasons for people living longer.

- **Class, gender and regional differences in life expectancy.** Social factors can influence your life expectancy, such as class, gender and where you live (region). For example, working-class women or men in unskilled manual jobs are twice as likely to die before the age of 60 than women or men in professional or managerial jobs. One explanation is that working-class people are more likely to have a poorer diet and lifestyle (unhealthier eating habits, more likely to smoke and less likely to exercise). Women tend to live longer than men because men generally drink and smoke more than women, and men tend to be in more stressful (linked to cardiovascular disorders) and dangerous jobs (health hazards, industrial accidents) than women. Also, those living in the South of England have a higher life expectancy at birth than those in the North of England and Scotland. One possible explanation is that there are more working-class people in the north, who, again, have poorer nutrition and lifestyles than those living in the south.

Ageing population

The UK population is ageing. With the decline in birth rates and the increase in life expectancy, there are fewer children and young people in the population and more older people. This has led to an increase in the average age of the UK population. In 1971, the average age was 34, but by 2014 this had increased to approximately 40, with a future projection of approximately 43 by 2031. This has produced an ageing population which means that the number of people aged 65 and over is increasing and the population of people under 16 is declining, with future projections showing that the over-65s will overtake the under-16s, and the gap will continue to widen.

Evaluation: the effects of an ageing population

- **Family size – the rise in one-person households.** An ageing population means a rise in one-person households. Women are more likely to outlive men because of their natural longer life expectancy and tendency to marry older men. This can bring emotional and psychological disorders for those living alone.

- **The rise in dependency ratio.** The young (under 16) and the elderly (over 64) need to be supported financially (through taxation to pay for pensions and social security) by those of working age, (16 to 64). As the number of retired people increases, the UK will have a high dependency ratio as there are more people not of working age, and fewer who are. The consequence of this is a rise in taxation to pay for social services, health care and pensions funds.

- **Ageism.** Attitudes towards old age can often involve negative prejudice or discrimination. For example, in terms of employment opportunity and workplace practice, older people may be treated differently (eg, they may not get a promotion). Some may perceive older people as being incompetent and a burden on the health and social care services.

- **Policy implications for state pension age.** Governments in the future will increase the state pension age (ie, raise the retirement age) to help finance the ageing population. For example, the average state pension age will rise from 62 for women and 65 for men to 66 for both men and women by 2020.

Migration

Until 1931, more people emigrated from the UK than immigrated to it, mainly to the USA, South Africa, Canada, Australia and New Zealand. From 1931 to 1961, net migration showed more people coming into the UK than leaving. During the Second World War, many people came into the UK either for economic reasons or to escape political or religious persecution (eg, European Jews). Post-war immigration (1950s onwards) mainly came from the New Commonwealth countries such as West Africa, the West Indies, India, Pakistan, Bangladesh and Sri Lanka, many of which were gaining independence from British rule.

With the influx of immigrants from coloured New Commonwealth countries (rather than the white Old Commonwealth), politicians decided to restrict 'unlimited immigration' into the UK. A series of Immigration Acts in 1962, 1968, 1971 and 1981, which were basically designed to take away the rights of British passport-holders if they were black rather than white, restricted non-whites. By the 1980s, immigration was predominantly white and the European Union had become the main sources of settlers in the UK, in particular Ireland, Spain and Germany.

The largest factor behind the increase in population growth until 1999 was natural increase/change (the difference between births and deaths). However, since then, net migration has been the main reason for the increase in the UK's population growth. Current trends show that inward flow (immigration) exceeds outward flow (emigration). In 2014, an estimated 583,000 migrants arrived to live in the UK, whilst approximately 325,000 emigrated. This leaves a net migration of +258,000.

Reasons for immigration

Pull factors: Immigrants have continually arrived in the UK over the centuries for economic prosperity or to improve their quality of life, to join their family, to access state welfare provision (eg, health, housing or benefits) or to study.

Push factors: Some may immigrate to escape religious or political persecution, and have become refugees (eg, Bosnians, Somalis and Jews) or because of unemployment and economic recession.

Reasons for emigration

Pull factors: The main reasons for migration have often been pull factors such as a better lifestyle, greater economic prosperity, better weather and less crime. Population destinations have been mainly in Europe, such as France, Spain and Cyprus, although some people have moved to Australia and the USA.

Push factors: unemployment and economic recession.

Evaluation: the effects of migrations

The effects of migration (mainly immigration) are:

- **Changes in family size.** As the migrant population in the UK increases, it will have an impact on family size. For example, Asian families (India, Sikhs, Pakistanis and Bangladeshis) are more likely to have an extended kinship network, whereas Afro-Caribbeans tend to live in single-parent families. The new influx of immigrants from European countries (eg, Poland and Greece) are more likely to have traditional smaller nuclear families or be living on their own (singletons), depending what stage they have reached in their lives.

- **Increase in cultural diversity.** Immigration into the UK has led to great cultural diversity, which has in turn led to more interracial and interfaith marriages and cohabitation than before. For example, fewer Afro-Caribbean men and women are married to fellow Afro-Caribbeans, resulting in mixed-race families.

- **Cultural identity.** Migration can lead to prejudice and discrimination. A large number of the native British population would like to see a tougher immigration policy, mainly because they think a multicultural society has led to Britain losing its 'British values' and own cultural identity. Some politicians, especially members of the Conservative Party and UKIP, want to see tighter immigration policies. Other, more extreme, right-wing political parties such as the BNP have strong anti-immigration policies and have gained a number of seats on some local councils.

- **Community divisions.** There is a natural tendency among some immigrants to join their own ethnic communities, and to choose spouses from their countries of origins, leading to the formation of parallel communities with little contact or identification with mainstream British culture. Indeed, in some cases the younger generation are growing up hostile to British culture (eg, extreme Islamic groups).

- **Social and environmental concerns.** Apart from issues such as problems of overcrowding in some cities, there is an extra burden on social resources (schools, NHS and welfare systems). For example, the present projected rate of population increase will lead to a requirement of about 1.5 million houses in the period 2003 – 2026.

Practice exam questions

AS Level type questions

1. Define the term 'birth rate'. **[2 marks]**

2. Define the term 'death rate'. **[2 marks]**

3. Define the term 'fertility rate'. **[2 marks]**

4. Define the term 'net migration'. **[2 marks]**

5. Define the term 'infant mortality rate'. **[2 marks]**

6. Using **one** example, briefly explain how migration may affect the age or structure of the population. **[2 marks]**

7. Using **one** example, briefly explain why women may choose to postpone having children until they are older. **[2 marks]**

8. Outline **three** factors that may affect the dependency ratio, apart from migration. **[6 marks]**

9. Outline **three** effects on society of an ageing population. **[6 marks]**

10. Outline **three** reasons for the decline in the infant mortality rate in Britain since 1900. **[6 marks]**

11. Outline **three** reasons that birth rates have fallen in Britain since 1900. **[6 marks]**

12. Outline **three** reasons that people may migrate to the United Kingdom. **[6 marks]**

13. Outline **three** reasons for rising life expectancy. **[6 marks]**

AS & A Level type questions

14. Outline and explain **two** ways in which the ageing population may contribute to family diversity. **[10 marks]**

15. Outline and explain **two** reasons that women might delay having children. **[10 marks]**

16. Outline and explain **two** reasons for, and the consequences of, the fall in the death rate since 1900. **[10 marks]**

17. Applying material from **Item (...)** and your knowledge, evaluate the view that an ageing population creates problems for society. **[20 marks]**

18. Applying material from **Item (...)** and your knowledge, evaluate the view that demographic changes are leading to more family and household diversity in contemporary UK. **[20 marks]**

A Level type question

19. Outline and explain **two** reasons for the changes in the size of families and households in the last 50 years or so. **[10 marks]**

The AQA specification: **Families and Households**

- The nature of childhood, and changes in the status of children in the family and society.

The exam requires that you are able to:

▶ Describe and assess how childhood has been socially constructed.

▶ Assess whether childhood has improved or not in contemporary society.

▶ Describe and assess the different views of the future of childhood.

Key term

- **Childhood** is viewed as the early stage of human physiological and psychological development, typically the time period from infancy to puberty, or before people turn 13 (although some consider it to last until people are 18 and considered legally adult). In contemporary Britain, childhood is considered to be a distinctive stage in life that is experienced before becoming an adult.

- **Social construct** means that certain things, in this case 'childhood', have been created and defined by society, rather than being a natural biological development.

Is childhood a social construct?

Childhood is viewed as a distinct and separate period of life, a time of innocent vulnerability that requires protection from the harsh realities of the adult world. It goes without saying that children are younger and biologically less developed than adults, but sociologists argue that notions of childhood are *socially constructed* (see above). This is because the responsibility, treatments, laws and status of children:

  — vary between different cultures (eg, western, non-western and developing countries).

  — vary even in the same societies (eg, as regards class, ethnicity and gender).

  — have changed through history (eg, pre-industrial, industrial and modern/future periods).

Childhood in different cultures

There is a wide variation in how children are viewed and treated across the world. For example, in European societies, the period of childhood is usually longer. In non-European and developing countries, childhood is a much shorter period, with some children taking on adult roles as soon as they are physically able. For example, approximately 150 million children (aged 5 -14) are involved in child labour with the largest number coming from Africa and China and boys and girls in this age group almost equally affected (International Labour Organisation, 2015). Even more disturbing is the use of children as soldiers in Africa, for example in Uganda, Chad, Congo and Somalia (www.warchild.org.uk). There are an estimated 250,000 child soldiers in the world today. It is estimated that 40% of all child soldiers are girls, often used as 'wives' (ie, sex slaves) of the male combatants.

Childhood in the same society

Experience of childhood is not the same even in the same society. In contemporary Britain, inequality based on social class, ethnicity and gender means that not all children have the same experience of growing up. For example, girls, particularly Asian girls, will often have a more restricted childhood than boys. Government statistics show that 27% of children living in Britain (2014) are defined as poor. Poorer children are likely to suffer more ill-health and disability and have fewer educational qualifications than those who are better-off.

Historical changes in childhood

Children in pre-industrial society (pre-1760)

Phillipe Ariès (1960) argues that in pre-industrial European society, childhood did not exist. His analysis through secondary sources such as letters, diaries and historical documents as well as medieval paintings demonstrated that children were treated no differently from adults: they were seen as 'little adults' and made to work as young as 7 or 8 years of age alongside adults (or be apprenticed out to learn a trade). Children were seen as economic assets rather than as a focus of love and affection. In the eyes of the law, 7- and 8-year-olds were seen as being criminally responsible. This means that they could be tried and punished for crimes such as stealing on a similar basis to adults. Aries argued that two factors explain why society did not regard children as objects of love and devotion:

— High level of infant mortality. There was a very high level of infant mortality, which may have led parents to be indifferent towards infants.

— Financial reasons. Children had to work in order for the family unit to survive, which in turn meant they were given adult responsibilities at a younger age.

Children in industrial society (1760-onwards)

Aries argues that it was industrialisation that influenced the social construction of childhood, that is, changed our attitude towards children. By the 19th century, laws and social changes had resulted in the emergence of 'childhood'. For example, laws were introduced that included banning children from working in mines and factories and which isolated most children from the 'real world' of adult work and responsibilities. The government also introduced a law to provide education for children up to the age of 10 (the Elementary Education Act 1870) and raised the age of sexual consent to 16, to cut down on child prostitution. Improvements in health, sanitation and diet led to a decline in infant mortality rates. This gradually led to children becoming objects of love and devotion, regarded as vulnerable and in need of protection, rather than economic assets. However, some working-class children ignored the new laws and continued to work in mines and factories, since their families were often dependent on their children's wages for survival (there being no welfare or state pensions).

Once the idea of childhood had been established in the 19th century, different notions of children and childhood emerged. Wendy Rogers (2001) argues that two dominant images of childhood emerged in the 19th century and remain with us today: that of the sinful child and that of the innocent child:

— Innocent child. The innocent child view suggests there is something wholesome and precious about childhood and that children should be protected from the nasty adult world and allowed the freedom to enjoy their time of innocence.

— Sinful child. The sinful child view assumes children are essentially selfish and unable to control their selfish desires. This is associated with the 'control view' of childhood, in which the job of adults is to control, regulate and discipline children.

Childhood in modern society (1960-present day)

It was not until the late 20th and early 21st century that major changes took place whereby children are now seen as a distinct category from adults. British society has become more child-centred in the post-war period, which means the welfare of children is very important in society: we spend large amounts of time, effort and money on a smaller number of children. In a child-centred society, children are seen as naive, vulnerable and in need of protection from bad things (eg, murder, death, violence and conflict). Parenting children the right way also became a concern for most adults who have children. A large amount of money and time is invested in children academically, socially and physically to prepare them for adulthood, and a string of laws have been passed to provide protection for children.

Why did the position of children change in the 19th and 20th centuries?

— **Industrialisation.** Formal schooling developed as a direct response to industrialisation. The 1870 Education Act introduced a basic system of primary education with the hope that literate educated workers would create a skilled workforce.

— **The decline of infant mortality rates.** More infants surviving meant parents had fewer children and made a greater financial and emotional investment in the fewer children they had.

— **Advances in specialist knowledge about children.** Advances in the field of psychology during the 19th and 20th centuries meant the promotion of ideas about the importance of the early years of child development.

— **Laws banning child labour.** From the 1840s, children changed from economic assets to economic liabilities, financially dependent on their parents.

— **Compulsory schooling.** The Elementary Education Act of 1870 made education compulsory from the ages of five to ten; this created a period of dependency on the family and separated children from the adult world of work. With the later expansion of education, children were obliged to spend a minimum of 11 years in school.

— **Contraception.** The availability of contraception means parenthood is now a matter of choice rather than economic necessity or biological accident. Families can have fewer children, investing more time and care in them.

— **Children protection and welfare laws.** The expansion of social welfare services and a number of acts have given children greater protection. For example, the Children Act (1989) sets outs parents' 'responsibilities' and protects children who are thought to be at risk, mandating action if necessary by involving the social services and the police. The Child Support Act (1991) is designed to protect children's welfare in the event of parental separation.

— **Laws about social behaviour.** The minimum age of a wide range of activities, from sex to smoking and drinking alcohol, reinforces the attitude that children are different from adults.

Has childhood improved?

Many would argue that the lives of children in the western world have greatly improved compared to the lives of children in earlier centuries and those of children in many other parts of the world.

Positive view

The 'march of progress' sociologists take a positive view of childhood and argue that, over time, the lives of most children have improved, and that the family, including society, is child-centred. This is because:

— Children's welfare has improved, in terms of their education, psychology and health.

— Infant mortality rate has declined; most babies now survive.

— Smaller family size means parents can afford to provide for children's needs

— Children are protected from harm and exploitation by laws against child abuse and child labour.

Negative view

- **Conflict theorists** (eg, feminists and Marxist) argue that the 'march of progress' view is idealised, and take a more negative of childhood. They highlight points such as:

  — Gender differences: (the way we see and treat girls and boys). Girls are more likely to perform domestic duties and parents often are more protective of girls, allowing them much less independence.

  — Ethnic differences: for example, Asian parents (eg, Muslim, Sikh and Indian) are more likely to be strict towards their daughters than white parents.

  — Class inequalities: for example, poor children tend to lack many of the experiences that middle-class children may enjoy (holidays, day-trips and activities).

Firestone (1979), a feminist, argues that childhood has not improved because inequalities exist between children and adults. Children are controlled and dominated by adults. For example, children do not have the freedom to choose whether they can work, what they do with their time, what they wear and eat, and whether they want to go to school or not.

Marxists would also point out the class differences in definitions of childhood over the years: it was mainly working-class children who were expected to work long hours in the 19th century, whereas upper-class children were the first to be 'coddled'. They would also argue that how we treat children is likely to depend on the economy and the needs of the means of production.

- **Functionalists and the New Right** see childhood as a natural stage in development and a time where children are vulnerable and under threat, requiring protection from the adult world. However, Melanie Phillips (1997), a journalist who supports the New Right view, argues that in modern society the culture of disciplined parenting is breaking down. She sees two trends as the reason for this:

  — Liberal ideologies. Liberal ideas that children have rights (eg, not to be punished by smacking) have undermined the ability of parents to establish authority over children, which in turn has undermined children's respect for parenting (and authority).

  — Media. The media and peer groups are becoming much more influential in shaping a child's identity than parents.

Philips argues that the above two trends are detrimental to childhood as they have encouraged children to become adults faster and simultaneously undermined the ability of parents to regulate their children's passage into adolescence and adulthood. As a result, the period of childhood innocence has been shortened as children are made to mature at a much earlier age, causing all types of problems, such as inability to cope with choices, leading to psychological disorders (eg, suicide and eating disorders).

- **Family relationships.** Childhood can be damaged by family disruption such as divorce, reconstituted family arrangements, and sexual and physical or emotional abuse. For example, the Child Protection Register contains approximately 50,000 names of children vulnerable to abuse, mainly from family members. Their dependency on adults and their inability to obtain legal paid employment mean they have little opportunity to escape unhappy family life.

- **Mass media.** Some sociologists argue that in modern society, children have lost their innocence and their childhood has been shortened though exposure to adult issues such as sex and death through the mass media and the internet. The media has also influenced many young girls' behaviour by encouraging them to envisage themselves as sexual beings at a much younger age than previously.

- **Children in other countries.** Children in developing countries will often experience childhood differently from those in developed or Western societies. Factors such as the trafficking and prostitution of children, child pornography, child military service and child labour will mean that children often experience their childhood negatively.

The future of childhood

Neil Postman in 'The Disappearance of Childhood' (1983) argues that childhood is disappearing in the 21st century and children are becoming more like adults. This is mainly due to mass media (eg, internet and TV) on which children are being exposed to the adult world, (eg, sex, drugs and violence) at younger and younger ages. The formerly secret aspects of adulthood have been revealed to children at a much earlier age, forcing them to grow up more quickly.

Palmer (2006) argues that rapid changes in technology and social attitudes are damaging children's development (eg, junk food, computer games, intensive marketing to children, testing in education and long hours worked by parents). As a result, children are deprived of a genuine childhood.

Nick Lee (2001) suggests that childhood has not disappeared but has just become more complex and ambiguous (unclear). Children are dependent and independent at some points during their growth. This is due to the increasing similarities between adults and children, which have led to a new social construction of childhood which at present is unclear. On the other hand, Grossberg (1994) argues that much of adult culture now increasingly enjoys aspects of 'youth culture', with many people in their 30s and 40s refusing to let go of their youth.

Conclusion

It is clear that being a child in the past was very different to being a child today, although how children experience their childhood will depend on the country they are born in, and what class, gender and ethnicity they belong to. Changes in the UK since the 19th century have led to the emergence of a child-centred society, which has had a positive impact on the experience and development of children. Changing technology and social attitudes now mean children are maturing much faster, but this may come at a cost. For example, UK youth are at, or near, the top of the international league table for obesity, self-harm, drug and alcohol abuse, violence and teenage pregnancies, which suggests they are not ready to cope emotionally and psychologically.

✔✘ Evaluation

✘ **Cognitive development.** Psychologists such as Piaget have shown that children develop mentally (cognition) through a number of different stages and are not capable of thinking in the same way as adults. The process of socialisation also indicates that 'childhood' is a learned concept: the young person learns how to be a 'child' and the adult learns how to create a 'child'.

✘ **Childhood not all a social construct.** It could be argued that childhood is not completely constructed socially. The physical and mental development of the young human being helps to define the roles and responsibilities they can take, and also the treatment they receive. The physical boundaries of age must play some part in determining what a child can do.

✘ **Exaggeration of children's lives in pre-industrial times.** Ariès has been criticised for his interpretation of childhood in pre-industrial society. It has been argued that in certain respects, children in medieval Europe were seen as different from adults. For example, there were laws prohibiting the marriage of children under the age of 12.

✘ **Poverty in less developed countries.** Although childhood is experienced differently in less-developed countries, this is mainly for economic reasons, that is, that children are essential for the economic survival of the family, rather than because they have a different social construction of childhood. For example, poverty and lack of decent work for adults forces many children into work, a factor preventing them from going to school and equipping themselves with literacy skills, even if being illiterate will further propel the poverty cycle.

✘ **Child abuse.** The child-centeredness of society does not necessarily mean that childhood has improved. Child abuse still exists, whether physical, sexual or mental. For example, the NSPCC claims that in 2014, nearly 50,000 children were on the Child Protection Register because they were said to be at risk of significant harm from family members. These figures emphasise the dark side of family life, of which children are victims.

✘ **Child-centered society.** Frank Furedi (2000) argues that a child-centered society has led to an age of 'paranoid parenting': an over-exaggerated level of constant fear and paranoia of the potential threats their children face in terms of health, safety and welfare (eg, parks, foods, cots, baby-sitters, pedophiles, gangs or drugs). This has caused parents to be over-controlling and more restrictive of children's activities (eg, playing in the park). This restrictive approach towards play stifles children's initiative and desire for play/adventure, which is important for the child's social and cognitive development. For example, for children to become responsible, they have to learn to make decisions for themselves, something they can never do under a parent's watchful eye.

AS Level type questions

1. Define the term 'child-centred society'. **[2 marks]**

2. Define the term 'social construction'. **[2 marks]**

3. Using **one** example, briefly explain how the difference between adults and childhood may be becoming less clear. **[2 marks]**

4. Using **one** example, briefly explain how there may be a 'loss of childhood' in contemporary British society. **[2 marks]**

5. Outline **three** ways in which adults may control the activities of children. **[6 marks]**

6. Outline **three** ways in which adults control children's time, space or bodies. **[6 marks]**

7. Outline **three** reasons why children have less power in society than adults. **[6 marks]**

8. Outline **three** ways in which the position of children can be said to have improved over the last one hundred years. **[6 marks]**

9. Outline **three** ways in which differences between childhood and adulthood are becoming less clear in society today. **[6 marks]**

10. Outline **three** ways in which childhood may not be a specially protected and privileged time of life. **[6 marks]**

11. Outline **three** reasons why the experience of childhood may differ between children in contemporary British society. **[6 marks]**

AS & A Level type questions

12. Outline and explain **two** reasons why childhood as a separate age-status is a 'relatively modern invention' **[10 marks]**

13. Outline and explain **two** changes in society which may be reducing the distinction between 'childhood' and 'adulthood'. **[10 marks]**

14. Applying material from **Item (...)** and your knowledge, evaluate sociological explanations of changes in the status of childhood. **[20 marks]**

15. Applying material from **Item (...)** and your knowledge, evaluate the view that contemporary families have become more child-centred. **[20 marks]**

16. Applying material from **Item (...)** and your knowledge, view that childhood is being lost in society today. **[20 marks]**

A Level type question

17. Applying material from **Item (...)**, analyse **two** arguments against the view that childhood is a fixed, universal stage. **[10 marks]**

18. Applying material from **Item (...)**, analyse **two** changes in the position of children in society over the last 100 years. **[10 marks]**

www.ingramcontent.com/pod-product-compliance
Lightning Source LLC
Chambersburg PA
CBHW080901030426

42336CB00016B/2975